A PLACE CALLED HOME

St. Martin's Press
New York

A PLACE CALLED HOME

TWENTY WRITING WOMEN REMEMBER

Edited by Mickey Pearlman

Book Design by Gretchen Achilles

ISBN 0-312-12793-6

Library of Congress Cataloging in Publication Data is available from the Library of Congress.

First St. Martin's Edition: September, 1996

10 9 8 7 6 5 4 3 2 1

P. x. Hershon, Robert. "The Driver Said." In *How to Ride on the Woodlawn Express*. St. Paul, MN: Booklinger, 1985. Copyright © 1985 by Robert Hershon. Reprinted by permission of the author.

Pp. 21-24. Kingston, Maxine Hong. "Our First Home." First published in Maxine Hong Kingston, *Hawai'i One Summer*. San Francisco: Meadow Press, 1987, pp. 5–8. Reprinted by permission of the author.

Pp. 25-39. Morris, Mary. Portions previously published in *Wall to Wall*. New York: Doubleday, 1991. Reprinted by permission of Doubleday.

P. 31. Bishop, Elizabeth. "Questions of Travel." From *The Complete Poems 1927-1979*, by Elizabeth Bishop. © 1979, 1983 by Alice Helen Methfessel. Reprinted by permission of Farrar, Straus & Giroux, Inc.

P. 171. Williams, William Carlos. "El Hombre" (2 line excerpt). From *Collected Poems: 1909-1939, Volume I.* Copyright © 1938 by New Directions Publishing Corp. Reprinted by permission of New Directions Publishing Corp.

P. 171. ———. "Preface, Book I" (first line). From *Paterson.* Copyright 1946 by William Carlos Williams. Reprinted by permission of New Directions Publishing Corp.

P. 177. ———. "Asphodel That Greeney Flower" (lines 25-27 from Book I). From *Collected Poems 1939-1962, Volume II.* Copyright © 1944 by William Carlos Williams. Reprinted by permission of New Directions Publishing Corp.

P. 191. Donohue, Denis. *Ferocious Alphabets.* New York: Columbia University Press, 1984.

P. 192. Brown, Rosellen. "Landing in Jackson." In *Some Deaths In The Delta And Other Poems*. Amherst, MA: University of Massachusetts Press, 1970.

P. 195. ———. "The Autobiography of My Mother." In *Street Games.* New York: Ballantine, 1981.

P. 197-198. ———. *Civil Wars.* New York: Viking Penguin, 1985.

P. 201-202. Brown, Rosellen. "Emigre." Reprinted by permission of the author.

Also by Mickey Pearlman

AUTHOR

WHAT TO READ: The Essential Guide for Reading Group Members and Other Book Lovers

LISTEN TO THEIR VOICES: 20 Interviews with Women Who Write

COAUTHOR

A VOICE OF ONE'S OWN: Conversations with America's Writing Women (with Katherine Usher Henderson)

TILLIE OLSEN (with Abby H. P. Werlock)

EDITOR

AMERICAN WOMEN WRITING FICTION: Memory, Identity, Family, Space

MOTHER PUZZLES: Daughters and Mothers in Contemporary American Literature

THE ANNA BOOK: Searching for Anna in Literary History

CANADIAN WOMEN WRITING FICTION

BETWEEN FRIENDS: Writing Women Celebrate Friendship

for Sandra Appleman:

grace and courage

Contents

"THE DRIVER SAID"

BOERUM HILL?
IT USED TO BE
GOWANUS
THIS AIN'T NO
NEIGHBORHOOD
IF YA *BUTCHER*
COMES TO YA *FUNERAL*
THAT'S A
NEIGHBORHOOD

—ROBERT HERSHON

Acknowledgments

Peace and gratitude to all those who have supported and cheered me on through the last nine books. To those names I wish to add a few whose encouragement—by phone, fax, mail, or actual proximity— helped make my long-term interest in home and place into *A Place Called Home:* Howard Bryden, Christine O'Hagan, Linda Pritchett, Barbara Ben David, and especially Marv Rayfield. It also helped to have the most talented, hardworking, and competent agent in New York, Anne Dubuisson, and the funniest, most "marketing-oriented" and trustworthy editor imaginable in the world of publishing: Michael Flamini, W.F.B.

This collection is also in memory of two fine young men: Matthew Munroe Henderson (1967-1995) and Leo Rosengart (1970-1995).

A PLACE CALLED HOME

``Hometown Gal: An Introduction''

MICKEY PEARLMAN

LIKE MANY AMERICANS of a certain generation, my now-dead ex-mother-in-law *schlepped* for three years by cart and wagon across Europe—from Minsk to Antwerp. There, at seventeen years of age and with three younger half-brothers to care for, she boarded a creaky, listing ship in steerage class, bound for New York.

Many years later her globetrotting son was planning a trip back to the then–Soviet Union and naturally offered to take her with him. She looked at him as if she had raised a three-headed child.

"*Why* I should go *there?*" she replied. "I *came* from there."

IN WHAT HAS proved to be a colossal case of naiveté, I thought this response both mildly funny and somewhat puzzling. Like most native-born Americans, especially those who like me were raised in the South, I had been breast-fed on the idea that *home* was *place—town, city, apart-ment, region, house, neighborhood*—and that even a northerner knew that anyone who "came from there" would grab at the chance to go back, at least for a visit! No doubt I had heard too many renditions of "Carry Me Back to Old Virginny" and "My Old Kentucky Home," repeated choruses of "Georgia" (my father's birthplace), and endless

1

singers wailing about how they wished they was in the land of cotton. Indeed, I assumed without too much introspection that feelings of safety, security, and emotional comfort grew naturally from the sights and sounds and scents of the familiar.

In my own case I knew this was not so. From the age of seven I lived on an island, called Rivo Alto (high river, in Italian), which jutted out from Venetian Causeway, a private highway with a ten-cent toll. That fashionable thoroughfare connected Miami, at that time still a small, southern, non-Latin city, with its more fashionable suburb of Miami Beach, a place reserved in the 1950s exclusively for white people whose black maids carried identification cards for travel after 6 P.M. My house sat at the top of a heavily wooded cul-de-sac where the road wound gracefully through a neighborhood of elegant houses hidden behind masses of purple bougainvillea. Many of these villas faced the waters of Biscayne Bay.

For all its beauty and luxury it never felt right, never generated those feelings of intimacy and warmth that emanate when the person and the place match. But in the narcissism of youth I *knew* in my southern heart that *I* was a special case; *I* was a natural northerner and urbanite born by mistake among the lethargic palm trees, pastel-tinted hotels, and alligator farms and surrounded by whining tourists in lime-colored slacks and fake Hawaiian shirts. (Has anyone counted the people in this huge country who are sure they were born in the wrong place?)

It took eighteen years to "escape," but only one semester at City College, near New York's Spanish Harlem, to know beyond doubt that I had indeed been on alien turf and very much dis-placed. I can still remember standing in the hallway of the English department at eleven o'clock at night, listening to a motley crew of underfinanced New Yorkers (some of whom had forty cents to spend *either* on a knish *or* on subway fare) argue about "Emerson and His Contemporaries." I exhaled twenty-three years of frustration ("Is it me? Is it them?") in an epiphany to rival anything in a James Joyce short story and realized that I had, somehow, magically landed in friendly territory. For the first time I felt not-"nuts" for being interested in all the "wrong" things and not-"sassy" (the pejorative adjective of choice for all intelligent southern women of my generation) for wanting to discuss and talk and argue for hours about certain subjects. I wanted to kiss the ground, as I imagined Catholics did near the grottoes at Lourdes, and to bless each mango and papaya at the bodega I passed near my subway stop on Upper Broadway. In later years when I found myself for twelve months in waltzing Vienna—where the population looks *immer gerade aus* into its inglorious past and wallows happily in a whipped-cream world of unrelieved nostalgia—I longed for the dingy CCNY cafeteria on 130th Street and the shouting matches between the Socialists, the Democrats, the Trotskyites, and the reformers—all of whom sat at different tables, barricaded by ideas. Again, when I lived for several years in an elegant, sandy suburb of Tel Aviv, where everybody above a certain age is from somewhere else, "glad to be here, not *there*," and people count out the price of tomatoes or knitting wool in their long-familiar first languages of Yiddish, Arabic, Hungarian, or even German, I was Not Home. Apparently, home was about people and the sometimes miraculous psychological, spiritual, and often unexplainable connections that happen between them. And home was where those people were—in my case closer to Shea Stadium than to the ruins at Caesarea.

So how did I forget all this when I chose the nineteen writers for this book, told them the subject was home and place, asked them to dig deep and to let the good times roll? I knew that Norman Rockwell images would not emerge in prose from this group of talented and edgy essayists even though the Christian Coalition was (and is) assuring America every fifteen minutes that we could all be linked, arm in arm, in a golden daisy chain if we'd only get our "family values" straight. I was not expecting visions of braided rugs before the hearth or kitchen walls dripping with potholders. But I must admit my surprise when I began to receive—by fax and snail mail—so many essays about childhood homes as places *to get away from.* Why were so many of the writers telling me that this "stuff" had been buried for a long time and that resurrecting it was painful and hard? Where was Home Sweet Home . . . be it ever so humble? Home, Home, at last? East or West, home is best? Where were the lilting and loving reminiscences of safety, succor, or comfort? Why was I hearing on a daily basis that this experience was "wrenching," "draining," and "exhausting"? (At the same time—since all writers to varying degrees depend on the idea of place—most of the essayists were telling me and themselves that "this should be easy, right? I am a writer of place, am I not?") As requested, these writers were looking back, and what was emerging in many cases were memories of anti-Semitism ("TV dinners filled with dog shit steaming in the snow outside our front door"), racism ("the memories: The swastika on the carport wall. . . . the words: Gook. Nip. . . . Yellow housenigger. Chink"), unloving or missing parents ("Because of Ruthie [the housekeeper], we were accompanied. . . . she seemed to keep us alive; without her, we would've certainly perished"), loneliness ("I come from the flat even plains of the Midwest where there is nowhere to hide"), and loss ("i go to where my mother is,/alive again and humming/in a room"). Even Marcie Hershman, who grew up in a "spacious, safe childhood home," wrote about a trip with her brother to Germany, "the land that had filled the nights and our hearts with emptiness." Forget Emerson; perhaps Henry James was right when he wrote that writers "start from the port of grief"; as a group they pay attention to pain—theirs and everyone else's—which is, indeed, their job, and this was an opportunity not to be missed.

Of course the loving descriptions of home did emerge, but they were often portraits of discovered places that had become home, sometimes in stark contrast to what had been left behind. Julie Smith, for instance, a native of Savannah, writes about her French Quarter neighborhood in New Orleans, Erica Jong works in a treehouse in Connecticut, Arlene Hirschfelder revels in her book-filled house in New Jersey, and Melinda Worth Popham describes her post-divorce digs in Los

Angeles. Indeed, the question of *who* feels comfortable *where* remains one of the eternal perplexities; I, for example, now live inside the ethnic stew of multicultural New Jersey where the owner of the local candy store, who comes from the western part of India (and encourages me daily to "have nice day"), speaks Gujarati, an Indic language; the pharmacist at the local A&P is named Rashda, not Rosie; the bagel store (green on St. Patrick's Day) is run by Italians and Salvadorans; the German bakery makes both hot cross buns for Lent and challah for *shabbat;* the local falafels are concocted by Armenians ("You have party for forty; we *deliver* the hummus!"); the Sunoco station operates in Turkish; the local Italian crossing guard knows *to the child* who is at Hebrew school or communion class and who is playing hooky; the Japanese and Korean kids go to nursery school at the Jewish Center; and the Greek grocer, when I am short a few bucks for grape leaves and spanikopita, reminds me that, "it's no problem; you got *credit!*"

In spite of the angst, several essayists did take a lighter approach and wrote about their seeming inability to get the carpeting down and the curtains up, as if decorating skills and furniture placement were a genetic inheritance missing from their individual DNAs. When Francine Prose recalls her beloved "seven month home" she remembers that she and her husband had "less than a thousand dollars left over from a book advance. My parents were barely speaking to me, they were sure I was ruining my life, having a child with a poor artist ... [and] absolutely unmoved and unimpressed by the fact that we were ... young bohemians in love." Kathryn Harrison's solution has been that she has taken "the ready example of my grandmother's home that opposed the world around it and learned to make a similar home within myself, an interior landscape into which I could disappear with increasing ease." Carole Maso, who lives "everywhere and nowhere ... built a home of language ... safe in the shelter of the alphabet."

Clearly this collection revolves around the idea that home is a lost-and-found collection, sometimes of non-disposable items that must be claimed. As Jill McCorkle explains, "the desire to go back and recreate really is not about being young so much as it is about finding the people you have lost." Or never knew. That is why Sandra Benítez visits her twin sister's grave in Maryland (the twin died when they were one month old) with a "shoe box, its lid secured by a wide rubber band, a jumble of photographs and mementoes representing flashes and fragments of my life. . . . *Mira*, Susana, I say. Look, a few home views." And sometimes you go back in order to find yourself, as Lois Lowry does in the essay that closes the collection: "My mother is smiling as she looks up from reading *The Yearling* aloud to a little pigtailed girl. . . . I can join them any time. The place is called Memory."

A FEW WORDS seem necessary about the role of the editor on this journey. I have put together many collections of original essays—on friendship, mothers and daughters, American and Canadian writing women, and characters named Anna—and it is always the editor's job to function as a supportive and demanding mommy (who also applauds) and to ask more from the writers even when they proclaim that the well is dry. An editor serves as a combination therapist/ benevolent dictator/Dean of Students and confessor, and this time it was my job to remind everyone, as Rosellen Brown writes, that "we all know that 'where you come from,' where you grew up, is a matter for the imagination—for anyone's imagination, not only a writer's."

In the end, producing these essays was not easy for most of the contributors; much of the sorrow you will read about in this collection has until now been unspoken. But no reader should see these essays as unrelievably painful because these deeply personal revelations are a gift from these writers to all of us. Every reader who has experienced and conquered real adversity will, I hope, be cheered and buoyed by the message that comes through so often—and so clearly:

Everyone leaves home and everyone finds a place to call home. Exodus, it turns out, is genesis.

Home Views

SANDRA BENÍTEZ

MY SISTER SUSANA died thirty-eight days after our birth. As identical twins, we had floated nose to nose in the dark watery haven of our mother's womb before it propelled us—me first—into a glare of lights and a dry Isolette. Susana died in hers. Alone in my narrow crib, I was left to go on. If home is abode, domicile, dwelling, residence, house, lodging, quarters, or room, then what is the womb, but the first one of these we have? And what is a twin, but a womb-mate? Susana and I. We burst from the same egg to spend mere months together, when, had fate been kinder, a regular lifetime would have not been long enough. On May 3, 1991, to commemorate the 50th anniversary of Susana's death, I travel to a Maryland cemetery to visit her grave. I have not been there before. I bring with me, stashed in a shoe box, its lid secured by a wide rubber band, a jumble of photographs and mementoes representing flashes and fragments of my life. For an afternoon, the sun warming the ground on which I sit, a perfumed breeze wafting from the cherry blossoms, I pull, at random, treasures from the box and relate their stories. *Mira*, Susana, I say. Look, a few home views.

* * *

IN MY OLDEST memory there is María Luisa. She stands proud, her hair a dark storm around her face. I was three when Dad hired her. We had left Washington, D.C., the place where I was born, and we lived in Mexico City, where Anita, my baby sister, made her appearance smack in the middle of an earthquake. We lived at the edge of Las Lomas, on Boulevard Virreyes. We had two other nursemaids before María Luisa came: An American lady, Mrs. Long, who had personal problems and who tried to solve them one day in the kitchen by downing a bottle of iodine. And there was Marcela, a young woman, who cared more about the lustful men who frequently dropped by to see her than about us.

After María Luisa comes into our lives, I steal into her room, which is in the garden shed at the back of the yard. She shares the room with Licha, the crotchety old cook who insists on slipping tacos into every one of our meals. Some nights, when the household is asleep, I tiptoe from the house and cross the yard under the moonlight to be with María Luisa. When I rattle the knob on the shed door, she rises from her bed and lets me in. She pulls me inside, scolding me for risking an encounter with Reno, our white bull terrier, who prowls the yard at night. María Luisa pats me on the rump and says, I should take you back right now. But she does not. Instead, she lets me climb into her cot, and though her cot is hard and narrow, it has been warmed by her and it is her warmth I seek.

When I lie back, María Luisa pokes the end of her blanket-serape under my chin while across the room Licha's snores rise and fall. María Luisa has wrapped herself in a rebozo. She sits like a shadowy angel on the edge of the cot and tells me things.

She tells me about color. She tells me red is the color we first are. She says, red is heart and red is fire, and adds, it is always good to wear a bit of red. Her own adherence to the rule is a little red pouch that dangles from a string around her neck. It is dark in the room so I cannot see it, but were I to lift my hand to her heart, I know that I would feel it there. In the pouch are bits of laurel leaf and rosemary. A hardened grain of *maíz*. A nugget of *copal*, thick as a thumb. I ask her about the color blue, because it is my favorite and because there is hardly any red in the things I have to wear. Blue is sky and blue is the night, she says. Blue is the sea. I've never been to sea, so I cannot truly picture it. I think instead of the color the sky takes when I lie out on the grass and look up. I picture all the blue behind the clouds, and soon I fall asleep as María Luisa's shadow watches over me. Always when this happens I awaken in my own room, in my own bed, and I do not know if it was only in my dreams that I was so clearly cherished.

MARÍA LUISA AND I take trips to the park. El Bosque de Chapultepec, the Mexican national park and forest, is not far from our house; some days María Luisa and I go, just the two of us, some days we take my baby sister. When we do, María Luisa carries Ani most of the way because Ani is only two. I don't like to see my sister in María Luisa's arms. When we reach the section of the park that contains the zoo, María Luisa puts Ani down and then she spreads a large cloth on the grass so we can sit and watch the tigers in the cages across the way. Because the terrain is uneven, Ani teeters on her chubby legs and María Luisa plops her down upon her lap. I stamp my foot, poke my hands into my sides at seeing Ani and María Luisa so intimate. It's my turn, I say, and try to push my sister out of María Luisa's lap. *No, niña, no sea mala*, María Luisa says, holding on to Ani. I stamp my foot again, for I'm not a bad girl. I try another ploy. Ani's not really my sister, I say, hoping María Luisa will believe this and drop Ani like a hot *tamal*. Besides, maybe what I say is true. I have seen other sisters playing in the park and they have looked one much like the other. In appearance, my sister and I are different. My hair is dark, my eyes are brown. Ani's hair is like corn silk, her eyes are very blue.

María Luisa ignores my comment. She pats the space on the ground beside her. *Sientese*, she says, and I sit next to her as she orders, my own chubby legs sticking straight out from under my pinafore. You had another sister once, María Luisa says. Remember what your mother says. You had a twin sister. Your twin sister and you looked exactly alike.

The fact that I had another sister is not news, but the idea that she looked just like me is something I've never fully grasped. When I look in a mirror, is my twin sister the image I see in the glass? *Cómo se llama?* I ask, because I've heard her name before, but I've forgotten it.

Susana, María Luisa says. She was named after your mother's sister, *la tía* Susana.

Where is Susana now? I say, looking over at Ani. If I can see this sister, why can't I see the other one?

Susanita is an angel, María Luisa says. You can't see her because she's an angel in heaven. She points up to the sky.

I make no reply. After a moment, I lie back on the cloth we've been sitting on. I look up at the sky, at the cottony clouds drifting by. I try to picture an angel in the clouds, an angel with a face like my own.

OF MY FIRST solo trip, I've been told this: That it was 1946, the year I was five, the year we moved to El Salvador. That I announced my departure to the family, explaining I was going away because living with them had become impossible; that I packed, quite methodically, a suitcase with clothes, a jump rope, and a cap; that I marched out the door and headed down the street toward freedom.

My mother has recounted this story many times and she always adds, "When you left like that, don't think you weren't watched. I kept an eye on you till you came back." I must have been all eyes myself. Certain details of that journey are still vivid in my memory: The door through which I escape is dark and carved and heavy; my suitcase is a small square with rounded corners and a thin handle. I wear a flouncy dress made of some slippery kind of fabric. My braids are very tight and adorned at the ends with bows. There are sandals on my feet. Oh, and I also remember this: as I walk away, my steps are sure and I'm not afraid. In my memory, I'm proud to be on a trip of my own devising. I pass the high walls of the estate across the street, the abandoned house that looms on the corner. When I reach *la doble via*, the wide avenue that leads to and from the city, I crane my neck. Look up and down the avenue. Buses lurch by, broad-beamed and open-sided. They belch black smoke and leave behind the stench of diesel fuel. An ox cart rolls by. A boy prods the beasts with a stick. A few dogs trot by. People hurry past, most don't look my way, but a few of the dogs attempt to sniff around me. I shoo them away. I sit on the steps leading up to an iron gate, ornate with grillwork. I tuck my dress carefully under me, keep the suitcase with my worldly possessions close beside. I watch the road and then, for the very first time, I feel profoundly alone. I spring to my feet. Pluck up my suitcase. Run all the way home.

I SIT AT the edge of the patio, watching the laundress do the wash. Mercedes Emestica is a sinewy woman with steely hair gathered into a bun. I'm barefoot as is she. In this, as in a number of ways, I try to imitate her. I want to come nearer, but I know she will brush me off. She is at the concrete washstand at the back of the patio where, after she wets and soaps the clothing, she lays it in the sun to bleach. It is this I want to do. I want Mercedes to hand me mother's dress or dad's white shirt. I want to carry them over, each a sodden, soapy weight, and lay them against hot patio tiles. When Mercedes does this, she spreads the clothing out with a foot. Mercedes's foot is very brown; the nails of her toes are small and rounded and short. They look like pearly buttons to me.

I walk over, ready to take a chance. Nana, I say, for I always call her this, *cuénteme un cuento*. I know that asking for a story is a way to engage her. She is rolling a ball of yellow soap across one of mother's skirts. Nana stops her scrubbing, but does not look my way. She looks instead beyond the patio wall, past the ruby bougainvillea froth-ing over it. *Había un vez,* she begins, her gaze gone soft. Once upon a time there lived a woman who was very beautiful. God gave her a child and he was beautiful, too. I lean against the side of the wash stand as she recounts again the story of la Ciguanaba. This legend is nana's favorite. It is the story of a woman driven mad by a man's love. So she can join him unencumbered, she casts her child away. God punishes her for this. You have abandoned your son, God says, when I gave him to you for keeps. As punishment, you will search for him until the end of the world. Nana rolls the soap ball back and forth across clothing. She looks at me, her eyes dark and fierce. She says, "At night, when you're in bed, if you listen very carefully, you can hear la Ciguanaba. Along the riverbanks and in the woods, she wails, *Ay, mi hijo,* oh, my child."

I shudder with delight, thinking I can catch, even in the daylight, the sounds of a mother's grief. Nana waves me away when I start to ask questions. I skip quickly across the patio so as not to burn my feet. Near the house, in a rectangle of shade, is the pole and perch on which *la lora,* the parrot, sits. I carefully avoid the white droppings peppering the ground around the bottom of the pole. *La lora* accepts with resigned patience her lot as my pet. Sometimes she lets me parade her around the patio in the dolly buggy. Sometimes she lets me cradle her and she will mold herself in the half-circle of my arm, her tail feathers stiff and green and quivering. I raise a finger to her and she blinks her papaya-seed eyes and gives a squawk. I blink back and whisper, You are my baby. I would never abandon you.

I REMEMBER ABUELITO, grandfather, in his white linen suit.

I remember his Panama hat. The supple leather of his shoes. The milky look of his hose.

I remember Abuelito roving about the house. At midmorning, he stands at the doorway and looks out into the street. Celestino,

Abuelita says, *¿qué te pasa?* I see Abuelito shake his head. I see him take up his hat, walk out the door, take the bus down *la doble via;* then the bus gets very small.

I remember Abuelito always comes back. Silently, he goes to his room. Takes up a pen. Sits very still in the chair under the window. Spills a trail of poems across the paper on his desk.

I remember Abuelito likes to salt his food. His fingers, graceful like a lady's, take up the shaker. He sprinkles meat, rice, vegetables, his milk. Abuelita clucks her tongue. Celestino, she says. *Mucha sal. Mucha sal.* Abuelito throws her a look. Sits the shaker down. Abuelito, I ask, why do you like salt?

La sal cura, Abuelito says. Salt cures.

I nod as if in agreement, but I'm perplexed.

I am nine. I cannot see what there might be in Abuelito's life that needs curing.

FIVE YEARS LATER and Dad says I have to leave home to continue my schooling. Dad says an American education is the best. Most of my Salvadoran friends are going to private schools in cities like Boston or Miami or San Francisco. I am also going north. I am going to my paternal grandparents' farm in Missouri.

Grandma and Grandpa are in their late fifties when they take me in. It must be quite an adjustment; their own children, my three aunts and Dad, left the farm years before, and here I come, a foreign girl they've seen only once before.

On the farm, on autumn nights, I stroll past the barn and stand at the edge of the pasture, beyond the brightness of the barnlight. I look out across the darkened fields remembering home. It's been weeks since I received any letters. I think of Mom and Dad and Ani, too. Mom and Ani are in their rooms, frozen at separate tasks as if in two different photographs. Dad is in motion, as if on a movie screen. He is alone in his VW, driving hard and fast. His orange "Bug" careens down a desolate, gravel road. In my mind, it's not that Dad is heading to yet another of his jobs. In my mind, it's that he's always heading away from home.

I turn toward the house sitting stern and reticent against the night sky. Light burning back in the kitchen forms an uncertain glow around the front windows. I think, in this world you make connections where you can, and start toward the light.

On winter nights, I burrow into a feather bed; curl my toes around the edge of the hot-water bottle Grandma tucks in with me. I listen to the moan of the wind, to the way it sets the plastic stretched across the windows to whistling. I picture the snow banked against the house and out along the fences Grandpa seems always to be mending. Lying in bed, I picture the cattle huddled together in the barn. I picture the ewes in the sheepshed, and I strain to hear their woeful bleating. Some nights, it's the cry of la Ciguanaba that I hear instead.

THE FARMHOUSE. ITS facade is rough to the touch and is the color of pigeon wings. The old house sits on a flat expanse of land that is not buffered from the wind. My room is at the top of the house. To reach it I go up a short flight of stairs, past a small door that is shoulder high and opens up to a space under the pitch of the roof that we like to call the attic.

Sometimes, when it is still day, I twist the wooden peg Grandpa made for a latch and swing the door open. In the attic, light filters down from the roof in bright dusty shafts. From the attic comes the ripe smell of fruit Grandma has set drying. I like to snitch apricots; their fruit is rubbery and tartly sweet.

Sometimes, when Grandma has gone to town and Grandpa is plowing the fields, I lift aside the length of fabric that curtains their bedroom door. I rummage through their dresser, fishing past underwear and the stiff squares of never-used hankies until my hand falls on the dresser-set put away in the third drawer. I take out the oval hand mirror. It is edged in mother-of-pearl and has a silver handle. I gaze at the image that leaps from a glass that is just the size to reflect only my face. It is my twin's face that I pretend to see. Hello, Susana, I say to the mirror. After a time, I look away, across the room and through the window, to the pasture and the puff of smoke rising from Grandpa's Farmall putt-putting across his land. I look back at the mirror. I think, if that is you, Susana, then who am I?

YEARS LATER, WHEN I'm twenty-one and waiting out the weeks before graduation and my wedding day, I walk up a street of my Missouri college town, kicking through amber leaves, my breath feathery before me. It's an early evening in mid-fall; the air is heady with the smell of smoke curling lazily from fireplace chimneys. I pass houses with wide steps and deep porches displaying lighted jack-o-lanterns with silly grins. I pass windows radiant in the yellow wash of just-turned-on lights. I think, this is how my life can be: a sheltered street; a welcoming house with home fires burning. In one house, a woman gazes dreamily out into the evening, her hands busy at a sink the window frame keeps me from seeing. In a backyard, children carouse and tumble in a pile of fallen leaves. I continue on, thinking that at this time of day it is only women and children who make up the world. Where are the men? I ask myself, and I think of my own man. How we'll soon marry. How with him I'll have all the home I'll ever need.

I'M LIVING IN St. Louis, Missouri. I have two sons under the age of five. One of the things I like to do when I have time and extra money is to shop for antiques.

In 1967, I have a mission. I'm searching for a trunk, the flat-topped kind. I want to redo one and use it for a coffee table. This is something I've seen in magazines: you take an old trunk, clean it up. Top it with glass.

I'm discouraged because for a long time I've not found the trunk

I want. I have seen numerous round-topped trunks, and even some flat-tops, but none that appear salvageable. In one antique store, however, I spot just the one. Since the shopkeeper is watching, I am careful to conceal my delight, lest he hike up the price. The trunk is flat, all right, and well preserved. Brass fittings hug the corners, leather straps hang at the sides. The wood appears to be oak. Canvas stretches under the strips and it forms rectangles over the trunk's surface. The canvas is soiled but looks scrubbable.

How much for that one? I ask, too excited to play the I'm-just-looking game.

The shopkeeper scratches his head. There's a little problem with that one, he says. It's locked, and there's no key.

I give the trunk a close inspection. A brass keyplate shaped like a fat exclamation point is fitted into the front. There is a hole in the plate for a key to slip in.

No key? I say.

No key, he says.

It takes me a moment to grasp what this means. So how much, I ask, trying not to think what the trunk might contain. I try not to picture coins, jewels, priceless oils. I fear he might look into my head and see the treasures too.

Forty bucks, he says, but since there's no key, give me thirty and it's yours.

This time I pretend to think it over, but then I say, okay, and soon the man and I are duck-walking the trunk between us all the way to the car.

That the heft of the trunk is lighter than I'd imagined is not lost on me, but I smile brightly at the man as I lower the car's hatchback and stash my purchase away. Enjoy, the man says. He gives a wave and I drive off. I feel that somehow I've been had.

It takes me a week to pick the lock.

I'm careful because the keyplate is scrolled and I don't want to mar the design. Into the place where a key would fit, I introduce the tip of a knife, a screwdriver, a hairpin. I worm these around, holding my breath, waiting for the little click that will tell me I'm in. My children watch the lock-picking with an eagerness of their own, but toward week's end their interest droops. Down in the basement where I've set up shop, they ride their trikes, circling me and the trunk. Christopher, the oldest, pedals by. He says, Mom is a burglar. Burglar, burglar, Jonathon, the little one, repeats.

Between lock-pickings, I scrub the canvas, sand and revarnish the oak. I saddle-soap the leather, paint the canvas the color of oyster shells, polish the brass until it gleams. From time to time, I raise the trunk on end, hoping to catch the sound loot makes as it rolls from side to side, but there is silence each time I raise it. It's then I picture bills, of the one-hundred kind, stacked so tightly they cannot be moved.

In the end, it's a metal file that does the job.

THESE THINGS I remember from the time I was crazy. The man shames me. One of his women calls. She leaves a message like, Are you there? Was that you last night at two A.M.? Back then, spinning in the vortex of a storm, I'm certain I'm crazy. My, but I'm neurotic, I think, as I throw an entire roast-beef dinner clean across the room. Oh, it's so good to slip my hands around the steaming beef. I heave the roast football-style. It sails across the kitchen and thunks the wall above the stove. On to the green beans, these thrown in fistfuls against the window overlooking the sandbox. I pick up the rolls and send little buttered missiles flying. Then there's the gravy. I dip a hand into the bowl and fling. Arcs of brown gravy hang for milliseconds in air before splatting against pictures and cabinets, the cookie jar and pans. Gee, but I'm crazy. Splat. Oh, but I'm loony. Splat. Splat. Splat.

PICTURE THIS. AN August night. A party in a house high on a hill overlooking the river. I'm on a deck, but my eye is on the inside of the house where the man is holding court. Even out here, I can hear his patter. The man is very charming. He tells of a recent trip. He talks about women. How some women can't resist him. What's a man to do, he asks. From inside comes nervous laughter. I turn away from the sound, look out toward the river. La Ciguanaba strolls by. I know it's her. I've seen her in my dreams. Tonight she doesn't wail. Tonight she laughs and there's a manic edge to her laughter. I turn away. Close my eyes to the sweet sultry air. I lean back against the railing. There's a crack of splitting wood and the railing breaks free.

I plunge backward into space.

In that moment, I learn that falling is another word for letting go. The man broke me. Over and over and at every turn and I'd keep coming back for more. I ask you, Susana, what was it that kept me shackled to such a lot? My sons. It was for them that I hung on. But no. That's not the truth. On that night, when the end finally came, I simply broke away. From him. From them. From what had been my life till then. That night I saw, in a crack of inspiration, that salvation always surprises, that it can come on a hot August night when the farthest thing imaginable is that you can learn how to fly.

THE TRUNK. WHEN I pick the lock, I discover this: burnt-wood boxes for scarves and gloves; hand-embroidered handkerchieves, lace blouses, a silky slip; a small leather purse, a beaded bag. There are letters with two-cent stamps and postcards with one-centers, all postmarked in the 1920s. There are dozens of valentines, some from Ina and Imogene, some from Wilson and Carl, all addressed to Helen Miller. One card has scalloped edges and features an accordion-folded heart that pops out when opened and is, most sincerely, from Tashido Sonada. In addition, there are granny glasses and a lorgnette. A collection of thimbles. Seed packets of alyssum, dwarf petunias, blue-nosed peppers, regal pink larkspur. Wrapped in yellowed tissue is a square of silk, an inky background sprinkled with red and blue flowers. And two objects I save for last to describe: a smooth round river stone, a long elegant feather from a very black bird.

A RUFFLE OF calendar pages to denote the passing years. Here are some of the lessons learned: Shattered vertebrae can mend if you put in body-cast and scalpel time. Your children will come back if you're truthful with yourself and honest with them. A broken heart is a stronger heart and it can love again. In every life there are many lives waiting to be lived.

FOR YEARS AND years, I wrote at a desk and chair set in the corner of the den, the place used also for TV viewing and the guest room. A week ago, I moved the desk and chair into a studio only minutes from home. I lugged in a work table, eight bookshelves, a ton of books, the rocker I nursed my babies in, a borrowed single bed to make up into a couch, an old kitchen hutch. I hauled in the computer, the printer, a borrowed file cabinet, notebooks, workbooks, journals, reams of paper. I toted in posters and paintings and a bulletin board. Boxes of treasures hoarded over time.

I've made a second home for myself in the studio. This is my sacred space. Here, the placement of every object has been carefully considered. Here, no telephone jingles. Here, no TV assaults my sensibilities. The outside world is not welcomed here.

Against a south wall is the wooden hutch I've converted to an altar. The altar holds candles, sacred images, and statues. Formal photographs and snapshots, stones, feathers, crystals and such. But the altar's focal point is a small silver tray on which rests a cloisonné box embossed with birds. The box is lashed shut by a length of violet cord. At each side of the box a small white dove is positioned. Both birds' wings are outstretched as if the birds are landing, or maybe just taking off.

IN THE STUDIO, Helen Miller's trunk serves as a coffee table. After almost thirty years, I've held her treasures close because fragments of her story are contained in them, and I have honored that.

I think of my family. Objects passed from hand to hand. Stories told, others not talked about, but known. Dear friends and acquaintances recount stories of their own. In public places, behind walls and doors, voices rise. Stories told float up and are deposited into the trunk of our collective unconscious. We have only to coax a lock to set the stories free.

AT SUSANA'S GRAVE, I replace the lid on the shoe box, stretch the rubber band around the box to hold the lid in place. I look out across the cemetery. No gravestones dot the place and it appears to be more like a garden with its cherry trees and willows, its hedges and all that rolling expanse of lawn. Round bronze plaques mark the sites. They are set directly into the ground above each grave. The deceased's name is etched in an arc around the top of the plaque. Running along the bottom, also in an arc, is the date of birth and the date of death of the deceased. My sister's plaque reads: Susana Jean Ables Benítez. March 26, 1941–May 3, 1941.

In the center of the plaque is a small round opening. If you poke a finger into it, you can lift the plaque up and turn it over. A bronze vase surprises you, if you do. When I'd first arrived at the cemetery, I'd brought a bouquet of lilies of the valley for Susana.

Now the time has come to leave. I set the vase aside and reach into the space above the coffin that conceals the vase when not in use.

It as if I am reaching down into Susana's grave.

I take from the earth, which for fifty years has rested directly over her, a pebble, a hardened clump of soil, a few sprigs of pale greenery. These treasures Susana offers me. Today, they rest in the cloisonné box on my altar.

To reciprocate, I search in my purse and come up with a treasure of my own. I poke a hand back toward Susana's grave. Patting it firmly in place, I deposit my offering directly above her coffin. Some day, I will return for a second visit. When I do, I will bring more stories, more home views. Some day, we'll be together again, Susana and I. Only a few hand-spans of packed earth between us.

Our First Home

MAXINE HONG KINGSTON

IT HAS BEEN a month now since we moved into our own bought house. So far, we've been renters. I have liked saying, "Gotta make the rent" and "This much set aside for rent" and "rent party."

A renter can move quickly, no leases, forego the cleaning deposit and go. Plumbing, wiring, walls, roof, floors keep to their proper neutral places under the sun among the stars. If we looked at each other one day and decided that we really shouldn't have gotten married after all, we could dismantle the brick-and-plank bookshelf or leave it, no petty talk about material things. The householder is only one incarnation away from snail or turtle or kangaroo. In religions, the householder doesn't levitate like the monk. In politics, the householder doesn't say, "Burn it down to the ground." I had never become a housewife. I didn't need to own land to belong on this planet.

But as soon as we drove up to this house, we liked everything—the cascades of rosewood vines, lichen and moss on lava-rock boulders, moss-color finches, two murky ponds thick with water hyacinth, an iridescent green toad—poisonous—hopping into the blue ginger, a gigantic monkey pod tree with a stone bench beneath it, three trees like Van Gogh's cypresses in the front yard, pines in back, an archway like an ear or an elbow with no purpose but to be walked through, a New England–type vestibule for taking off snowy coats and boots, a dining room with glass doors, only one bedroom but two make-shifts, a bathroom like a chapel, a kitchen with a cooler—through the slats you can look down at the earth and smell it. And—the clincher—a writer's garret, the very writer's garret of your imagination, bookshelves along an entire wall and a window overlooking plumeria in bloom and the ponds. If I could see through the foliage, I could look downhill and see the (restored) hut where Robert Louis Stevenson wrote his Hawaii works.

What thick novels I could brood up here with no interrupting chapter breaks but one long thought from front to back cover.

We found two concealed cupboards, one of them with seven pigeonholes; the artist who painted in the garret must have stored brushes in them, or perhaps, here, a sea captain or his widow kept his rolled-up maps. The person who once sat at the built-in desk (with a Formica top) had written in pencil on the wall:

eros
agape
philos

Promising words.

But when we talked about housebuying, both of us thought about dying. The brain automatically adds twenty years of mortgage on to one's age. And *mortgage* derives from *mors, mortis,* as in *mortal. Move* was one of the first English words my parents ever used, such an early word I thought it was Chinese—*moo-fa,* a Chinese American word that connotes "pick up your pants and go."

Renting had begun to feel irresponsible. Our friend who teaches university students how to calculate how many grams are gained or lost on a protein exchange, how much alfalfa turns into how much hamburger, for example, told us about the time when each earthling will have one square foot of room. This friend quit the city and bought five acres in the mountains; a stream runs through his land. He will install solar energy panels and grow food, raise a goat, make the five acres a self-sufficient system.

We heard about a family who had all their teeth pulled, bought their own boat, and sailed for an island that's not on maps. If we owned a vacant lot somewhere, when the world ends, we can go there to sleep or sit.

Coincidentally, strange ads were appearing in the real estate section of newspapers: "Ideal place for you and your family in the event of war, famine, strike, or natural disaster."

The advantages—to have a place for meeting when the bombs fall and to write in a garret—outweighed the dread of ownership, and we bought the house.

The writer's garret is a myth about cheap housing. In real life, to have a garret, the writer has to own the house under the garret and the land under the house and the trees on the land for an inspiring view.

On the day we moved in, I tried walking about and thinking: "This is my tree. This flower is mine. This grass and dirt are mine." And they did partly belong to me.

Our son, Joseph, looked up at Tantalus, the mountain which rises straight up in back of the house, and said, "Do we have to rake up all the leaves that fall from there?"

At the escrow office (new word, *escrow*), we signed whatever papers they told us to. Earll read them after we got home, and so found out that this land had been given to E. H. Rogers by a Royal Hawaiian Land Grant. "We don't belong on it," he said. But, I rationalized, isn't all land Israel? No matter what year you claim it, the property belongs to a former owner who has good moral reason for a claim. Do we, for example, have a right to go to China, and say we own our farm, which has belonged to our family since 1100 A.D.? Ridiculous, isn't it? Also, doesn't the average American move every five years? We just keep exchanging with one another.

The way to deal with moving in was to establish a headquarters, which I decided would be in the dining room, a small powerful spot, surprisingly not the garret, which is secretive. The Headquarters would consist of a card table and a lawn chair, a typewriter, papers, and pencils. It takes about ten minutes to set up, and I feel moved in, capable; from the Headquarters I will venture into the rest of the house.

Earll assembles and talks about a Basic Kit, by which he means a toothbrush and toothpaste. "The Basic Kit is all I really need," he keeps saying, at which I take offense. I retaliate that all I need is my Headquarters.

Joseph's method of moving in is to decide that his bedroom will be the one in the attic, next to the writer's garret, and he spreads everything he owns over its strangeness.

As at every place we have ever moved to, we throw mattresses on the living-room floor and sleep there for several nights—to establish ourselves in the middle of the house, to weight it down. The night comes black into the uncurtained windows.

I attack the house from my Headquarters and again appreciate being married to a person whose sense of geometry is not much different from mine. How do people stay together whose eyes can't agree on how much space there should be between pictures?

The final thing that makes it possible to live in the house is our promise to each other that if we cannot bear the weight of ownership, we can always sell, though we know from fifteen years of marriage that this is like saying, "Well, if this marriage doesn't work out, we can always get a divorce." You don't know how you change in the interim.

Looking for Home

MARY MORRIS

SOMETIMES IN BROOKLYN, where I have lived for the past four years, the sky turns rosy pink with bands of lemon yellow and I'll know that I've seen this sky before. Perhaps I saw its muted pastels in a book read to me as a child. Or perhaps I am being wrapped in a soft blanket by my father who puts me in the car and drives me to a cornfield off County Line where from the hood we watch the sun set somewhere across the Mississippi. When I see that sherbert sky now as I walk home from the store, I am a child again, small, protected, my head nestled against someone I can no longer recall.

The doorbell rings interrupting my thoughts. I'm sure it is Darrell, the homeless man in our neighborhood who has been ringing doorbells for the past year or two, and I am reluctant to go. Every day when he rings my bell I have to listen to the long story he has to tell. About his mother dying when he was ten or twenty or three. About the room he is about to rent, the job he has just lost, the pair of pants he is going to buy. Sometimes he has a daughter; sometimes he doesn't. But he swears there's a ninety-year-old grandmother in Queens who can vouch for his character.

Months ago he gave me his grandmother's phone number, but I-put it in a drawer. I don't want to get more involved than I already am in his life. Darrell always wants money to rent a room or to go to his sister in Virginia or his brother in Baltimore. To hold him over until his welfare check arrives or because it was just stolen. He'll hold up a bus ticket and say he just needs the cash to get out of town.

There is always a long narrative, an explanation, a story about who he is and what he's been through and how if I'd just help him out this one last time, until he gets on his feet, he'll find the way to pay me back. Often I give him dinner and a small outside job to do, walking the dogs or sweeping the steps. In return, he has brought me gifts of apricot soap and a pink sweatband.

Yesterday he was happy, showing me that he had showered and rented a room with the money he was making from his job on a loading dock on Wall Street. He only needed ten dollars to make the down payment on that apartment, which I lent him. But today he is not so happy. In fact, he is crying, banging his head against the wall of my house. "I've done something bad this time," he tells me, shifting on his feet, wiping his eyes.

Then he tells me that he murdered a man last night in our neighborhood, not far from my house. "Miss Mary," he says, tears in his eyes, "I've never murdered anybody before, but this time I did. He jumped me and I'm still a man and I've got my pride."

Darrell stabbed the man in the neck with a piece of glass from a broken bottle and now he has to get out of town. The police are looking for him and this will be the last time I'll ever see him. If I lend him what he needs, he can escape. Later I will call the police and they'll tell me what I already know—that no one was murdered where we live—but for now I give Darrell the twenty-five dollars he asks for, plus ten for food, because Darrell is living proof of what it means to be lost, to lose your way. Darrell is delusional, but there is a poignancy about him for me. Like all good storytellers, he is searching for home.

I WAS EIGHTEEN when I left home and every year for many years I was sure I would return. My parents often asked, though not too often, when I planned to move back. And when things were difficult for me, during some hard years, they assured me there would always be a place for me. But I never went. I went for visits. For a week or so at a time. I went and stood by the shores of Lake Michigan where I'd been a girl; I stood with my back pressed to the tree which had been bent back in the wind along the bluffs. This was where I told myself my first stories. Half delusional myself, I was a pioneer girl defending her fort, a shipwrecked sailor, an orphan in flight. Or I was grow up and traveling in a strange land.

My tree is gone now, having eroded with the bluffs, and long ago someone put up a fence, but I still drive thirty miles out of the city whenever I go home and go to the end of the street where I grew up and gaze across Lake Michigan, which is where my life began.

When I think of Illinois, I am overwhelmed by certain sights and smells. My feet dragging through autumn leaves, ants crawling in the peonies, dead fish in the lake, the smell of fresh water, the crunch of the bodies of the seventeen-year locust. A line of girls walking to school in identical saddle shoes and camel's hair coats. The wind in my face as I bicycle home from school. Peanut butter and marshmallow sandwiches sitting on a plate. My mother frying chicken, oil splattering on her hands. S'mores and sweet, sticky fingers.

I come from the flat even plains of the Midwest where there is nowhere to hide. But I grew up along the shores of Lake Michigan, near the bluffs. I had this flatness behind me but the lake ahead and it was as if I grew up in two separate worlds. All the trails the Potawatomie made led to the lake and many of those trails are the roads people drive on today. I have read that the shores of Lake Michigan have as much magnetism as the North Pole. I have always felt charged, drawn as if by some physical necessity back to the bluffs of the lake where I was born. Pulled back and repelled at the same time. And I know that this land has shaped me.

TWENTY YEARS AGO I sat on the island of Crete, reading the *Odyssey*. Looking up from my book, it occurred to me that the *Odyssey* had grown out of a specific landscape—a world of islands and circles and things coming back, returning to where they began. Such a circuitous route and such an episodic narrative could only grow from a landscape of islands and water. Tolstoi could only have written his novels from the expansive Russian terrain; Austen required England with its gentle enclosures. Willa Cather needed the prairie, just as I need the northern shores of Lake Michigan. The mountains will produce different stories than the flatlands. Islands will tell different tales than vast expanses. Swamps are full of mysteries; lakes produce possibilities.

For a time I contemplated writing a doctoral dissertation on the migratory patterns of midwestern writers. Why all the renowned midwestern novelists—Twain, Dreiser, Cather, Hemingway, Fitzgerald, West—wrote their masterpieces upon leaving home. Each migrated east or west before they could write their great novels of home. I wondered why it was that southern writers—Flannery O'Connor, William Faulkner, Eudora Welty, and more contemporary southern writers such as Richard Ford—write essentially from their front porches, the houses and streets where they were born.

Southern writers stay put whereas midwestern writers have to leave. The South, of course, has a deeper culture, more grounded historic roots. But the Midwest, for me anyway, is more a place of childhood—frozen ponds, forests, and ravines. Christmas cards make me think of home. The Midwest, as a friend once said, is a good place to be from. It is a good place to remember.

STORIES FROM HOME reach me and I guard them, keep them in a safe place like precious gems. The love affairs, the divorces, the face-lifts, the aging athletes who drink too much. The wife of a friend dies of breast cancer. My neighbor, now ninety-seven years old, sits alone in the house where she's always lived, deaf and blind. A scandal has occurred—a strange suicide on the Chicago Northwestern Railroad tracks, the result of a love triangle. I grew up with everyone involved. Illinois follows me around like some bad deed I've done, like some stalker I can't shake.

GOETHE ONCE WROTE that all writers are homesick, that all writers are really searching for home. Being a writer is being on a constant search for where you belong. In my own life I have found this to be so. Once I was living in the West and I met a man who came from a valley called Puerto de Luna, or Gateway to the Moon. He had lived in that valley all his life and so had his ancestors before him. He took me on a tour—the sinkholes, the decaying abode churches, the path Coronado took as he searched for the City of Gold. He showed me the house in which he and his father before him had grown up. This landscape was his vision. This geography was in his blood.

But my family are Jews, Russian Jews at that, and we have been called the wanderers of the earth, though our wandering was forced upon us not by nature, but by hardship and necessity. A purple plant with aimless reaching tentacles has been named after us, the Wandering Jew. My own family, which lived for troubled centuries on the steppes, mingling with Tartar blood, and in the farmlands of Ukraine, has been scattered like seeds and what is left dissipated in deaths, lawsuits, family feuds. It is only by chance that my tribe has landed where it has. I have heard of a psychological disability whose symptom is restlessness. The inability to stay put. The need to move on.

I have spent hours pondering where my own final resting place will be. If I were to die tomorrow, I have no idea where I'd go. A family plot in the Midwest, a place on the East Coast near the sea, or ashes sprinkled on a forest floor, tossed along the Lake Michigan shore or perhaps a Long Island cove. I have a fear of fire and do not want to contemplate cremation even in death, but this seems an easier choice than to pick one place where I must lie.

Recently my mother informed me that there is no room for me in the family plot. A distant cousin with no particular claim has taken my spot. So my choices are limited even more. Besides, do I want to lie beside them for eternity? It is more like me to be tossed in the wind.

I have always admired those who know when they have come home. A woman once told me this story. She had been driving along a country road when her car broke down. She knew no one in the area so she got out and walked. She walked until she came to a long driveway lined with trees and she could not see the house. She followed the driveway until she came to an old boarded-up farmhouse with green shutters and a wrap-around porch. The porch had a swing that looked out over the valley. She sat in that swing and rocked until the sky turned orange and the sun was setting. She knew that this was where she belonged. She has lived there ever since, some thirty years now.

But I am not that way. I have lived in too many places. I've seen too much of the world. At times I want the desert, other times the sea. I long for the changing seasons, but cannot say no to a Caribbean breeze. Sometimes I want the feel of asphalt under my feet; other times I long to breathe country air. I think I will never stop somewhere and say this is my home. This is where I belong.

Often I have dreams that take me home. I am in a jungle or on a train. In the jungle, surrounded by parrots and monkeys, it begins to snow or the train makes an unscheduled stop or the car I am in breaks down. Always it begins to snow, billowy, thick flakes, and I feel myself shrinking, growing smaller. I am in a snowsuit, my hands in mittens. Tracks appear, human tracks, and I follow them to my white house on Hazel Avenue and I go home. Up to the front door but I always wake up before I'm inside.

The house I grew up in was sold long ago to a man who has

married a woman half his age. An American flag flies on the lawn, white wrought-iron furniture sits on the front porch. They have built a cage for a dog that howls into the night. I know this because when I am in Illinois I visit my neighbor and from her kitchen I spy upon my former life. I try to envision someone else sleeping in the room where my father tucked me in. Where I read my first books, whispered my first secrets to girlfriends on the phone. Now a stranger lives inside that life while I wander, still searching for the tracks that will lead me home.

MY HUSBAND AND I go to Paris for a getaway vacation but walking the streets of Paris—Saint-Germain, the Place Vendôme—my thoughts turn to home as if some centrifugal force is always pulling me back there wherever I roam. The words of Elizabeth Bishop come to me here from her poem, "Questions of Travel": "Should we have stayed at home and thought of here.... Should we have stayed at home, wherever that may be?"

It was my mother who first brought me to Paris some thirty-three years ago. It was she who made me learn French in school and take lessons with Mr. LaTate, whose head jerked uncontrollably to the side whenever he spoke. Later I spent my junior year abroad here. It has taken me twenty-seven years to return to Paris after my junior year abroad. I believed then what I do not believe now, that you could actually get away. "You take yourself with you," my mother said, when she put me aboard the SS *France*. It was a long time before I understood what she meant.

Perhaps I can only come back now because I have been able to go on. Like a lover you can meet for coffee only years after the affair has ended. In Paris my husband and I sample Camembert, café au lait, good Bordeaux, fresh baguettes and croissants. My husband has never been here and I am his guide. In the mornings we sit in cafes and write in our journals. We move without encumbrances, without itinerary, dog, assignment, or child.

At first I am adrift, lost in this open-endedness. I cannot seem to function without the contradictory demands that are my life. I am having trouble with this intensity, this concentration of emotion. I have grown accustomed to feeling my life tugged in a dozen different directions. Now I have only myself and my husband and the quiet garret where we are staying. What has drawn so many to Paris—its cafes, its meandering sidestreets, its pause—is what suddenly frightens me. I prefer New York with its frantic pace and real assaults to this place of inner risks.

Though we wanted this trip for so long, I miss my daughter, my garden, my dogs—what I have come to call my home. I don't, however, miss the disarray of my life. Why can't I put things away? I wonder. Why can't I throw anything out? And why on this trip did I misplace things—a raincoat, my backpack, and twice our tickets and passport—along the way?

The first time I left our tickets and passport in the handicapped bathroom stall in Newark Airport. When it was time to board, I realized what I'd done. Racing back, I pounded on the door as an elderly woman smoking a cigarette locked herself inside. "I'm sorry but I've left some papers in there," I shouted. "Don't worry," she called back to me, smoke rising from the stall, "I'll flush it."

Perhaps I didn't want to go anywhere. Perhaps it is getting harder and harder to leave home, "wherever that is," as Bishop says. We walk along the Seine, past Nôtre Dame. A plaque on a house catches my eye. A quote from a letter written by Claude Claudel to Rodin—"Il y a toujours quelque chose d'absent qui me tourmente." There is always something missing that torments me. On a whim, as if you can recapture something lost, I look up my French "brother" in the Paris phone book and to my surprise he answers.

In 1967 and 1968 I lived in Paris. I recall it as the loneliest year of my life. I lived in the thirteenth arrondissement on the Rue Xantrailles in a large middle-income housing complex with a woman named Joelle and her son Jean-Michel. Joelle had lied on her application to have an American student live with her. She said that Jean-Michel was only fifteen when in fact he was nineteen and I had just turned twenty. I thought it might be nice to have a young, French brother, but when I arrived at the apartment on the Rue Xantrailles, I was greeted by a young man with silky blond hair, smoking a pipe. We had rabbit stew for dinner and I was sick the entire night.

Jean-Michel was always home studying as I was and he spoke to me at all hours about Proust and politics and dreams. We walked through Paris on rainy days under an umbrella and ate in Vietnamese restaurants and almost made love but never quite. We smoked our first cigarettes together and listened to melancholy Serge Reggani songs as the sun set on the balcony of the apartment where we lived. Then Jean-Michel decided he couldn't date the girl living in the next bedroom so he broke up with me, if you can break up with someone with whom you share a bathroom.

A few weeks later he brought home a girl named Valerie who had brown hair and doe-like eyes and seemed not very interesting to me. But Jean-Michel shut his bedroom door and played music to her on a long Sunday afternoon while I smoked and listened to Piaf and stared at the gray Parisian sky. Afterwards I began to wander. Trips to Italy to visit my college roommate in Naples, to London to see an old friend. Then Jean-Michel went to America and I went to Jerusalem.

The story grows complex here. A lost address book, a handsome student who offers me lodging, a near rape, a night in the bus station. There is even a Greek Orthodox priest in this part of the story who finds me weeping on my suitcase and leads me into the old Arab quarter to a hotel called the Casanova. I can still see the beard of the priest, the long cross dangling from his neck. I left the Casanova to have breakfast and sat down and ordered an omelette. The young man across from me picked up his newspaper and the headlines read, "Martin Luther King Assassinated: Civil War in America."

I asked to read his newspaper, my hands shaking, and the man asked me to join him. He was a rabbinical student from Los Angeles and we dropped acid on the road to Haifa and climbed into the hills where the prophet Elijah had preached. Then he followed me to Paris where the May 1968 Revolution was taking place; the Sorbonne was flying the flag of anarchy and a two-story poster of Mao hung in its courtyard. We fled Paris, leaving on one of the last planes out of Bourget.

When I reached Illinois after being away a year, I brought with me this young man named Elliott, English for Elijah, the prophet of God. I lit up a cigarette in front of my father and said I planned to marry Elliott and watched my father's face cave in. He still called me Pigeon then, a name he'd given me as a child because I was so restless, always fluttering around. Now anger cracked his face.

The young man flew to Los Angeles and I followed him a week later, my father driving me to the airport asking if this was what I really wanted to do. I arrived in Los Angeles as Robert Kennedy's body was being transported down Olympic Boulevard. Then Elliott and I dropped acid in Disneyland. We took a ride that carried us into the crystal of a snowflake and I saw myself surrounded by snow and then growing smaller and smaller, more compact, as we traveled that snowflake.

Afterwards on the Sabbath I burned a cigarette hole in Elliott's mother's bedspread and she wept not only over the hole in her bedspread but also over our smoking on the Sabbath; I was exhausted so I flew back to Illinois. At dinner in a restaurant my father asked me if I wanted a glass of wine or a screwdriver and for some reason I started to weep. I wept in the restaurant bathroom and I wept in the car home and I got into bed and wept for two weeks.

When I stopped crying, my house was sold (this had been long planned by my mother) and we were getting ready to move into an apartment in the city in a building my father's architectural firm had designed. On the day we were to move I woke to the sound of my father trimming the hedges and mowing the lawn. The new apartment wasn't finished and doorknobs kept falling off, locking us in empty rooms. My brother and a friend were arrested at the Democratic National Convention in Chicago for handing out bread and the police broke their fingers.

I returned to college to help my roommate through an abortion. And my dog who had always lived in a house in the country barked when she was left alone. The neighbors complained so my mother gave the dog to the checkout girl at the A&P and my childhood was gone.

I LOVED MY house, the one I grew up in. I loved its white walls and wood trim, its sturdy white brick and picket fence. Its green shutters and big lawn. When our house was built, the carpenter brought us the head of a deer he had killed. We stuffed that deer head and put it on the wall of the basement playroom. For my whole childhood I lived under its glassy stare.

Once we visited the house when it was being built according to my father's design. I was very little but I can remember the smell of sawdust and fresh paint. I stood with my father, blueprints in his hand, as he examined the structure of our house: patting the beams, trying to shake an archway.

My mother wanted a closet somewhere and my father stared at his blueprints, shaking his head. When they weren't looking, I found a razor blade. I had never seen a razor blade before so I drew it across my skin, cutting a line along my forearm. Blood flowed down my arm, soaking into the unfinished wood. My parents screamed, horrified, and the bloodstain was ignored and eventually carpeted over. But this thought has always been a comfort; a part of me remains.

FITZGERALD WRITES IN *The Great Gatsby,* "When we went out into the winter night and the real snow, our snow, began to stretch out beside us and twinkle against the windows, and the dim lights of small Wisconsin stations moved by, a sharp wild brace came suddenly into the air. We drew in deep breaths of it as we walked back from dinner through the cold vestibules.... That's my middle West—not the wheat or the prairies or the lost Swede towns, but the thrilling, returning trains of my youth and the street lamps and sleigh bells in the frosty dark and the shadows of holly wreaths thrown by lighted windows on the snow."

I had a dozen friends and we walked to school together every morning and we walked home every day and often at lunch as well. We walked, dragging our feet through the leaves or huddled against the cold. The best time to walk was in the fall because we could collect horse chestnuts along the way. In inclement weather we prodded our parents to drive us, but it was difficult to secure a ride. Sometimes we got a ride in the rain, but we always walked in snow. Cups of hot chocolate and a warm entrance way awaited us as we stopped to pick up the next friend. I can still feel the burning of my frostbitten skin, the numbness in my toes, the gnawing sense that we were going to be late (and we often were).

Once we had an ice storm—a silver thaw, it was called. We had an unusually warm January; then it began to rain, a steady heavy rain as the temperature fell slowly into the night and we woke to a world glazed over, covered in ice. We were children so what did we care if the power lines were down and a disaster had been declared. We put on our skates and skated in the streets. My mother kept a fire blazing in the hearth and for three days we lived like pioneers.

Recently I attended my thirtieth high-school reunion. It was held at Rainbow's Bar and Grill in Highwood, Illinois—the town of a thousand bars because the rest of the North Shore is dry. Rainbow's is owned by the first boy I ever loved who loved me back. He proved it thirty-four years ago by throwing eggs at my house (which my father made him clean up) and by blushing and ducking down corridors when he saw me coming his way. We went to dances together called "Moonlight and Roses" and our parents drove us as we sat in the backseat. Then he got his license and we'd drive into the farmlands and down to the lake, his arm wrapped around my shoulder.

He had aged well and something between us was still there when we said hello. Dennis came from literally the other side of the tracks. His father owned a moving and storage company and I have a picture of my parents at a costume ball dressed as Rafferty Moving and Storage movers. Among the many things Dennis said to me that night was that he loved my house. It was a house I knew I'd never live in, he told me, but I was always happy there. I loved your basement; I loved sitting on the back porch. I still drive by it, he told me, and say to myself, that was Mary's house.

THREE YEARS AGO my husband and I bought the house I live in now—a sturdy brownstone in a historic neighborhood of Brooklyn. In the backyard an oak tree soars that was probably planted when the house was built. I wanted a home, I told my husband when we began looking, a place of my own.

Before moving into the house I dreamed it was on a golf course and full of flying fish that kept smashing themselves into the walls. I didn't want to buy this house, though when I saw it I knew that I would live here. I wanted to cook in its country kitchen, gaze at the oak tree out back. I wasn't sure if I would call it home because home for me comes out of a place of memory, not geography.

IT IS DIFFICULT to say if my childhood was a happy or an unhappy one. My parents will say it was happy but I was moody. I might say other things. Anyway it is too complicated to go into here and besides I don't really want to. I read once that Harvard did a study and found that creative people recall their childhoods as unhappy even if they were happy. It is true my father had a temper, I will say that, and it was unpredictable and my mother has her own complexities, but he is ninety-three now and my mother is eighty-three and I've made my peace with them.

Recently I sent my father a copy of a new manuscript in which there is a character who goes to sleep as a child without stories or song, and my father wrote me an eight-page critique in which he reminded me that I never went to bed without a story or song.

It's fiction, Dad, I told him.

My father is a good storyteller and I was raised on his tales of the prairie and Hannibal and Chicago. When his baby brother was born my father raced across a vast stretch of prairie to tell their nearest neighbor. Now that prairie is Rogers Park. He remembers being tied to his brothers when the snow came and the wind howled so none of the brothers would wander off in the blizzard and freeze.

When he turned eighty, he called and said, "Mary, I just had this dream. I dreamed about the night before we moved to Hannibal where my father had taken over a dry goods store. That night before we moved, I was maybe five years old, I slept in a big feather bed between my aunt who was very fat and my uncle who was very skinny and they put a cover over me and I was squashed between them and I couldn't breathe. I never remembered that night before we moved to Hannibal until just now," he said. "When I woke up from the dream, I could breathe. You're a writer; maybe you can understand. My whole life lives inside me."

AFTER SPEAKING WITH the police, who confirm my suspicion that no murder occurred last night in my neighborhood, I rifle through drawers and locate the slip of paper Darrell gave me with his grandmother's phone number. Though I have had the number for weeks, I only choose to call it now.

A young girl answers. There is a TV in the background, a morning game show. I ask for Mamie Jones and an old woman answers. When I mention Darrell she starts to cry. She tells me that he went to private school and college. Where did it all go wrong? Why won't he come back and live with her and his sister and nieces? Why doesn't he get cleaned up and find himself a job? He was doing fine until his mother died just last year.

A few days later I run into Darrell in the street. He is a bit sheepish as he explains how he lost the money I gave him so he couldn't leave town. I tell him no one was murdered and he seems visibly relieved. By dinnertime he has rung my bell and I offer him a plate of food, some clean underwear, and five dollars. He says he has a new job at Key Food and promises to pay me back with his first paycheck.

I close the door on Darrell and wonder where he goes in this city when he is not making his rounds. Shutting my eyes for a moment, I can see myself driving aimlessly through my town, down the alleyways where I used to drive, knocking people's garbage cans down, past the train station where the loafers hung out and Leo's Delicatessen and McDonald's by the highway and Strike and Spare where sometimes Dennis and I lingered after the bowling was done. I can see the sun through cornfields, the moon over the lake. I can hear the water lapping as I follow the Indian trails.

Then I shake myself back into this house and this world and this place where I now live and return to the stories I write—the ones that take me home.

Outside In

KATHRYN HARRISON

"DO YOU THINK maybe you could get a chest of drawers?" my husband asks. He is not being sarcastic. For the first time in my life I face the task of filling an empty house. It's a second home, a place to be used only during the summer and for weekends, but still we need furniture on which to sit, sleep, eat. We need shower curtains, wastebaskets, wine glasses. We need a refrigerator and a stove. Though I am in my thirties and the mother of two children, though the summer house will be the fifth home I share with my husband, I have never before had to consider all that goes into a home. What is required, and what is comfort. So far I've shown little aptitude for the task. I bought appliances and beds, a dining table, chairs and a couch, but then inertia set in. Or is it paralysis?

MY IDEA OF home—like many of my ideas—begins with my grandmother, who raised me and who was herself raised in Shanghai almost a century ago. "Forty coolies!" was her abbreviated reference to life in Shanghai, where she and her sister were cared for by British governesses on an estate in the city's International Settlement. My grandmother would shake her head as she spoke the words, *forty coolies,* spoke them with wonder, not embarrassment. At the turn of the century, Shanghai was home to many Europeans, expatriates who created their own little Englands and Germanys and Frances and whose households were served by Chinese labor that was unimaginably affordable. To illustrate, my grandmother would tell this story: One day, an old groundskeeper fell from the top of a ladder while pruning a tree on the family's estate. As he fell, he grabbed for the ladder and pulled it over with him. The head gardener came running from the greenhouse, picked up the ladder, dusted it off, and left the groundskeeper where he had fallen. When asked by my great-grandfather why he would pick up the ladder and not the man, the head gardener shrugged as if the answer were obvious. "Man old, ladder new," he said, and he bowed and returned to the greenhouse. In China, life was cheap, and, my grandmother would have added, dirty.

"The filth! The filth!" was the second most frequent of her invocations of the country in which she lived until she was seventeen. In an age without vaccines or antibiotics, in a place where outbreaks of yellow fever and cholera and typhus were common, dirt meant danger. From my grandmother's childhood home, "night soil" was collected by one of the under-coolies (out of forty, one was designated for shit work, literally) and carried out to the street in the morning to be collected by an ox-drawn wagon when it passed on the boulevard. These wagons, called *kongs,* took human excrement to the rice paddies where it was used as fertilizer, guaranteeing the contamination of waterways and the spread of cholera. My grandmother's only brother died before his second birthday, and according to family lore what he died of was dirt. What killed the little boy was not so much meningitis subsequent to a teething infection as it was having been born in China, where, even as the only son of an Orthodox Jewish family, he died uncircumcised because my grandmother's mother once saw black crescents of dirt under the Shanghai rabbi's long fingernails and was so frightened by the sight of them that she decided to wait until she could take her son home to a rabbi in London.

Seventy years later, if you were to put a plate of Chinese food before my grandmother, she would vomit. Traveling with me through Chinatown in the back of a taxi, she covered her eyes. And if she didn't readily offer her hand in greeting to an Asian person, it wasn't racism or snobbery—although my grandmother could be an imperious woman and did not question her right to any of her wealth or possessions—but a fear of contagion that never diminished. Her family bought ivories and porcelains, silk rugs, jade, cloisonné; they decorated their homes in Shanghai and later in London, Nice, and Los Angeles with these things. But that was the extent of their interaction with China. Much of the food they consumed was imported from England. Even the cows and the chickens were brought to them over the oceans—a long journey for livestock. "Buff Orpingtons," my grandmother said the chickens were called. She spoke the name with rapture. "White and beautiful!" she said. What she meant, I knew, was *white and clean.* Vegetables were grown on the family's own land and scrubbed before eating with carbolic soap, a poisonously antiseptic detergent made from coal tar. Decades later, when washing anything she considered particularly dirty, my grandmother would whisper the words "carbolic soap" to herself and would shake her head with longing. Clearly, nothing could be dependably laundered without it. For me, a child born in Los Angeles in 1961, the words had a quaintly ridiculous ring to them; and yet just last winter, when our children succumbed to a particularly virulent and tenacious stomach flu, I found myself collapsed, despairing, over our washer. I knew that if only I had carbolic soap, the germs would perish.

In Shanghai, my grandmother remembered, she once glanced into the kitchen window of a hotel and saw a Chinese pastry chef patting a piecrust flat on his bare, sweating belly—an unsavory way to prepare food in any time or place, but one made more so, my grandmother assured me, by the incontrovertible "fact" that Chinese bathed only once a year. Her own ritual of hygiene, to which I listened from outside her tightly closed bathroom door, included such vigorously loud scrubbing and frantic splashing that it sounded as if she were trying to lather up a tiger rather than her own assumably cooperative limbs.

Every day that she lived in China, my grandmother learned that a home was erected in opposition to the world around it. That was the kind of home she made in Los Angeles, that was the home in which I grew up. When she married another displaced British subject, a man whose mild personality was eclipsed by her fierceness, she made a life with him that confined rather than supported, and that invited rebellion from, my American-born mother. In an inspired flight of defiance, my mother found my father, who was raised in El Paso, Texas, and who had a Baptist preacher for one grandfather and a Methodist circuit rider for the other. My parents were as ill-suited to one another as might be imagined, and their marriage was short-lived. When it was over, my mother gave me to her mother as the replacement daughter she believed would buy her freedom from my grandmother. "You were supposed to ransom me," she explained once, during a rare attempt to explain the history of her troubled relationship with her mother.

In that the same woman raised us, neither my mother nor I experienced the typical Los Angeles childhood. My grandmother emphatically disapproved of almost all things American and encouraged me to form myself in contrast to the children around me. American children stayed up too late, talked back, ate what and when they pleased, accompanied their parents to adult functions, wore vulgar clothing, watched too much television, chewed gum, went to bed with wet hair, slouched at table, slacked off on schoolwork, etcetera—all of which was the fault of their permissive parents.

My grandmother, whom I called Nana, was a vertiginous, intoxicating combination of extremes. At once strict and indulgent, she always put me to bed early, but only after I'd eaten a caramel custard or some other treat she had made especially for me. When I was ill she was gentle, and I remember her sitting by my bed all night when I had an asthma attack. But this patience was elicited by weakness. She tolerated no insubordination, and I remember, too, that when I "back talked" she slapped me across the face. She was not a nice woman, nor a kind one. She was passionate, and in turn she inspired strong feelings in everyone who knew her. Because she had great reserves of tenderness for orphans and strays, both human and animal, I suspect she loved me all the more for having effected my abandonment.

At the time of my birth, my parents were both eighteen and had been married for only a few months. My mother brought me and my father home to my disapproving grandmother, who immediately launched a campaign to oust my father. He planned to be a preacher, and a preacher, Nana argued, would never be able to support my mother in the style to which she was accustomed. Having raised a spoiled, dependent child, my grandmother knew this threat would frighten my mother. When my mother displeased or thwarted my grandmother, Nana hardened herself against her own child, and until my mother was dying, I never saw my grandmother give her more than the most perfunctory of kisses. Instinctively, if not consciously, I knew there was danger at the hands of someone so potentially ruthless. Afraid that someday I, too, might fall from grace, I ended by making myself my grandmother's servant. But that was later. First I was her pet, and her audience.

"Tell me a story," I'd beg. "Please!" The world my grandmother created around me was so expansive and exotic that as a young child I didn't feel my imprisonment in her home. Nana's memories of Shanghai were vivid; her life had included such adventures as traveling from Paris to Har Bin, China, on the Orient Express. She'd married late, at forty-two, after years of tantalizing indiscretions, many of which, she hinted, involved aristocracy. Her father's disapproval of her companions made her a target for blackmail by the chauffeur and the butler. Nana had a past that was easy to romanticize, and she would pull my head into her lap and stroke my hair as she told me stories, many of them frightening and tragic and funny, often all at once. Her taste for detail was gothic, her language strong. I remember how her eyes narrowed in assessment on the afternoon she decided that I was at last old enough to hear the stories that involved sexual indiscretions. It was the same winter, I believe, that she let me have coffee in my milk at breakfast. My grandmother had been the center of attention at every party for all of her life, and as an old woman she happily squandered her narrative gifts on me. "I wish I'd been a writer," she'd say to me, sighing at the end of a story, and not until I was much older did I realize that she always intended to seduce me with her words. My grandmother kept me jealously to herself and never planned to let me venture far beyond her skirts.

To encourage immunity to the outer environment, I was sent to a prep school whose motto was "College begins at two." At that age I was taught to offer my right hand to the school's headmistress while plucking at the side pleat of my gray jumper with my left and bending my knees: in other words, at two I learned to curtsy like a proper British child. By the time I had graduated from high school, I'd worn successive sizes of the same navy wool uniform blazer and white oxford shoes for fifteen years; I'd taken six years of Latin, eaten countless Bird's custards and Peak Freens and scones spread with Tiptree Seville Orange marmalade. I'd hidden a decade's worth of smoked tongue sandwiches from my classmates and made my way through thousands of Sunday dinners of roast beef, Yorkshire pudding, boiled potatoes, and green beans cooked until they were gray. I spelled color *colour*, said tomato *tomahto*, and my grandmother could be assured that I was not an "American brat."

Of course, increasingly, I longed to be exactly that. At school I was as desperate as any other child to fit in and so being American seemed essential. Brattiness, too, offered seductions to a child raised on didactic British storybooks that featured such cautionary heroines as rude Polly, stigmatized by large Ps and Qs sewn on all her clothing, one for each Please or Thank You she forgot to say. I saved my weekly allotment of television for Friday night's *The Brady Bunch* and *The Partridge Family*, because the children in those shows seemed quintessentially American. Based on reports from classmates, *Love American Style* and *Laugh In* would have served me even better, but, as my grandmother made clear, those shows were so vulgar that they were broadcast late at night when decent children were sleeping.

I spent a lot of time alone as a child. Too much. The characters in the books I read were too real to me, as were the people in the old photographs in the boxes upstairs: my grandmother and her sister and cousins in Shanghai and in Hong Kong, picnicking on the shores of Lake Como in the Italian Alps, swimming in Nice. There were others of my quiet grandfather in Germany's Black Forest, fishing in British Columbia (where his brother had become a Royal Canadian Mounted Policeman), and working as a timekeeper for the railway in Alaska. He told me about "Six Mile Mary," an Eskimo woman he'd known, and in Mary's picture, she was wearing a sealskin coat and smoking a long-stemmed black pipe. All these people and places were both fantastic and real, and increasingly, the place from which I understood them and myself to be was *Not Here*.

IT IS ONLY as the mother of young children, and thus the supervisor of play dates and sleepovers, picnics and trips to the zoo—most of which my grandparents were too old and frail to provide—that I begin to perceive my own childhood with any perspective. I realize now what a willful and lonely and fanciful child I was and that I regarded myself as two halves *other:* the known, deliberate otherness based in my grandmother's past, and the otherness of my father's side, too dangerous to discuss. I saw my father only once as I was growing up, and knew nearly nothing of his life. If I heard his name, it was usually in the context of one of the relentless, vicious battles between my mother and grandmother, arguments that, until I was five and my mother moved out, went on without interruption.

I was frightened by the fighting, and to escape it I withdrew inside myself. I took the ready example of my grandmother's home that opposed the world around it and learned to make a similar home within myself, an interior landscape into which I could disappear with increasing ease. This flight was aided, unexpectedly, by my religious instruction. On weekends I was remanded to my mother, who insisted on Saturday ballet classes and on Christian Science Sunday school, an indoctrination that stressed mind over matter with chilling effectiveness.

This is me, this is you. This is me, this is you, I would whisper to myself when I sat at the kitchen table, eating breakfast. Or perhaps I only thought the words: a first prayer, a determination to draw a line between myself and the women I loved. Christian Science doctrine ennobled my desire to ignore anything in my environment that troubled me; it raised denial, that most primitive of human defenses, to a form of worship.

If it became dangerous later on, living inside my head served me well as a young child. I was happy when immersed in fantasy, in storybooks, and later in textbooks. And I loved school, where I was encouraged to be self-contained and where I grew increasingly agile at expressing myself in words, especially those written on paper. It was in school that I began to create another home—abstract and lacking in material dimension but utterly manipulatable by me—on the page.

WHEN I WAS eleven we moved from our increasingly shabby big house to a smaller one in a less expensive neighborhood. The move had been postponed until my grandparents could no longer pay their property taxes, let alone keep the place in repair. My grandfather had invested money unwisely, and my extravagant mother, who could always solicit a loan as a surrogate for love, had been wasting it with a vengeance. The new house was, I thought, ugly. It lacked the imaginative details of the one we left, one my grandparents helped design and that included hidden closets and stairs and leaded glass windows made from the round green and blue and brown bottoms of old bottles. In its whimsy, the first house encouraged escape, but the second was just another landscape. To pay her debts, Nana sold many of her Chinese carpets and antiques and replaced them with more practical, serviceable things. Having long been spoiled by eccentricity in both family and furnishings, I found my new terrain's ordinariness itself confusing. For a year after we moved, I awoke bewildered each morning; I didn't recognize my bedroom with its blue carpeting and one too few windows. The worst of it was the wallpaper chosen by my mother, with climbing vines of blue roses. *Roses are not blue, roses are not blue,* I thought as I sat up in bed, another in a growing litany of negatives that guaranteed safety: *not here, not them, roses not blue . . .* My dislike of the wallpaper allowed me to take pleasure in its destruction, which came courtesy of the cats.

At one time during my adolescence, my grandmother had seventeen cats, and even when the feline population dipped to eight or ten there were always two warring factions: an older generation with full run of the house and a younger one corralled in two rooms— my bedroom during the day, and the den during the night. These rooms were separated by a staircase, up and down which the cats were herded with the incentive of a meal awaiting them at their destination. The runs were dramatic, if uneventful. Skirmishes between the older and younger packs were infrequent, but my histrionic grandmother screamed a lot anyway. "Oh Schatzie! Oh Jessica! Tomita! Come here! No! No! She'll kill her! Oh! She's got her by the neck! . . ." In my role as grudging shepherdess, I sometimes drove one herd into the other, hoping for diversion, but no more than hisses were exchanged. The cat wars were largely imagined by my combative grandmother— perhaps in my mother's absence the house was too quiet for her.

By the time I was fifteen, the blue-rose wallpaper was hanging in shreds around three "cat trees," from whose highest perches cats and kittens rappelled down what was left of the drapes, using their nails to catch threads and swing to the floor. There were two litter boxes and, most difficult to explain to an outsider, bits of raw meat were stuck to the door frame, the chairs, and any intact wallpaper. For the cats my grandmother ordered pounds of beef heart and lambs' kidneys from the butcher and picked it up fresh every other day, and she cut the meat by hand into little square pieces. Raw organ meat has an adhesive nature, and she got the stuff onto her hands and sleeves so that she unknowingly anointed whatever she subsequently touched with flecks of raw meat that dried and stuck with surprising tenacity. If I tried to peel one off the wall, the paper came with it.

My grandmother and I began to quarrel with one another, about the cats and about her fears that I was going to "be like Cecily." Cecily was my grandmother's older sister, whom I resembled in bookishness and an early disinterest in boys. Because Cecily had been a lesbian, my grandmother interpreted intimate female friendships as dangerous and interrogated me rigorously as to what I did over at friends' homes. Our inevitable fights often ended in a kind of draw in which she would scream, "I took you in! I took you in! You ungrateful girl! Don't you understand, I took you in!" To which I'd respond, "Why don't you throw me out, then! Just throw me out! I wish you would!"

We said these things but (or because), obviously, there was no place else I could live. The first time my mother had an apartment that included a room for me was the year I went to college. I used the closet to store clothes I no longer wore, a gesture we both understood as polite. My mother, who never remarried, was a woman so obsessed with a material sense of order that her apartment was tidy to a degree I found unwelcoming. For years she had been locked in a relationship with an alcoholic who never divorced his wife (with whom he had a son my age, a male mirror to my fury and alienation), and superficial order was what my mother needed to shroud the waste of her youth and beauty and intelligence. I see this now, if I did not before when I was treading carefully over carpets that bore vacuum tracks, looking up to see myself in a mirror polished so mercilessly that my reflection seemed not so much a face as a composite of smudged mascara, stray hairs, and misplaced freckles. I slept at my mother's only a few times. I remember that after she'd gone to bed, I'd lock myself in the bathroom, sit on the counter with my feet in the sink, and squeeze clogged pores on my nose and chin until they bled.

I WENT TO college with all the things I cared about packed in an ancient steamer trunk that had once held my grandmother's belongings on her many overseas journeys. The trunk was faded and battered, and I liked what it seemed to announce about me—that for me the vanished past was as real as the present, the Shanghai of my grandmother's wonderfully wrought tales perhaps more real than the city in which I was born, the Los Angeles of sound stages and false fronts. Inside the trunk were books, bedding, and clothes. When I graduated from high school I was released from fifteen years of wearing a uniform, the same thing every weekday, with a few supplementary clothes for weekends and evenings, and when I began college I was so absorbed with accessorizing my body that I gave little thought to the room around me. I was a junior before I'd acquired the typical coed's posters and rug.

I took three years off between college and graduate school, time spent largely in Los Angeles, where both my grandfather and my mother were very ill, dying—he of digestive problems that had worsened with his advanced age, she of breast cancer. It was a time given to memorizing rather than to grief, which makes its own appointments. I stayed near home, trying to learn all I could of what—who—would be taken from me. I wanted to be left with at least an accounting of what was lost. But my deathwatch required a form of self-imposed anesthesia. What I felt penetrated only so far; I didn't allow it to touch me, hidden, as I was, deep inside myself.

One day I came home from the hospital to have tea with my grandmother, but when I entered the kitchen, Nana didn't have the kettle on the stove, there were no cups or cookies on the table. She held a sheaf of papers in her lap. "Why didn't you ever show me these!" she said.

"What are they?" I asked.

"I found them in your desk. Years' worth! And you never showed me one. Why!"

I took the papers from her when she handed them to me: twenty-four honor-roll certificates, one earned each quarter of every school year from the seventh grade through the twelfth. "I don't know," I said.

But I remembered bringing them home from school and, without showing them to anyone, hiding them in the drawer of the desk where I'd earned them. When the stack got too high, I threw out the thick envelopes in which each had been presented to me. My school life—the life of the mind, of writing papers and earning the grade-point average that ultimately made me valedictorian—was private. I did my homework alone, behind closed doors, and when my grandfather offered me rewards for straight As, I turned them down. The report cards, the certificates, and the letters of acceptance to all the colleges to which I applied (had Nana looked, she would have found those in another drawer) were documents of the life I guarded, defensively, against my family.

"I'm surprised you went through my desk," I said. "You shouldn't have."

My grandmother put her face in her hands and wept.

IN GRADUATE SCHOOL I met the man I would marry, though when I arrived in Iowa City I was still preoccupied with the past, not thinking of the future. I went to the University of Iowa's housing office to pick up a list of possible rooms to rent. The first, owned by Mrs. K, a widow, was listed at $140 a month, furnished. It was at the top of her small house on Ronald Street, and its ceiling sloped steeply over the twin bed on one side and the chest of drawers on the other, so steeply that you could not prop a mirror on the dresser, nor could you sit up in bed to read. The bed's frame was iron, its mattress very soft—getting out of it would mean rolling out, toward the middle of the room where the ceiling was higher. The room's molding, baseboard, and doors were all painted mustard yellow, a choice inspired, I concluded, by the wallpaper, whose design of black and green and orange and yellow paisley was so hideous that it made my shredded blue roses, still hanging in my grandmother's house, look almost pretty. The walls and ceiling of the room were covered in sickening, bilious swirls printed so poorly on the paper that their black outlines missed their colored middles by as much as a quarter of an inch. To look more than passingly at this two-dimensional rendering of nausea, or of desperate depression, induced eyestrain and then vertigo.

The toilet and shower were on the first floor, which Mrs. K. shared with the downstairs boarder, a slight Korean woman studying engineering. And there was, Mrs. K. showed me, an auxiliary toilet (she called it a "stool") in the spider-infested basement. Set in the very middle of the cracked concrete floor, among cobwebbed boxes and broken, mildewed chairs, it had a plastic shower curtain drawn around it for privacy.

I agreed to take the room, and thus to share a tiny kitchen and eating area with A., the other upstairs boarder. A. had the nicer bedroom, painted blue with a large window alcove and hanging plants. The weekend I moved in, A. was visiting her family, so all I could glean of her was whatever was suggested by the few personal effects in the room. The bookshelf by the bed, neatly made, tucked tight, held a King James translation of the Bible, eleven self-help books, one

Adele Davis cookbook, a variety of analgesics, and a box of pink, scented Kleenex. On the back of her door hung pajamas and a plaid bathrobe. When A. herself arrived, she told me she had been an undergraduate for seven years, so far, without declaring a major. I soon learned that the work that absorbed A. more than her studies was the maintenance of a detailed health log, a daily, sometimes hourly journal of her premenstrual symptoms and a condition newly highlighted by American doctors: TMJ, or temporal-mandibular-joint syndrome, which A. felt was contributing to her incapacitating headaches.

A. and I did not become friends, but this was not simply because we shared no mutual interests. I wasn't ready for any form of intimacy. The fall I came to Iowa was that of my mother's death after three years of widespread cancer, years that provided the greatest intimacy we had ever shared: one of bedpans, catheters, sores that would not heal, oxygen tubes, and so much medication that we followed a written dosage schedule for months without memorizing it—there were too many pills. My mother's humiliating and painful disintegration required enough morphine and psychological armor that although we touched more often than before, we rarely spoke.

After it was over, I lay on Mrs. K.'s metal bed and looked at the paisley wallpaper and observed that for the first time in my life I lived in an environment that reflected how I felt, at least in those months following my mother's death when I was as flat and as dizzy, as blearily black and brown and green and yellow as the terrible walls around me. I went to classes, did the work required of me, socialized halfheartedly with other students, walked up and down and around the few streets of the college town, and came home and closed my bedroom door behind me.

I lived in Mrs. K's upstairs room for almost a year before I ventured into the world beyond it, an emergence that began, tentatively, at night, while A. and Mrs. K. and the Korean girl slept. I made tea on the burner and drank it at the little table placed between the refrigerator and the sink. If there had been an oven I would have done what my grandmother forbade, set it to broil and rested my cold feet on its open door. I examined the food A. kept on her shelf of the refrigerator. Sometimes I tasted what she brought home from her parents' house, slices of turkey and cold potatoes left over from family dinners. I'd peel away an inconspicuous shred of flesh and chew it slowly. Rather than go downstairs or into the horrible basement, I peed in the sink, and by that feral gesture, I made the communal kitchen mine. I felt a mean delight in doing something I knew would horrify A., whom I had begun to hate for losing herself in obsessive worries about her body. Would I have had more compassion for her suffering were I not myself enduring the tenth year of chronically relapsing anorexia, of my own secret notebooks given over to calories consumed and exercise accomplished? "Ten years," I'd whisper to my reflection in the mirror, trying to frighten the woman I saw, the one who had spent a decade within the careful confines of self-denial, within a deliberate internal architecture assembled to protect and contain. I hated A. because she provided a vision of myself more valid than the one I saw in Mrs. K.'s mirror, its silver back peeling off in circles and offering a fragmented image no more reliable than that cast back by a pond's ruffled surface.

Can you find yourself in a mirror the way you can in the eyes of those around you? When, on our third date, my future husband came up Mrs. K.'s stairs, his expression of dismay helped me to really see the room in which I lived. He spent one night on the awful bed, and the next day he handed me his house key. We never discussed our living together before I moved in any more than we talked about marriage or parenthood before they were done. Certainly we loved one another, but we had loved other people. Our bond was that we recognized each other, completed one another. I knew with whom, if not how, to make a home, and took it as a betrothal when we shelved our books together and discarded the duplicates.

*   *   *

WE MOVED FROM Iowa to New York with a small U-Haul truck filled with boxes of books, a bed, and two desks and five thrift-store chairs—all of which were worth less money than the amount we spent to transport them. Their value was that they were ours, they were what we shared. C. drove the truck; I flew ahead of him to find an apartment in New York City. The place I chose was in Brooklyn and included a tiny garden in which C. grew tomatoes and basil, cucumbers, squash, and even a few token ears of Iowa corn. The garden was crowded, but inside, the rooms were only half filled by our things. A friend donated a couch, and we bought a table and bookshelves at IKEA, a superstore of Scandinavian furniture, affordable because mass-produced and unassembled. The apartment never lost its haphazard, junky quality, and we lived in it for only two years before we married and then moved.

As we sat together at C.'s parents' dining table, addressing envelopes for wedding invitations, his mother suggested that I register for gifts, a chore I put off because I thought I was uncomfortable suggesting to friends and family what they might buy for us. Or was it the deeper discomfort of having little sense of what made a household? When a good friend realized that I might never accomplish the trip alone, she forcibly accompanied me to Bloomingdale's. I'm not efficient in department stores, especially not in furnishings. Vistas of beds and sofas invite stupor. I could easily sink into their cushions, fall as deeply asleep as Dorothy in the narcotic embrace of the poppy field separating her from Oz's Emerald City and from what she longs for: to find a way home. Beyond the beds were housewares, table after table set with empty plates and glasses and looking to me like a judgment, a sneering jibe at someone who for so long had refused food, especially in company. If what I ended up selecting proved useful, it was only that I responded, zombie-like, to sensible promptings.

Once we were married, C. and I moved into a brownstone that

my grandmother helped us to buy and that included a ground-floor apartment in which she lived for the last two years of her life. Her furniture, shipped east from Los Angeles, overflowed its rooms into those above, making it unnecessary for me to have to fill up a house; this amounted to another reprieve.

PARENTHOOD NECESSARILY TRANSFORMS people, and when I became a mother I was able to create, slowly, a room around my daughter. It began with her crib, which looked entirely out of place in the room that adjoined our bedroom, a room that we had supposed might be a library or study. When our daughter was born, the walls were decorated with skulls I'd collected from desert road trips through the Southwest—deer, ram, and cow—the shelves filled with grown-up books. In the middle of the large, shabby Oriental rug, the crib, festooned with mobiles and stuffed with pastel toys, appeared as an unexpected mirage of babyhood. Even I could see that it looked alien, adrift. Long before she could talk, our daughter expressed her clear dislike for the skulls, and I took them upstairs and replaced them with framed illustrations of Babar.

Some parents find themselves recreating what they cherished from their childhoods. The rest of us helplessly react against old hurts. Bit by bit, I decorated our children's room as my own childhood bedroom had not been: whimsically. Increasingly we've given our house over to our children. They eat at a table at which I used to eat only holiday meals, sit on chairs on which I sat only if they were covered with a towel. My grandmother used to keep her dining table covered with fitted felt-backed pads, and if I am allowing our children to destroy its finish, it's not so much in keeping with any plan of retribution as it is irresistible. My permitting our children to use the house and its contents is my reentering the space of home—a vicarious passage back to rooms in which a grown-up standard of behavior was held over me during my childhood.

As for the summer place, it still isn't finished. In apology for the missing chest of drawers, I bought a twelve-pack of plastic hangers at the market. What clothes we can't hang or throw over the pole we drop on the closet floor. I leave my underwear and nightgowns in my suitcase, as if to announce what I feel, that I've only just arrived. The children, who are not yet tall enough to reach hangers, each have a box to hold their clothes.

I suppose I could have gotten dressers at IKEA, where we got the beds, but I didn't want all the furniture to match; I thought they would look like motel bedrooms. At least, that's what I told C. afterwards, but at IKEA I was speechless. I fought the dangerous desire to lie down in the guise of testing the firmness of a mattress, and I tried to complete one of the little white cards we were given at the entrance to the immense warehouse. It looked like a miniature golf tally and came with a stubby eraserless pencil, but was intended to be filled with the stock numbers and descriptions of the items we wanted. C. asked me questions, simple ones like, "How about this?" which I met in glazed silence. When I could manage it, I shrugged my shoulders. At some point C. took off in frustration, alone. I sat in a chair the color of oatmeal and watched over the children, who used the bunk beds as gym equipment until he returned and I gave him my score card, unchanged from when he last looked it over.

The one room of the summer house that is fully outfitted is the one in which I write. It has a bookshelf, it has a table and a chair. A neighbor, after visiting several times and noting that the walls were still unadorned, invited me to select those I wanted of her paintings, stored in her basement. Sensing my inertia, she escorted me home with three, her favorites, and watched as I dazedly drove nails into the plaster. "How about here?" she said, trying to guide my hammer to the blank white wall of the study that my chair faces, but I resisted. I hung her picture on the wall I never see, the one at my back. Though I have learned to provide what my family needs, I myself still live in my work. I make the page my home, just as I did when I was a schoolgirl writing book reports and history essays. I carry drafts out to dinner, to movies, even to the market. The box that holds a novel in progress has become like a snail shell—the physical manifestation of my thoughts in which I learned to live so long ago. I sleep and feed on words, walk through words, sit and lie among them. When I travel, I open my folders on planes and trains and in unfamiliar rooms in countries whose languages and food are unknown, and I feel at home, immediately comfortable.

There are dangers to interior castles, I know. I find my thoughts often return to the one frank conversation I had with my mother in the last year of her life. In trying to explain why she had always been so remote, my mother told me that inside herself she had discovered a fortress, something she had built brick by psychic brick to defend herself against my grandmother. "The problem is," she said, starting to cry, "I don't know the way out. I'm stuck inside myself."

What were they made of, my mother's internal walls? An obsession with order and cleanliness, with polished surfaces and tasteful things placed just so. Hers was a system, like my own anorexia, that delivered safety in perfection, but that necessarily, purposefully left no openings. And what of a writer's walls of language? Must I remain vigilant to make sure that what I've built inside myself continues to be a home and not a trap? Or is it safe to assume that if words can make a wall, they can also make a door, the passage out, or, for readers, in?

The Seven Month Home

FRANCINE PROSE

I HAVE RETURNED to that house so often in my dreams that I sometimes wake up surprised to remember how briefly I actually lived there. I lived in that house in Red Hook, New York, in the Hudson River Valley, from the tenth of March to the fifteenth of October, 1978. The precision with which I remember those dates, after almost twenty years, must surely have something to do with the clear sharp corner my life turned during the short time I called it home.

It was an old house, pretty, though you might not think so as you veered round a curve on a country road through a cluster of frame houses, your headlights shining directly into the living-room window. White clapboard, early nineteenth century, a plain functional two-story rectangle paralleling the road, it was divided down the middle into a two-family dwelling. Howie and I (and later our son Bruno) lived in one half; the other half was occupied by an elderly furnace repairman and his wife whom we almost never saw except when he built huge bonfires in our common backyard—which he did disquietingly often.

Inside, the house was full of what I now know are called

charming period details, features that inspire decorating magazines to interview homeowners on what was saved and what was lost during restoration projects. Everything, it seemed, had been saved, which was a kind of miracle after the decades the house had spent as a strawberry farm (the sign for the roadside fruit stand was still in the small barn in our backyard) and some recent tough years as a rental property for groups of Bard College students.

There was a double parlor, an elaborately carved and mirrored wooden mantelpiece, wideboard floors covered with paint, an enormous primitive kitchen with windows on three sides. But the house's glory was the wallpaper, perfect and uncorrupted and different in each room: museums of Victorian cabbage roses, yellow daisies, delicately flowered patterns, elaborate ribbon borders, perhaps fifty or sixty years old. Many of our friends (this was an era when people dropped by and stayed for a week) reported sleeping more soundly than they had in years because (they said) the guest-room wallpaper was the same as the paper in their childhood bedrooms; obviously this couldn't have been true for all the people who thought so. None of the floors were level or anywhere near the same height: you walked up and down steps to get from one room to another.

The house's antique systems were considerably less charming and considerably more of a problem. It was comforting to live so near a furnace repairman, even one whom we suspected of being a bit of a pyromaniac. And Howie kept the rest of our house together, more or less. Before he patched the hot-water heater it shot steaming geysers across the basement. Once, as I turned on a light, I touched the switchplate and—the next thing I knew—I found myself on the other side of the kitchen.

The electric shock worried me more than it might have if I hadn't been pregnant. Naturally, I couldn't help thinking that enough voltage to blow me across the room might not have been good for the baby.

* * *

THAT MARCH WAS harsh, for the Hudson Valley. There was a foot of snow on the lawn when we first drove up to the house we'd rented, sight unseen. We sat in the cab of the pickup truck that contained all our earthly possessions. We were parked outside the freezing-cold house into which we were moving. I was wearing a raccoon coat. We were waiting for the delivery truck to bring oil for the furnace.

It seemed impossible: how warm we'd been, just two months before. We'd spent the fall in India, where we'd made an extremely strenuous and almost nonstop marathon journey from the mountains and lakes of Kashmir down to the ancient temples on the beaches south of Madras. I'd been feeling fine—quite normal, really—throughout most of the trip, so I assumed that the reason I wasn't menstruating must have had something to do with the stresses of travel. When I got back to New York, I thought it might be a good idea to check with my doctor—who told me I was pregnant. Four months pregnant, in fact.

Part of the reason I hadn't figured this out on my own was that I was so emaciated—from the heat and the diet and travel. And for one terrible week, soon after we got back to New York, there was some question that the antimalaria pills I'd been taking might have had what the doctors called, chillingly, a "teratogenic" effect on the "fetus."

When it turned out to be unlikely that any such damage had occurred, we were so exhilarated and relieved that we somehow forgot to worry about the many disturbing and chaotic aspects of our lives: we had no house, no jobs, no prospects, only a Siberian husky and a few possessions that we'd boarded with friends when we gave up our part of a rental loft in Manhattan. We had hardly any money, less than a thousand dollars left over from a book advance. My parents were barely speaking to me, they were sure I was ruining my life, having a child with a poor artist and not with some doctor whose steady income would allow me to continue writing my little novels

in some degree of security and comfort. They were absolutely unmoved and unimpressed by the fact that we were reckless, romantic,
young bohemians in love.

Now that I'm a parent, I have more sympathy for their fears
than I did then; and now, as someone who is more often a host than
a guest, I have infinitely more compassion for the tolerant friends
whose hospitality eventually ran out. We overstayed with friends in
a Manhattan loft, then drove down to Florida and overstayed with
friends there, then took bumpy Route 81 up to Binghamton, New
York, and stayed with Howie's parents in their cozy trailer, until we
realized we couldn't keep this up, this constant moving and over-
staying. By that time, even *I* couldn't fail to notice that I was really
pregnant.

We asked around and learned that a former landlord—we'd
spent a summer in the Hudson Valley—had a house he was trying
to sell, and which he was willing to rent.

Our landlord was a member of a community of artists, many of
whom are now Buddhists, but who were at that time firm believers
in Werner Erhardt's Sensitivity Training, in property acquisition, and
real estate investment. We were allowed to rent the house for almost
nothing, provided we understood that it could be sold at any minute.

So the house's surface plainness and profound mechanical problems seemed oddly reassuring. Because for much of the time we lived
there, few prospective buyers came by—and only one ever returned
for a second look.

For an attached house, right on the road, it was so cut off from
the world it could have been a tiny island, floating in midocean. On
that first day, ours were the only footsteps in the snow as we trudged
back and forth, lugging kitchen equipment, pillows, my typewriter,
Howie's art supplies, a portable TV, a few books, and a bed, getting
so involved in our work that we were startled by the screech and
belch of the oil truck arriving.

The furnace fired up at once. Amazingly, a hot wind gusted from the grates in the floors and ceilings. We thanked the delivery man. We closed the door. We sat on the floor. We were home.

IN THE COURSE of those long, lazy months, I got to know the bedroom wallpaper intimately: its pale gold background, its flower buds so small they turned into flecks in the distance, abstract pinpoints of carrot and brown beneath a border on which a gold rope looped improbably between golden chalices. The bed was like a chrysalis, in which I hibernated and waited, alone or with Howie, dozing, sleeping, watching TV talk shows, reading long Victorian novels and *People* magazine. I listened to the blues: Big Mama Thornton, Irma Thomas. I thought that the baby kicked more when I played Robert Johnson and Blind Willie McTell.

I wrote at a desk in a sunny corner room with a white-painted wood floor and white and yellow wallpaper. On the bumpy pickup-truck ride from New York to Florida, I'd started thinking about a novel about a butcher who wins his wife in a card game—a book that would eventually turn into *Household Saints.* I wrote quickly, but then I got horribly stuck because I was approaching a section in which, I knew, a baby would be stillborn, and, like many writers, I have always worried that what I imagine and write would come true.

Actually, I was writing about a pregnant woman driven into a state of superstitious dread by the superstitious terrors of the community around her. Perhaps not coincidentally, this was the time when newspapers and TV reports were full of new research results on all the things that could harm unborn children; every day, it seemed, scientists were finding out the negative effects of some deceptively innocuous substance—wine, coffee, antihistamines, antibiotics—that I'd consumed during my first trimester.

I found an obstetrician in Poughkeepsie, a doctor out of a vintage TV series: sixtyish, handsome, old-fashioned, kindly, reflexively patronizing to his women patients and comfortingly unimpressed by the scary new research. For better and for worse, his every gesture and word communicated the fact that he'd been helping women have babies for almost forty years.

Once a month we drove forty minutes south to my doctor's appointment in Poughkeepsie. I would try to imagine what it might be like, driving in the same pickup truck with a baby in a car seat between us, and Howie would try to imagine driving that road if I went into labor suddenly and we didn't have forty minutes.

If our life in that house seems like a dream, perhaps the most dreamlike part was that any single sustained dream could have combined such anxiety with such intense langorous sweetness. Everything about our daily existence felt stupified, bludgeoned, and at the same time dramatic, romantic, and thrilling. We were in love in the way that feels like a two-person trapeze act, and the fact that I'd gotten pregnant seemed like a triple flip, some daring stunt never before attempted . . .

Much of what we did in those days had a certain in-your-face aspect. I dressed in oversized men's tuxedos for contrast with my long hair and huge pregnant belly, or in an antique embroidered satin skirt that I'd bought in India, a brilliant pink, full and clearly made to be worn, with only slight adjustments, through the whole nine months. At a garage sale, I bought a set of throwing knives and got reasonably good at hitting a target on the barn wall because I liked the idea of myself as a knife-throwing pregnant woman. All that bravado was necessary to help us not worry more than we did, especially when the landlord came by to collect the rent and, as gently as possible, reminded us that the house was still on the market.

I remember the seven months we lived in that house much more clearly and in sharper detail than whole years I have spent since then, certainly whole semesters. I recall that we ate lots of mussels, because they were so cheap, no doubt ignoring warnings about the toxins concealed in their bivalve hearts. I remember who visited, and who didn't, and the eruptions of drama that from time to time blew holes in the tense, thrumming surface of our daily lives.

One night a bat flew into the house; we trapped it in a spare bedroom, from which it mysteriously vanished. And when we went to search for it, we discovered that some previous occupant had hung a crucifix just inside the spare-bedroom window.

One night strangers knocked on the door, two tall men who were vaguely acquainted with our landlord. They were Buddhists, just down from a retreat in Vermont; against our better judgment, we asked them to stay for dinner. It was a horrid evening; they were both raving drunk. One of them was very hostile and kept making remarks about deformed newborn babies. The other had been a sculptor, he had given art up for the Buddha, and as way of thanking us for dinner, gave Howie all his sculpting tools, crates of hammers and chisels, blocks of marble, and slabs of wood.

DOWNSTAIRS, IN THE house in which we live now, in which we have lived for seventeen years, an hour southwest and across the Hudson from our house in Red Hook, is a framed drawing that Howie began on the night our son Bruno was born. It's a copy of an old photo, a male and female nude, recognizable but blurred to strikingly contrasted areas of dark and light. Around the edge of the drawing, like a sort of frame, is a series of numbers. I'd gone into early labor; Howie was timing my contractions, writing the minutes down, and the numbers got sloppier, more and more frantically scribbled as the intervals between them diminished.

As it turned out, we had more than eighteen hours to make the forty-minute drive to Poughkeepsie. Bruno's birth was long and difficult, but he was fine, we both were fine, nothing I'd done had harmed him. The astonishing surges of passionate love we felt for this child were so intense, ecstatic, and all-consuming that it wasn't until I got home—after two days in the hospital—that Howie thought to tell me: a man had come by to see the house and returned the next day, and it seemed fairly likely that he might be planning to buy it.

Bruno was a week old when the buyers stopped over again: this time, two pleasant young men who had been attracted by the house's low price and charming period details. They obviously felt guilty about buying a house out from under a couple with a newborn baby. But then, we also felt a little guilty about not telling them about the serious plumbing and wiring and heating problems we'd promised the landlord we wouldn't mention.

After that, things must have happened quickly—though it all seemed to take forever. My parents fell in love with their new grandson and offered to lend us the money for a down payment on the house we had found to buy on the other (less tony and expensive) side of the Hudson: a house with seven acres, a guest house, and a large barn that Howie could use as a studio, a place that fit our needs so well that we have lived here—comfortably, happily—for almost two decades.

ON THAT SECOND moving day, our second in seven months, we needed a twenty-foot van to transport the possessions we'd accumulated during our brief stay at the Red Hook house: items we'd bought at garage sales, things we'd been given by friends and relatives who'd taken pity on our situation, the substantial wooden sculptures Howie had made with the tools he'd got from the renegade Buddhist.

And of course now we had a baby between us in the pickup, the same truck in which, a few months before, we'd been easily able to transport everything we possessed.

In the months that separated that simple arrival and complex departure, those months transfigured by youth and hope, joy and terror, when everything was overwhelming but nothing seemed like a problem, we were kept busy waiting—and getting ready. It was as if we were practicing to have real lives, a real home, a real family—and as if somehow, during those months, real life sneaked up and found us.

Our lives had formed around us, as if we belonged to some species of coral, or a family of sea creature whose very being is indistinguishable from the dwelling in which it lives. That house was our first real home together, the first place to which our son came home. And in my dreams, when I walk through those beloved familiar rooms, I feel certain that we still live in them, and that the crooked, charming, crumbling old house has always been our home.

From Chicago to Chickawaukee

ARLENE HIRSCHFELDER

I GREW UP believing a house was not a home unless it had at least one room that looked like a small library. I did not realize at the time, so overwhelmed was I by the power emanating from my father's library, that it was not only the books that made this room a place of both imprisonment and enchantment. What I did know, even at age five, was that the only room my father lavished any attention on was his library and that he paid more attention to his books than he did to his neurologically impaired patients in his downtown Chicago office. His patients knew they were never to doubt his diagnoses and his books never talked back or questioned his judgment.

Twice, in the two homes I grew up in on Chicago's South Side, I watched my father, the son of a Russian carpenter, take up fragrant boards of hardwood and build, shelf by shelf, from floor to ceiling, an altar to his beloved books. He placed each tome carefully in its place as if it were a jewel being set in a priceless bezel. Later, as a college student and then as a mother of two children, I saw him repeat the same ritual in the two upscale apartments my parents lived in that faced Lake Michigan. There, as in many sacred places, both book-lined apartment libraries faced east toward Jerusalem as befitted the shrines my father had created.

My father lived in his library world seated at his mahogany desk in a thronelike carved wooden chair with curlicued legs. Here he was king. He barricaded himself behind the desk with neat piles of medical texts, medical journals, medical articles, stacks of correspondence, and patient files. An arm's length away, two telephones, a dictaphone, and a radio tuned to a classical music station stood ready for his royal touch. Medical books filled easily half the library. Bound in burnt umber, dark brown, and black leather, these hefty four-inch-thick volumes contained descriptions of every part of the body. Books about hearts and lungs lined up with texts about brains and the central nervous system. Countless books explored epilepsy, Parkinson's disease, and multiple sclerosis.

Silence reigned in my parents' homes, except when my father, who loved the sound of his own voice, was lecturing us or talking endlessly to patients and other doctors on the telephone. The only other sounds in this kingdom were those of classical music—symphonies, concerti, and arias. Along with his photographic memory, he could identify pieces of music and their composers after hearing only a few bars. But he was, unfortunately, tone deaf to my emotional needs. He silenced us at the dinner table, our only opportunity to talk to him each day since he left for hospital rounds before we got up for school and came home late from his office every night. Discussion over the roast beef was a no-no since the only opinion that counted was his. Although neither we nor his patients were allowed to question him, it was obvious that their grand mal seizures and brain tumors would always take precedence over our problems.

Many days after school, when my father was doing hospital rounds or was at his office, my sister and I amused ourselves in the library. She liked to thumb through the medical books of anatomical illustrations (she later became an artist), but it was the history books that drew me like a magnet. Stretched out on a sofa in his room, I studied the great Chicago fire or the history of Rome. My father loved history, and after he retired from private practice, he began a second career as a historian. His pièce de résistance was creating a permanent hall of fame of the "founders of neurology." He installed more than 180 photographs in the corriders of the University of Illinois Neuropsychiatric Institute. Putting the exhibit together connected him in some way to the greatest thinkers in his field over the past 350 years, but I think his fascination with neurological greats stemmed in part from his drive to be crowned in history along with other neurologists like Alois Alzheimer and James Parkinson who discovered the degenerative diseases named after them.

When I wasn't reading one book or another in history, I liked to look at my father's volumes about Judaism. Once in a while, I traced the grooves in the ornate gold-embossed cover of the Bible or touched the silver filigree covers of old prayer books. I discovered that in the Judaica section, my father had made a place for a blue-violet velvet bag, embroidered with silver Hebrew letters, that once held my grandfather's *tallit,* a special prayer shawl worn by Orthodox Jewish men. I figured that if I gave him gifts involving medicine or Judaica, the two shrines at which he worshiped, I might reap some approval and a portion of the attention he bestowed on his medical practice and religion. One Chanukah I gave him a small Vermeer-like oil painting of an old Jewish man wearing the same traditional blue-and-white prayer shawl as the one folded inside the bag. Another time it was a small decoupaged wooden plaque with an image of the Greek physician Hippocrates, his idol, glued onto it. I spent hours breathing in the sulfuric fumes of one lit match after another as I burned the edges of the wood and then shellacked the picture so many times my father could see his reflection in it. He seemed to like the plaque, but he never saw my reasons for making it.

As I had subconsciously absorbed other ideas from the ruler of the house, I realize now that I swallowed this message early, surrounded by all those books: that spelling and reading and writing were just about as important as breathing and eating. In his study, my father was always writing an article for a medical journal. Like all good teachers, my father reinforced this message into my adulthood. Whenever his resume was updated, the latest entry added by a patient secretary, a copy, thirty pages long and listing hundreds of articles, arrived in the mail. It was only a matter of time before I started to mimic this behavior. Before I turned thirty years old, I had written a master's thesis and my first article in a social-studies journal; for twenty-five years, I realized recently, I had sent him copies of each new book by me, waiting in vain for his kudos.

It was not until I earned undergraduate and graduate degrees that my father was willing to trust his kingdom to me. On my first visit back to Chicago, he steered me to his library, pointed to a stack of medical articles at least four feet high, and commanded me to file them alphabetically, by author, in three-ring binders. It pleased my father that I could sit for hours hunched over articles with titles like "Generalized Cortico-reticular Epilepsies: Some Considerations on the Pathophysiology of Generalized Bilaterally Synchronous Spike and Wave Discharges" and "Nonictal Symptoms Associated With Severe Electroencephalographic Epileptiform Abnormalities" and put each in its rightful place. It pleased me that I could finally show off my academic skills.

As is required with some shrines, my sister and I made pilgrimages to our father's library throughout our childhood. Unlike the hajj, the at least once-in-a-lifetime pilgrimage some supplicants make to Mecca, our journey was nightly and obligatory. Every night, before we went to sleep, we traipsed to the library. The ritual consisted of kissing his majesty good night; he sat there fully dressed on his throne and we, his little princesses, dressed for sleep in nightgowns our parsimonious mother bought off racks in sample shops set up in people's basements, paid court to him. Once when we were little girls, we went off to sleep without our usual show of affection. He woke us up and ordered us out of bed. Standing at attention, we were informed that we must never forget to place that kiss on his cheek.

When we were young and worshiped our father, the ritual seemed relatively easy, relatively effortless, and relatively innocent. But when we became teenagers, and less inclined to revere him, kissing dad every night became more onerous—since we were not allowed to startle the ruler while he was doing his correspondence, reading or writing some medical article, or dictating letters at his desk. Such an interruption set off an explosion and his whiplike tongue left scars we could not see, but felt years later. At all costs, we tried to avoid disturbing him, so we invented a variety of intricate maneuvers to get Our Father to acknowledge our presence at the threshold of his study so we could enter it and kiss him goodnight. Sometimes we waltzed around the entrance like dancers at Roseland; more often we stood silent but with pounding hearts outside the library door. After the kiss on his cold, lifeless cheek, we fled his territory, glad to exit without a fuss. The days became weeks, then months, finally years, and they multiplied into decades. But even as grown women, we still made the nightly pilgrimage to the library. We still pressed our now grown-up mouths onto his still-rigid cheek and then raced out, relieved of our duty. It never occurred to us to revolt, but once in a while we had a reprieve. When our father was angry at us, he went into a deep freeze for days and we were persona non grata in his chambers. During that time, we were freed from our nightly obligation.

Our mother accepted the quotidian ritual as she did everything else. She never uttered a word or questioned his dicta. She never tried to intervene. She never explained his motivation for turning a kiss into an obligation. Unlike my sister and me, my mother rarely went into my father's room. During my childhood and adolescence and in later years, when I returned to visit, she did invest a great deal of energy in trying to extricate him from his inner sanctum. Every night I remember her calling to him from their bedroom, pestering him to leave the library and come to bed. Her attempts inevitably led to a tirade and I pleaded with my mother to stop irritating the king. He was determined to stay up half the night no matter what she said, and I detested listening to him berate her. Once, however, when I was about ten, she finally lost control. In the library. While he sat on his throne. Whatever fury was bottled up in my mother finally exploded. Frantically, she grabbed piles of cream-colored files and flung those sacred medical histories every which way as if she were destroying the limbs and torso of someone she hated. Papers tattooed with my father's inky black script floated to the floor, and then my silent and powerless mother fled the room, the house, her rage, and me.

During my childhood and adolescence, I never saw my mother read. When she was not cooking or cleaning, she preferred to spend time with her plants. Year round she nurtured dozens of plants with an innate expertise that trained horticulturalists might envy. With her plants, my mother was queen and they her happy subjects, and in her domain there was no tyranny. Her touch worked magic and plants grew, blossomed freely, and had babies, and the babies had babies, all of which she replanted. My father never showed any interest in her green thumb. At the time, neither did my sister or I. But many years later, I studied pottery one year at Washington University and although I never mastered the wheel, I created several hand-built clay pots glazed in celadon green to hold my mother's ferns and cactus plants. I have no way of knowing—my mother has been dead for two years and a new queen reigns in court—but I hope that those pots still contain her beloved greenery.

Outdoors, during spring and summer my mother grew beds of red roses, pink and white petunias, and yellow snapdragons. Once she showed me their snapping "mouths," prying open the two lips that gave these spiky flowers their name. But like the snaps whose lips are usually sealed, so my mother sealed hers too. She talked soundlessly to her flowers, caressed them with her hands, and they responded and bloomed. She touched her flowers more than she touched her children. She never told me how to grow the flowers that gave her companionship. I learned that myself after my husband, children, and I settled into our first house in New Jersey. Indoors, I set celadon-green glazed pots filled with arrow and spider plants and sansevierias in a good southern exposure and doted like a parent on rubber trees and hanging baskets of pothos. In my own library, I plowed through books about annuals, perennials, roses, bulbs, trees, and weeds and taught myself how deep to dig, what plant food to add, how much to water, and what words to say.

Researching garden books in my own library reminded me of my father's study and my passionate need to know about things. During the school year, I was a fixture in the elementary-school library. I can still picture myself taking Anna Sewell's *Black Beauty* off the shelf. Like that horse that "got used to" bits, bridles, and cruppers, I too learned to endure the constraints at home. I learned from Black Beauty to heed his mother's advice: "the better I behaved, the better I should be treated and that it was wisest always to do my best to please my master."

I turned to the world of books for the conversation, wisdom, and emotional nourishment that my parents neglected to provide. Lucky for me, I grew up at a time when bookmobiles arrived almost at my doorstep. In the summer, one of these traveling libraries regularly parked in my neighborhood. I ran alone down the block eager to grab the latest Nancy Drew mystery off the shelf, take it home, retreat to a quiet corner, and ride along with the spunky girl detective. Nancy's adventures enabled me to escape, if temporarily, from a home that had more rules than a jail. By the age of ten I had read all thirty-one volumes in the series and I am still attracted to sassy female detectives. Fortunately, now there are many more to choose from. I chase around with Kinsey Millhone, Kat Colorado, Kay Scarpetta, and Sharon McCone, envying their adventurous, assertive, and courageous spirits.

I never needed to be freed from the realm of books, the one positive inheritance from my Chicago homes that made years of emotional silence, inflexible demands, and unjust punishments bearable. When my first job took me to the third-floor reference rooms of the New York Public Library, I entered a new kingdom, this one so filled with books that the power of my father's study dwindled like the receding landscape from a plane. I had books delivered from the stacks, and week after week I read autobiographies written or spoken by dozens of Native American people. I spent so many hours in the American History Room working on a bibliography with hundreds of entries that a friendly librarian arranged for a pass so I could eat in the staff cafeteria, an unheard-of privilege at the time. This kindness saved me hours of standing in line to retrieve my black pea jacket from the public coatroom; besides, in the early seventies, the library's Fifth Avenue neighborhood was not exactly a mecca for quick and decent places to eat. And, while it lasted, my lunchroom pass made me feel that I was finally, finally at home. And this time someone had invited me in without making me stand with my lips puckered at the door. It was more than sandwiches that fed me when I gained access to the New York Public Library's inner sanctum. The pass gave me an acceptance that made me forget how starved I was for my father's approval during those umpteen times I managed to enter his domain.

The pass was just the beginning. The lunchroom notwithstanding, everyone is welcome to study at the New York Public Library, but not everyone finds her own books printed in the catalogs or listed in databases on the library's computers. Every few months, while I am waiting for books to be delivered to the Main Reading Room, I pass the time in the Catalog Room seated before one of the computer terminals. I either punch in my name and bring up my own titles or track down journals where reviews of my books have appeared. It pleases me that not only has the New York Public Library acquired all ten of my books but also that its librarians steer readers to several of my works listed in the library's Indian Studies bibliographies stationed in a rack at the entrance of the Catalog Room.

After twenty-five years, I know every nook and cranny of the quarter-acre-large Main Reading Room, a place as familiar to me now as my own home. And when I am sitting at one of the twenty-one long wooden tables, elbow to elbow with other serious researchers amidst the sculptures, murals, bronze work, wood carvings, and plaster relief, I feel serene and nourished again and again by the contents of books. I can return to those blissful days on the sofa when the king happened to be away from his royal room. And I have learned finally that one of my greatest pleasures is portable. Now any library gives me great pleasure, especially my own. Not surprisingly, when we bought a house in Teaneck, New Jersey, the first order of business was building shelves for all the books my husband and I had accumulated. It was time to get rid of the just-married version—made with heavy, ornamental gray concrete blocks, one resting carefully on top of another, separated by long boards of hardwood painted white—and to close the open closet we used for our children's library.

Although 90 percent of the books in my childhood homes were contained in my father's study, in my home there is no altar, there is no throne. Books spill into every room. In fact, most of my books can be found in the living room in floor-to-ceiling mahogany-stained plywood bookcases. In the dining room, a wicker bookcase houses cookbooks. Piles of *New Yorkers* are in one bathroom and back issues of the *New York Times Magazine* are in the other. My study, an eleven-foot by six-foot porch attached to the living room, teems with materials that cover every available surface, including the floor. My study is wide open and my computer room has no door and I am pretty easygoing about loaning out books. No cards or due dates. Just a promise the book will be returned and my own reminder system—the borrower's name and book titles jotted down on a slip of paper and tossed into a manila file buried under letters to be answered and notices of books to be bought. When students of mine cannot find assigned books, I lend them mine. Nine times out of ten, they get returned. Recently, a student's dog ate one of my out-of-print books, but a computer search eventually turned up a copy in better condition than the one I loaned. Once in a while, when a borrower permanently disappears with a book that cannot be replaced, I feel bereft, as though I have lost a friend.

CHICKAWAUKEE STREET. NO number. Look for the Christian Science Society of Martha's Vineyard at the corner. Turn left or right depending on whether the ferry docks at Oak Bluffs or Vineyard Haven. Drive to the end of the paved road. Ride a few feet on a stony, unpaved road past a tangle of garnet-stained trumpet vines, ivory-colored wild carrot, and periwinkle-blue chicory. Angle left onto a sandy path cut through a canopy of trees and low-lying wild blueberries to a clearing. In this place stands a sizeable, modern two-storied redwood house situated in the midst of black oak and pitch pine trees that encircle it like a nest. Marlene's cab found this rental house in East Chop on Martha's Vineyard sixteen summers ago. In the dark. Our car has found this place like a homing pigeon for the past fifteen summers.

I overheard my daughter call our Chickawaukee rental place "home" in a conversation she had with a friend and it might as well be since we have celebrated so many birthdays and anniversaries here, sitting on goldenrod-yellow chairs pulled up around the electric-blue Formica Parsons table. Chickawaukee feels like the home I have always envisioned. Our parents, siblings, cousins, friends, and our children's friends have trekked here. At times, our open-door policy has resulted in crowd scenes. We have stored cribs and babies in the oversized walk-in closet (with the door open, of course) attached to the master bedroom located on the upstairs level. We have stepped over snoring teenagers in sleeping bags camped out in the narrow hallways on the downstairs level. At times, we've sandwiched four bodies in a tiny bedroom designed for two. Sometimes, we have crammed in so many bodies you could hear the house groan.

In part, Chickawaukee feels like home because we care for the place as though it were our own. At the end of our rental period, the stove sparkles; towels, washcloths, and sheets lie perfectly folded and stacked in the downstairs linen closet; and the appliances look untouched. We scoop up every grain of sand in the house, a considerable feat given its ubiquitous presence on the island. It costs us at least two precious days of vacation to tidy up and return the place to a pristine condition, but our dedication to fastidious housekeeping has paid off. When the people from whom we had been renting Chickawaukee for six years sold it to new owners, we, like the fixtures, were part of the deal.

Every summer, I fill the car with cartons of books and files containing research materials for my latest writing project; stacks of unread issues of the *New York Times, People,* and *Reform Judaism;* the latest novel by Louise Erdrich or James Welch; Brandeis and University of Chicago alumni magazines; and half a dozen good mysteries. There's also a bagful of Berol color pencils, sticks of oily Cray-pas, and quality drawing journals.

Why I bother to lug up Tony Hillermans, Sue Graftons, and Karen Kajewskis does not completely escape me; I intuitively make a house a home with my own library of books. It's really not necessary however since Martha's Vineyard is a literary paradise. Not only is the house on Chickawaukee stocked with dozens of paperbacks, but there are enough bookstores and town libraries to keep readers occupied for weeks. Some of my favorite authors even live on the island and often give readings at one of the community centers or the small college affiliated with off-island institutions. And Martha's Vineyard boasts its own mystery writer, Philip Craig, whose character, ex–Boston cop Jeff Jackson, would rather be fishing than playing detective. I grab up each new Craig mystery in the series to savor the evocative descriptions of the island and of the clamming, angling, and sailing that has made the Vineyard a mecca for vacationers.

Often getting into Vineyard Haven turns into a hassle because traffic clogs the streets and parking comes at a premium. Fortunately for me, Chickawaukee just happens to be three short blocks from the

Book Den, a used bookshop for literary browsers. I can walk there and mull for hours over out-of-print art books and esoterica. Some book in Native American studies that I can't live without or some art book whose flower drawings make me teary always surfaces. I have bought more photography books for my husband than he can count. With my latest treasures in hand, I walk less than a mile into Oak Bluffs and sit in the Old Stone Bakery sipping coffee, munching on a corn muffin filled with tart cranberries, and read my latest find.

As gradually as the tides change, we have shifted from vacationing on the Vineyard to living there. No more obligatory daily trips to "wavy" (South) beach, the famed long stretch of the Atlantic Ocean at the south side of Martha's Vineyard whose powerful surf you hear long before you see it, or "quiet" (State) beach facing Nantucket Sound where you can swim without battling waves. No more production lines turning out dozens of peanut-butter-and-jelly sandwiches and plastic sandwich baggies filled with sliced carrots and celery to be packed along with bags of Cape Cod potato chips, pretzels, and chocolate-chip cookies in a heavy cooler. Now I rarely budge from the table on the upstairs porch, tripled in size several years ago, where I read for pleasure, write chapters for my latest book, or draw sunflowers. Only authors reading their books or a good movie tear me away from my perch nestled among scented pines.

Planted safely on the Chickawaukee porch far from Chicago, I have had plenty of time to think about how I fled my father's palace, but not its priceless contents. His love for books captured my attention, though books have not monopolized my life as they ruled his. As a child, books shielded me from spirit-crushing criticisms, incessant angry outbursts, and prolonged hostile silences. As an adult, books have helped me soothe the wounds on my psyche. Books about the Native American experience and the ways in which Native people have struggled and prevailed against brutality have especially empowered me to try to transcend my early childhood experiences and to move forward.

In my rented castle on Chickawaukee, I have redesigned the architecture of my Chicago life. Once I lifted the windows on my own awareness, other changes came easily. I opened the doors to peace of mind, slammed others shut on crushing memories, and permitted myself to walk across the threshold to a better place.

Coming Home to Connecticut

ERICA JONG

HOME IS THE place where you feel safe, where despite disquieting news that arrives by cable or optical fibre, you can leave the door on the latch and wander outside in your old terrycloth bathrobe and a pair of muddy clogs to check on whether or not the brave arrows of the crocuses are poking through the snow.

As a child, not knowing there is an alternative, you never really appreciate home. As a young adult, home is where you want to leave as soon as possible, brandishing a new driver's license and a boyfriend.

Only in midlife—our sexy new euphemism for dread old middle age—does home beckon seductively again, inviting you to pleasures running away can never supply. Home is where your books are. Home is where you keep those bell-bottoms from the sixties that might just come back in time for your daughter to wear them. Home is where you know all the quirks of the plumbing but they comfort rather than irritate you. Home is where you get out of bed at 3 A.M., wink at the full moon through the bathroom skylight, and go back to sleep perfectly contented, knowing no demons can follow you here. Home is where the trees are all part of your history: the weeping cherry planted for your daughter's birth, the Scotch pine that once was a

Christmas tree—or Chanukah bush—the birch that was hit by lightning and came back the next spring, the oak that seemed to die the winter you were divorced but revived three years later with patience and pruning.

Home is where the same bird's nest on the front door lintel receives new robins' eggs year after year after year. Home is "something you somehow haven't to deserve" says Robert Frost in "The Death of the Hired Man." Amen.

I travel so much that often I wake up with a start, wondering whether I am in Rome or Hong Kong or Auckland, but in my house in the hemlock woods of Connecticut I always know I am home no matter how jetlagged.

I bought it exactly twenty years ago: my first house with my first real writing money. I carried my daughter into it in my arms when she was three days old. Built on an outcropping of rock hanging vertiginously over a river valley, it is made of old Vermont barn beams, fieldstone, and glass. It has never been "decorated." It contains instead the collections of my life: my grandfather's paint-splattered easel, my father's old upright piano, my former father-in-law's ancient Royal typewriter (an amulet for Molly), antique quilts bought on drives to Vermont, majolica plates sent home from Faenza, wine glasses I watched being blown in Venice, a motley—and precious— assortment of family portraits painted by my painting family.

I have a writing room on stilts—a tree house connected to the main house by a raised breezeway. The breezeway is lined with shelves that contain all my books in foreign editions. My desk wraps around me in a U-shape. It is always piled high with books for the current project. (Only between novels do I clean my desk.) On a raised platform facing a wall of windows, my desktop is polished oak the width of an old tree. A wall of poetry books is to my left and all my archives of photographs and manuscripts are in the cabinets. I am never happier than at my desk in Connecticut. This is where I heal and dream.

In the fall, the squirrels play acorn-football on the roof of my study. In the spring, birds nest in the eaves and wake up with the first pink light of dawn. I even enjoy having insomnia in the country so that I can be up before the birds are and await their serenade.

From the deck of my tree house, I can see the white-tailed deer tiptoeing up to eat my roses. They wait until the tender buds appear, then chomp them savagely, leaving the bushes bare. I do not shoot. Every year, I vow to put in a deer-proof fence, but I never do it. At least the deer leave the mountain laurel and the blackberry brambles to me.

Midsummer will come and there will be blackberries glistening up and down my driveway and throughout my woods. Like the deer, I will burst their redness upon my tongue, searching for ruby jewels amid the thorns.

I know I am home because Poochini, the Bichon-frisé, has curled up on the stair-landing between the first and second floor. I know I am home because Basil Bastet, the Russian blue who looks like an ancient Egyptian cat-goddess, is racing up the huge ficus tree in the living room, looking for a perch in its swaying top. I know I am home because my desk is heaped with fresh legal pads and stacks of marked-up books. I know I am home because my heart is calm and my pen is moving over the page to its tranquil beat.

Last summer I put in boxwood hedges to fool the deer. (Deer apparently hate the aroma of boxwood as much as I love it.) I replaced the roses the deer had decimated and prayed for the best. I planted peace roses, pale yellow with blushing edges. Last spring, I had the roof redone. Cedar shingle-chips rained all over the decks for months, imparting their tart aroma on top of the resinous smell of the hemlocks.

I have been planning to build a pool for almost twenty years. But the cycle of a writer's economic life is such that by the time I have paid the taxes on the last book and the bills that accumulated while writing it, there is *never* enough money left! I live on that seesaw (best known to freelance artists) between flush and broke—so I am glad to have the house even if it lacks a swimming pool.

The pool is no minor matter since the house is built on ledge, so blasting will be required to gouge a pool out of the cliff. Every year it gets more expensive.

"I'll build it next year," I say to myself, before turning to the next writing project. If only I could *write* a pool! I imagine it as an outdoor Roman bath surrounded by pillars bearing statues of the world's most inspiring women. Sappho, Boadicea, Elizabeth I of England, Mary Wollstonecraft, Colette, Emma Goldman, and Golda Meir would look down upon my swimming mermaid self. In the summer, it would be a *tepidarium*, in the winter, a *caldarium*. I would swim naked of course, attended by towel-bearing young male masseurs.

What's wrong with this picture? The pool doesn't match the house—which is homey and warm, if not humble. It's a cocoon for writing, dreaming, sleeping, having long talks with my daughter, entertaining friends, and making love. The hot tub on the deck doubles as a cauldron for witches' brews. It has known several incarnations in twenty years—from redwood wine cask to insulated fiberglass that keeps the water hot all winter.

In that tub I have planned my life and books for as long as I can remember, summoned (and dismissed) lovers, and conjured up adventures. I wouldn't trade this magic house in the woods for the Mount, Hadrian's villa, or San Simeon. Its spacious simplicity suits me. The house has mothered me as I mothered Molly, my books, and—dare I say it?—many men.

I suspect there is one more house in my life, but where the ultimate one will be I don't yet know. Near the sea, but whether the Adriatic, the Aegean, the Atlantic, or the Pacific, I haven't yet decided. In theory, it is drastically modern, a glass Bauhaus box with futons instead of beds, tatami instead of rugs, and a raked sand garden imitating eternity.

The truth is, I admire such houses, but I could never live in one. What would I do with the clutter of manuscripts, pictures, collections? What would I do with my walls of books? What would I do with family and friends, arriving to paint landscapes on the deck or compose contemporary concerti at my father's old piano in the guest room? What would I do with all my autographed first editions?

Words can build many houses. I am thankful that this one is mine.

Secret Places

JILL McCORKLE

MY FIRST CLEAR vision of home came when I was five and my
sister, who was eight, ran away. "You may visit me," she said,
"but this is my permanent home." She made a grand gesture with her
arms to encompass this two-by-two foot mound of pinestraw on
which she squatted behind our lagustrum bushes. The front door of
our house was not more than five feet away. She emphasized "permanent," looking so old and wise to me as she sat there in a pink
nylon car coat that I would inherit in a couple of years and a navy
knit cap pulled low on her forehead like a convict. She had her
schoolbooks and Bible; she had a little jug of water, a box of Nilla
Wafers, and the yellow blanket she had slept with her entire life.

"Permanent means forever," she explained as she stretched out in
her new home. I marveled at her courage and envied her solitary space.
It was the same way I felt ten years later when we left her in a dorm
room complete with mini-refrigerator, hot plate, and the freedom that
comes with independence. But that day, as I squeezed behind the
bushes with her, I didn't picture her living in that new space so much
as I envisioned her *not* being in that pale blue room we shared—her

side orderly, mine littered with paper and sticks, rocks, gum-ball prizes, and assorted bits of beloved junk.

I couldn't imagine Jan's twin bed empty at bedtime; and I couldn't imagine missing her lengthy bedtime ritual, the one that involved wrapping her feet up in the yellow blanket. I watched this process with great interest from my own bed where all of my stuffed animals and dolls were gathered for the night. My dad often sat between our beds in the darkened room to tell a story or to hum television theme songs or commercial jingles for us to identify. When he finished the games and ventured back into the lighted part of the house, we played I Spy to the noise of the television and the running water in the kitchen. Then Jan made up songs and sang until we both fell asleep. She lay on her side, rocking back and forth in rhythm to her song; I lay on my back with one knee up going back and forth like a windshield wiper. For years it was like having a jukebox. I made requests and she sang them. She was especially well versed in Burl Ives songs and other elementary-school, music-teacher favorites like "Yellow Bird," "Mexican Woodpecker," and "I Love to Go A Wandering ..."; eventually she could do the whole soundtrack of *The Sound of Music* and *Mary Poppins* with a few choice selections from The Beatles and Herman's Hermits. Without the bedtime music I might never have slept again.

But I didn't have to worry about her absence for long. My cat, Goldie (a creature who once hitched a ride up under the car axle across town to the First Baptist Church only to find his way back home two weeks later), crept behind the bushes and sprayed Jan's blanket. Just as quickly as I had been invited into her new home, I was asked to leave and to take my stinking cat with me. I assured her it would pass, the mildest bit of kitten gas, but Jan went off in search of our mother, Clorox, and the washing machine. Even after several washings—which the fraying blanket couldn't afford—the primitive smell of an animal marking his turf remained. And, without that blanket Jan was forced to forsake her freedom and move back in with me. She went right back to drawing that invisible line innate to all children. She dared me to let my junk spill over; she demanded that I get rid of the dummy I had made out of stuffed paper bags and named after a boy she liked in her class. She ridiculed Buzzy, the rubber snake that I kept in a jar of water on my dresser.

Jan needed a private world, her own space, and her attempt, though brief, to strike out and find one inspired me; I had been seized by the desire for independence. Actually what I loved most was the *idea* of independence; I liked packing bags much more than I liked going anywhere, the great romance promised by a backpack or a ho-bo's stick or a footlocker packed with essential items for camp. I liked the idea of self-reliance, everything you might ever need reduced to the space of a neat little container. I liked camping cups that folded flat as a compact and rain hats that could be reduced to the size of a quarter. I envied Jeannie on *I Dream of Jeannie* all tucked down inside that comfy bottle of hers. She could see out but they couldn't see in. I envied turtles and the simple compactness of their lives. My daughter once referred to when she was inside of me and described at great length the television within my womb; I think I always imagined that turtles had more than their organs tucked away in their shells, that they had whole little apartments.

I wanted to step into the dioramas I made from shoe boxes, one end covered in wax paper to let in filtered light. I made landscapes, rooms, homes that were secret. I loved to hear my mom tell the story of when she went to first grade with a little doll in the cigar box used to hold her pencils. She got caught playing with the doll when she should have been listening; instead of taking note of the lesson to be learned in that story, I took a great sense of kinship—I knew exactly why she needed that doll there. I also felt a strong identification with my dad's stories about how he played under his childhood home, an old house with enough crawlspace that he could create a whole town there in the rich black dirt. I was inspired by the notion of a secret place, one inhabited by me or by a doll I was responsible for or even by a creature of the imagination. Sometimes a scrap of paper with a secret message tucked away somewhere is enough to satisfy the urge—the little scrap a reminder and representation of something much larger than life. I imagine it's the power a person feels walking away from the Wailing Wall, or even contributing to some lengthy graffiti.

Permanence. From the moment I heard that word and discovered its eternal power, I was hooked. I wanted permanence, and with that desire came the habit of recording and saving. To this day I have an old burned-up piece of coal that I picked up on my very last day at Tanglewood Elementary School. I gripped my friend Susan's arm and held up that piece of coal and said, "This piece of coal will make me think of right now for the rest of my life." And it does. I see the back of the school where the women who worked in the kitchen came and went through the heavy screened door, their laughter rising over the clanging of pots and utensils, the smell of soapsuds and disinfectant and those big lard-filled biscuits that they served every day. I think of Susan standing there squinting into the sun, her long blonde hair pulled back in a ponytail. The crossing guard was down on the corner in her navy blue suit, ready to direct us into summer. Our only possessions that day were the Peanuts lunchboxes that we swung back and forth while we talked about the three months ahead of us. I would go to Myrtle Beach and ride the Swamp Fox roller coaster and to Fort Fisher (a Civil War site) so that I would have something educational to write about in the fall when we went back to school. She would go to Sliding Rock in the North Carolina mountains and to Colorado, where (she would write on a picture postcard) she saw snow. We would both spend hours at Woodside Pool, bleached and burned by sun and chlorine, while we pretended not to notice the boys our age as they cannonballed into the deep end. Many afternoons we would escape the heat, choosing instead the cool darkness of my den where the air conditioner rumbled and the black-and-white television delivered rerun after rerun of *I Love Lucy* and *Andy Griffith*. When

I think of that day—of Tanglewood and Susan, the way our town looked then—I think of home.

I HAVE BRUSHES. Black rubber brushes, one with bright blue bristles and the other with orange. Who knows when they were bought or why. They look like old scrub brushes but my grandmother kept them tucked away in the eave of her back porch. My sister and I used them to brush down the porch railings and posts (for our horses) and then we spent hours riding the range while the grown-ups gathered in the sideyard or on the front porch. A whole world is conjured from these memories: my grandmother in her kitchen, the whirr of her upright mixer as she made a pound cake, the smell of fatback and biscuits, faint traces of kerosene from the free-standing heater. That heater's little glass door served as a make-believe entrance to a tunnel that led beneath the cool darkness of the house and beyond, through her garden where the rows of corn were thick enough for a good game of hide and seek, where our feet quickly blackened with the rich turned earth and our pockets filled with found marbles and bits of broken glass, on down Second Street, a steady stream of screams and yells, as the neighborhood itself was being driven down, no longer the safe, quiet place it was when my mother was growing up.

When I was in junior high my grandmother moved, taking the rubber-backed brushes and all of her other belongings with her. The smells from the old house followed her to the new, making the transition much easier for me to accept. Not long after, the old house burned, speeding up the inevitable process of neglect and vandalism. And yet for me, it's still there, even when I ride by and see the cinderblock laundromat that has replaced it. The house, the used-car lot across the street, the old warehouses in the distance. The pecan trees that shaded the yard all of the years my grandmother was there.

The harder transition to make was when my grandmother moved to a nursing home. That was not her home and she never accepted it as such. By then she was often confused about time and place, and it seemed a wonderful bit of grace that she could escape the institutional setting for hours at a time, traveling over miles and years to her childhood home, to the first time she met my grandfather, to a more recent visit from a neighbor. She might be intent on finding the right shade of thread to sew a button on a dress that my aunt wore in high school or she might be looking for a ride across town to the Cash n Carry where she would buy a big country ham and a hog head. I made myself her audience as often as I could. I sat and listened while she fixed her sharp blue eyes on me; sometimes I was her mother and sometimes I was my mother and on occasion I was her niece who had committed suicide years before. From time to time, I was me, but as she got further and further from the present, I was needed to fill the role of someone long absent from her life. She would often look from her bed into the hallway and see her father in the image of some unknown man passing by. Her father died when she was eleven.

I became obsessed with her mental travels. I caught myself wondering about the things she said, the scenes that she seemed to relive. "You sit in the front of the wagon, now Annie," her father told her. "I have to go to the bank for some money," and she searched the side of the road, the riverbanks, banks of dirt where the downtown area was being built. "Wasn't I foolish?" she asked in a whispered voice. "To think my daddy might dig up some money there by the river." Even now when I think of the story being told and retold, I see it happening with the vivid clarity of a movie, as if somewhere out there she is riding in that wagon beside her father and searching the banks of dirt.

One day my grandmother was especially cheerful and when my mother asked what had happened to make her feel so good, she said, "Oh it was so wonderful. I went home last night and everything was just as I had left it." More than anything, I wanted to believe that she had been there. I had just completed a novel in which I had relied heavily on her old house and furniture, the smells, the placement, the light through her kitchen window and how it changed month to month. My wish would be that every scene from our lives is preserved on a neat little stage and all we have to do is step in. Sometimes I get the strong feeling that I can pick up the phone and dial my grandmother's number and she will be there, not in the nursing home, not in the new house, but there in the old house. Or that I could dial my dad's parents and somehow in the process resurrect another house long torn away and the years that people spent living there. They would answer in strong young voices, old age peeled away from their faces like a mask.

I REMEMBER THE wonderful smell of my home, always most clear when I wasn't there and fully immersed in it. My home was the pine paneling of our den where I could see animal faces in the knotholes. It was Prell shampoo and my dad's cigarette smoke, the tins of pipe tobacco that lined a shelf. My mother's Windsong. Saturday night T-bones, the plastic of a new Barbie doll. It was air-dried bedsheets and clothes fresh from the clothesline; old fabrics my grandmother had fashioned into quilts many years before.

When I was seven my dad, who was working at one of the local textile mills, had a wooden shipping crate for a knitting machine delivered to our house. He needed a toolshed, but no sooner was it placed in our backyard, fashioned with a door and small push-out window, than I moved in. All of my secret items—a piece of red plastic that looked like a ruby, a button from my grandmother's house that looked like a diamond, a Blue Wedgewood plastic tea set, moth-ball-smelling dress-up clothes—went with me. My dad never even tried to stop me, but instead gave me the key that fitted the padlock he had bought for the door. It was mine.

The biggest event of the playhouse—the time when others were invited in—was my annual Christmas party. I first went out into the woods that separated our house from I-95 and sawed down a small pine tree with one of the white-handled serrated steak knives used for the Saturday night T-bones. Then I spent a day or two decorating: cast-off ornaments, things I found in the yard, paper and glue. I also took that time to shop and buy presents (the best present I ever got my mother for this occasion was a little plastic bottle with a genie inside of it). And then it was time for the party. Invitations were sent. Food was prepared (Little Debbie snack cakes or Hostess Twinkies served on the small plastic plates). I often used something other than my teapot for serving the Coca-Cola because it was still stained and strong-smelling from a batch of wine my cousin and I attempted to make in the heat of July. The party began with a welcome to my family—squeezed in and sweating even though it was December—and continued with refreshments and the gifts. Then I asked that we all sing a carol or two, after which my mom rushed back inside to finish cooking supper and my sister dashed in to the telephone and television, relieved to be able to breathe and get back to her life. The best part of the party was getting ready for it and telling them all how good it was going to be.

The last year that I had the party I was in the fifth grade. It was that same year that, much to my horror, all of my friends got things like hot rollers, lip gloss, vinyl boots, and record players from Santa Claus. I had gotten a new Liddle Kiddle and a ballerina doll named "Tippy Toes." I didn't tell anyone what I had gotten and I kept that doll hidden at the back of my closet until a decent enough period of time had passed that I could give her away. Somehow I felt shamed by her; worse, I felt forced to feel shamed by her. By spring that worry had been replaced by others; I was leaving the safe comfort of Tanglewood School, going to Joe P. Moore School where I would be joined by hundreds of other kids from all over town. And on the last day, I picked up my piece of coal and put it in the wooden box that my grandmother had given me years before. It was a candy box, a gift from my grandfather though she couldn't remember when he had given it to her. Also in the box, which was kept on the shelf in the playhouse, were the magnet that I had kept under my desk throughout fifth grade, a flag given to me by my mother's first cousin who by then was dead, a savings stamp book that I would cash in long before it earned any interest, and my dog's baby teeth.

In sixth grade the collecting continued: the plastic red Coke cup saved from a high-school football game where I sat with my boyfriend. Photos of Margot Fonteyn as the dying swan that I clipped from *Life* magazine. A rubber-band chain made by my boyfriend, who was adept at both killing flies and hitting me in the head from across the room. Chains made from pop-tops and chewing-gum wrappers. Eyelashes that I had wished on and carefully wrapped in toilet tissue. December came and went, paving the way for my first Christmas without a doll, a Christmas with lip gloss and fishnet stockings and a sleeping bag to take to slumber parties. My parents were about to begin converting our carport into their bedroom, so much of that spring was accompanied by the sounds of saws and hammers as a moonlighting fireman did the job. Then for the first time my sister and I parted ways and I moved around the corner to my much smaller new room. I got used to it quickly, this space of my own, and I no longer needed to slip out into the backyard for a moment of silence. When I think of home and my room, it is the late afternoon light I see most clearly.

It was years later when my parents described that year to me. My mother said my dad nearly drove her crazy asking if the invitation for the Christmas party had arrived. He in total honesty said that it broke his heart. It was hard for me to believe that I had really *forgotten* to have the party, and yet nowhere in my memory could I find the moment when I had contemplated sneaking the steak knife and heading out into the woods. I really had forgotten, just like that.

When I was a freshman in college, the playhouse was completely eaten with termites. It had to come down but my dad was having a horrible time doing it. He was back in Lumberton, sitting out on the picnic table, crowbar in hand, but he couldn't begin. I was in my lime-green dormitory room with a spring breeze blowing in the big window, the phone cord twisting as I leaned to watch students jogging past. That's what I had been doing myself and stood there in gym shorts and sneakers, my boyfriend impatiently pacing around in the hall while I reassured my dad that it was okay to tear the house down. He had called two other times already, each time beginning with: "Are you *sure* it's okay?" And in that moment I remembered all that I had forgotten before, all of the times that he hinted about a party, suggested that I go out to the playhouse, made mention of its status— the termites or water damage—as if he were updating me on the health of an old friend. The house had meant as much to him as it had to me. It was, and I was, after all, his creation.

My dad was a man in tune with nature and he often took his cues from the world around him. He later told me that while avoiding the task, sipping a beer and getting very sentimental, he watched a mother bird giving flight lessons. He always told me that I could never put it in a book, it would sound so phony. But there he was and it happened. He had the sign he had spent the afternoon waiting to see. Before constructing the next building (one of those prefab aluminums) he poured concrete for the base where he wrote my sister's and my names. He wrote the dog's name. He wrote my mother's and his own.

TWO YEARS AGO, as he was dying of cancer, my dad said, "Everyone needs his own little box to put things in." He had one. But was he referring to his dresser drawer, where he kept a rubber frog my mother gave him when they were dating and other reminders of his own childhood? Was it the box on the shelf in his closet with other old letters and pictures? Was it his wallet, where he carried pictures of Jan and me as children and a folded-up note that I had once written to Santa Claus? The little statements and metaphors guided him through, leaving me now to wonder if the "box" was really a box or our house or maybe even his way of seeing his whole life. Once in the morphine confusion he asked us where he was, only to be told "home." "My home?" he asked in great bewilderment, and with re-assurance, he sighed the sigh of contentment, the relief that follows a long trip back.

MY MOTHER JUST put their house on the market and the ad in my hometown paper reads: "adorable and affordable." Real estate adjectives cannot do justice to a person's life. She called just yesterday to say that it was so hard to say good-bye, that when she walks into the backyard all she can think about is the playhouse, the names in concrete, the dog who once dug a cave between two trees, Easter-egg hunts, and Jan's home behind the bushes.

I JUST HAD a prefab pine shed delivered to my backyard. The men assembled it in an hour and a half. I have yet to paint it and wire it. It will be my new office, a mere one hundred feet from my house and the laundry and telephone. Lately I just go in it to breathe in, to smell the pine wood that conjures the old place. Just the other day my daughter turned to me and said: "Have you ever noticed that people's houses have different smells?" I said, "How about ours?" "It smells like home," she said. There are no words I'd rather hear from her. Home is a creation, and if built correctly, is a permanent possession. You carry it around in your suitcase or purse, your journal or jewelry box. You carry it around in your pocket.

BEFORE MY DAD's death, I often heard myself at readings or in class or at a cocktail party saying with great confidence that I would never choose to go back through high school and college, that I felt good about the knowledge that comes with age, that I would in fact choose to be ninety rather than go back. But now I see that the desire to go back and recreate really is not about being young so much as it is about finding the people you have lost. For them I would go back; I would pay closer attention to every second. I would remind myself what a gift just being there can be.

For me my dad will always be there in his chair in the den, or out in the backyard swing with my mom, or between our beds humming his familiar tunes. The voice never changes; the smell of pipe tobacco is constant. My mother's leaving our house won't change any of that any more than my grandmother's move stopped me from thinking of her in her original kitchen where she bathed me in the sink and where I remember a red polka-dotted mixing bowl under her upright mixer. For me that is home and for the rest of my life I will think of my grandmother standing there in front of the window, her African violets on the sill, the front of her dress dusted in biscuit flour. I will hear my dad's car pull up, hear his familiar walk up the back steps, his key in the lock. I will hear his voice, young and strong and clear.

It's not the place as much as what I have taken away from it; the images and smells and sounds. There is a feeling, like having a secret; it's powerful and wonderful and it's what keeps people and places alive. It's why people have the urge to go back and why they tell stories. It is my wish above all others that my children will love me so much that they will want to step back and recreate me, that they will cast my image in some permanent way, perhaps the bedtime ritual where we whisper and tell stories or maybe me painting the shed, the mysterious wooden box that my daughter is already asking to share.

Malibu DPs

MELINDA WORTH POPHAM

"HOW SOON COULD you leave? my husband said.

I glanced at the level of my wine. "Five minutes. What's
the hurry?"

"Leave Chicago is what I meant."

"Oh, *Chicago?*" I took a slow sip, thinking of all that would have
to be done—and knowing I'd be the one who'd have to do it. "Two
weeks," I said, foolhardy in my eagerness.

It was Halloween night, 1977, and we were having a drink at
the brand-new Ritz Carlton on Michigan Avenue. Eight years of Chicago had been more than enough. Now that business reasons no
longer held my husband hostage there, we were champing at the bit
to move back to California. Five acres of oceanfront land in Malibu
awaited us, but for months our getaway plans had been foiled by our
Chicago house having found no buyers. Now we had decided to just
up and go.

A month later, living in a rental house on Point Dume in Malibu,
I called a writer friend in Chicago to tell her I was so happy it worried
me. Might not such unabashed happiness dry up the wellspring of
my writing? How on earth could a serious writer live in Malibu? After

all, as former Malibuite and *seriously* serious writer Joan Didion observed, its very name is "a kind of shorthand for the easy life."

Then came the voracious fire season of 1978. A brush fire in the hills took off and headed straight for the ocean thirteen miles away. Feasting en route on gated estates and an orchid nursery, by the time it jaywalked the Pacific Coast Highway and snacked on million-dollar beach shacks it had polished off 197 homes in all. It skirted Walt Disney's widow's pink villa but swept across our lot two doors away. We looked at our blackened land and the burned-down houses immediately to the left and right of our house site and, rank novices though we were at wildfires, knew that our house, had it been built, would have been gone.

The fire season was followed by the rainy season. Mountains and hillsides denuded by fire of soil-holding vegetation loosed floods, house-high boulders, and mudslides onto houses and the highway. By now, I realized that Malibu was made to order for natural disasters and that life there would prove very real. I was secretly glad to find that Paradise had a down side to it. Now I could stop worrying that Malibu was not a fit place for a serious writer.

Over the course of my seventeen years in Malibu, I became a veteran of so many encounters with brush fires, floods, sinkholes, mudslides, rattlesnakes, and landslides that at times, I had to wonder if the license-plate frame that says, "Malibu—a Way of Life" referred not to the sybaritic lifestyle but to the roster of natural disasters.

Two years after our land burned, a massive landslide permanently buried the road to an interim house where we were living, then, later on, that house burned to the ground. Though the interim house on Rambla Pacifico was no longer ours when it burned down, it bore such powerful "place-where" associations for me that it seemed in some way to still belong to us. To see the place where I had been pregnant with my two children, the place where my son William had pulled on cowboy boots for courage to face preschool and my daughter Lilly had sneaked crayons into her crib to scribble a mural on her wall during naptime, to see that place reduced to nothing but a chimney and a homeless hearth made me feel robbed of something I had considered mine.

But it wasn't until my friend Cory's house burned to the ground that I grasped what it means to lose your *actual* home. During the two and a half weeks that she and her husband, daughter, and cat lived with us after the fire, I saw what it means to be displaced persons—DPs, as they were called in World War II. And what I learned stood me in good stead when, less than a year later, I, too, became displaced.

After I decided that, for me, "marital dissolution" was a lesser evil than remaining in a marriage beyond resuscitation, I began to realize that my situation bore a striking resemblance to Cory's. We were both burn-outs: she, from the place she had called home since 1976; I, from my marriage of twenty-four years.

Perhaps it should not have come as news to me that a home lost in a wildfire would resemble a marriage gone up in smoke. After all, both situations pull the rug out from under your life and require you to start over again from scratch; both rank right up there with the death of a loved one on the experts' lists of life's greatest stressors.

THE FIRE THAT would eventually burn down Cory's house in Malibu broke out at 1:30 P.M. on Tuesday, October 26, 1993, in Thousand Oaks, in the San Fernando Valley, when an arsonist succumbed to the twin temptations of tinderbox chaparral and an arid Santa Ana wind.

An hour later, over on the ocean side of the Santa Monica Mountains in Malibu, the sky had taken on that eerie coppery luster that means a wind-propelled Santa Ana fire is heading your way. During a Santa Ana condition, the normal ocean breeze gets stopped in its tracks by a topsy-turvy pressure system that sends a hot, dry wind barreling off the Mojave desert. Like a car going the wrong way on the freeway, that wind's got nightmare written all over it.

I stayed up most of the night to watch the nonstop fire coverage on TV, but reports on major wildfires in Altadena and Laguna Canyon overshadowed those on the Thousand Oaks fire, which would ultimately burn 43,251 acres but destroy only 66 houses compared to 151 in Altadena and 366 in Laguna. Now as I tracked the rapid advance of "our" fire, I tried to gauge its distance from our house, and that made me think about how danger is often measured in terms of distance. I was thinking about the state of my marriage as well as the approaching fire. I thought about how, with a house, the closer the fire, the greater the threat; but between husband and wife, the wider the gap, the greater the danger.

When the TV reports began mentioning names of neighboring canyons and roads, I wondered if it was time to get out my fire checklist and start packing up. Frustrated by the scanty news of the only fire I cared about, I turned off the TV and went outside. I ran my finger over the table on the terrace and picked up a light dusting of ash. I checked the sky for stars and sniffed the air. No stars, but it was windborne smoke, not fireglow, blotting them out. I went to bed knowing that, if evacuation did become necessary, county sheriffs would cruise along the highway sounding sirens and rousting residents. It was 3:00 A.M.

Which, it turns out, was exactly when Cory woke up to check the fire—not on TV but out her bedroom window—and saw flames cresting Boney Ridge just to the north. She woke Bryony, her eleven-year-old daughter, and drove her to her parents' house twenty-seven miles away. Her husband Nick began hooking up garden hoses in strategic locations and stockpiling water in bathtubs, sinks, buckets, and trash cans. By the time she got back home around 5:00 A.M. the wind had shifted.

I called Cory first thing Wednesday morning to ask how things were looking at their place.

"Better," she said. "But not good."

She had tested their fire pump and discovered that it wasn't working. With their most crucial piece of emergency equipment out of commission, their capability for self-sufficiency was shot. This was an alarming setback since they would be on their own to fight the fire. Fire engines would not venture up their narrow, dead-end road; there was no city waterline way up there.

Even so, she sounded, at that point, as if she was taking the threat of losing the house seriously—but not *too* seriously. Her tone of voice suggested disbelief that her house, the house she and Nick had built, the very house in which she was presently standing and talking on the phone, might, within hours, burn to the ground. She was packing up, but her efforts lacked a felt sense of dire necessity. She was just going through the motions.

Two hours later, I called back to ask if she wanted us to come help. Her voice was breathless with urgency. She said the wind had shifted again, it looked like they were going to lose the house for sure, and it would be a big help if my husband John could come up with his Jeep and take out a load of their stuff.

I might as well say right here and now that I had a selfish interest in not wanting Cory's house to burn down. Much as I enjoyed our dinners together at Zooma Sushi, our standing TV date on Oscar night, and the family 4th of Julys we spent at our place watching fireworks over the ocean, what I liked best of all was being at Cory's place.

Her place was so synonymous with her—the way New Mexico was with Georgia O'Keefe—that I could not imagine it not *being* there any more. Over the years, going to Cory's had always been a respite for me, like taking a getaway vacation in the midst of daily life. To go up to Cory's for lunch, borrow one of her warped straw hats or an old sweater, settle in on the glider, and take the first swig of an afternoon beer was *sui generis* bliss—and I am not even partial to beer.

I met Cory in 1978, soon after moving from Chicago to Malibu, when I rented space for my typewriter on the sun porch of an architect's office above a liquor store and hamburger stand on the Pacific Coast Highway. She was working there as a draftsman while boning up for the board exams to get her architect's license. She was twenty-eight, I was thirty-four.

To my midwestern eye, Cory was Malibu through and through. She went around barefoot, drank herbal teas from interesting mugs, and at lunchtime climbed over the wall behind the Union 76 station to sit on Las Flores Beach and eat what was then called "health food." A willowy five-eight but strong as an ox, she had an uncultivated, appealing, maverick attractiveness. Whatever self-doubts her idiosyncratic looks may have caused her in adolescence—someone once described her hair as "touchingly thin"—they had come irrefutably into their own in womanhood.

The first time she invited me for dinner I could tell from the directions—a row of rural mailboxes at a certain junction; a series of paved and dirt roads; a small handpainted sign—that her place was going to be off the beaten track. But I did not know until I arrived that she lived atop a mountain in a tepee and a humpy little Airstream trailer.

She showed me around her acre and introduced me to the menagerie of animals she kept for milk, company, and eggs—Kurdi the Goat, Betty Kitty, Jack the Dog, some laying hens, and a rooster. Her view took in a big slice of the Pacific Ocean and the canyon clear up to Boney Ridge. Her only neighbor in shouting distance was Jack Nicholson, but he arrived only now and then to use his hot tub with friends. The remoteness of her land was what had put it within her budget. Construction on the house she had designed would have to wait.

I was thrilled to know someone who lived alone in the mountains in a tepee and a trailer, and I was bowled over by the gumption of a single woman in her late twenties buying herself a piece of land on which to build a house—her very *own* house. She was a first for me.

WHETHER IT IS an approaching firestorm or a failed marriage staring you in the face, the first question is whether to stay or to go. It is the hardest decision of all. Which is better? To abandon a threatened house or try to save it? To pull the plug on a lifeless marriage or stay on in the false hope it might somehow be revived? To face an inferno with a water bucket and a garden hose or get the hell out of there?

In divorce, 75 percent of the time it is the wife who wants out. In wildfires, too, it's the women who get out, taking the children with them, and it's the men who, even against bad odds and their better judgment, stay to try to save the house.

Once you have decided you cannot save your house or your marriage by staying in it, then comes the decision of *when* to go. Do you hang on until the eleventh hour, hoping for a shift in the wind or a change of heart, or do you get out immediately? Most people, I think, stay as long as they possibly can—and probably longer than they should. And when they finally do bail out, and even when there should not have been any question about it in the first place, they still feel terrible about leaving.

For Cory, staying in order to save the house was not an option. The stucco house might have withstood the fire, but her arrhythmic heart might not have withstood the stress. Nick planned to see it through as long as my husband John and Cory's brother-in-law George were willing to help. Their plan was to remain inside the house during the firestorm and scoop water from trash cans to douse any cinders that got under the doors. In the event the windows blew out and the interior of the house caught fire, their last-ditch plan was to jump in the pool and hope for the best. Swimming pools have saved many a place setting of good china and silver from fire, but a firestorm sucks all the oxygen out of the air, leaving the people who jump into a swimming pool with nothing to breathe when they come up for air.

George instigated their last-minute exit when he said, "Do you realize that if we stay we'll die?" So the three of them came out, and when they got to the mouth of the canyon they discovered Cory standing there. She had been waiting for two hours with wool sweaters and borrowed fire extinguishers, which the sheriff at the roadblock had not allowed her to deliver.

When I saw two sets of headlights coming down our driveway, I set three more places at the table. Cory, Nick, and John came through the back door like shell-shocked survivors of something they could not talk about. Nick drank two glasses of water, then, turning to face the kitchen sink, said in an emotion-clotted voice, "I figure it must be burning right this minute."

"I'm just glad you didn't get yourselves killed trying to save it," Cory said.

Though the four of us kept both TVs going to pick up reports on the fire, Cory and Nick went to bed late that night still not knowing if they were overnight guests or homeless fire victims.

The next morning Cory went to see if, by some miracle, the house was still standing. She called me from the bank of free phones set up for fire victims at the corner of the Pacific Coast Highway and Yerba Buena Road.

"Well, it's gone," she said.

That afternoon, as I was driving my twelve-year-old daughter Lilly home from school, I told her that Bryony's house had burned down and that they would be staying with us for a while. Knowing how Bryony loves sweets, Lilly expressed her condolences by making her a chocolate cake with white frosting and a drawing in decorating icing of a house with red and yellow flames coming from the roof and windows. She surrounded the burning house with birthday candles.

Both Cory and Bryony made silent wishes over the cake before Bryony blew out the candles, and although she blew out all of them in a single breath, none of us felt inclined to cheer her feat. When Lilly cut the cake, Bryony asked for the big piece that had the window of her room on it and Cory took the piece with the front door and the address.

It was while we were sitting around the table after eating Lilly's fire cake that I first saw a frozen look come over Cory's face—the kind of look that accompanies a trapdoor sensation in the stomach when you remember something extremely urgent you are helpless to do anything about—then she shrugged as if she were shaking off an injury that hurt more than she was willing to acknowledge.

"What was that?" I said.

"I just remembered something important I forgot to save. Oh well, nothing I can do about it now."

This was an anguish she would have to go through time and time again, because loss of home, no matter how abrupt and total, is not an all-at-once, one-fell-swoop experience. The loss becomes bigger and bigger with the specific memory of each and every irreplaceable item that is gone.

I already knew that Cory had had to abandon almost everything in her studio—her building models, files, architecture books, computer, and clients' house plans—because when her caterer neighbor's house had been more imminently threatened than her own, she had filled her car with the caterer's cookbooks and kitchen equipment; then, as fate would have it, Cory's house burned down, and the caterer's did not.

There were certain things I longed to know if she had managed to save—the family christening dresses displayed on dowels in the upstairs hall; her grandfather's weathered-leather knapsack that had hung in her studio; the cardboard model of her house she had shown me in 1978 during my first dinner in the tepee; the Mexican Santos sculpture; the watercolor she had painted in Florence—but I was afraid to ask about them. Likewise, when friends or family members toured my post-divorce home for the first time, I saw their faces light up at familiar things they hoped I would get to keep, but no doubt there were also things whose absence they registered but, out of kindness, refrained from asking about.

The morning after Cory had seen the concrete slab of the foundation covered with the cremated remains of her home, I came out to the kitchen at 7:20 and found her using the breakfast counter as a makeshift drawing board.

"How long have you been up?" I said.

"Since 5:30. I couldn't sleep."

"I'm not surprised."

"It wasn't *that*," she said. *That* being her burned-down house. "I was too excited to sleep."

"You were? Why?"

"I kept thinking of all these ways to make the house better this time."

Later that morning I met Cory up at the site. Driving through that bleak, blackened canyon should have prepared me for what it would look like at Cory's, but the familiar creates a template in the mind, and when that template does not overlay the reality of what you are seeing, when the two are so at odds as to be meaningless, you are left with a sense of profound disorientation, a kind of mental stammer. When Cory first told me the house was "gone," I did not understand that she was saying that where there had once been a house there was now nothing.

What she pointed out to me, though, as we walked around her site that morning was not the devastation but the possibilities of renewal. She snapped off a charred eucalyptus branch and showed me the hint of life still within it. With widespread arms she framed the view of Boney Ridge she could get by positioning clerestory windows at the top of the staircase. She also noted some of the fire's ironic oversights, like the *New Yorker*, its edges browned and curly like a pirate's treasure map, sticking out beneath the puddle of what appeared to have once been a sewing machine.

But every now and then her anguish broke through. At the thought of the sorry, sizzling deaths of her chickens and Bryony's goldfish, she waved the air and shook her head as if scattering bees from her hair, then quickly changed the subject to how she might connect the studio to the house.

About this time the insurance adjuster arrived on the scene, picking a high-stepping, shoeshine-worried path through the charred, mangled mess on the slab, and I left. I had already seen more than enough.

BY THE SUMMER of 1994, I knew that my marriage was as gone as Cory's burned-down house. The hostile silence that had come to encase us like an icy carapace had reached the state of permafrost. It was the *ad absurdum* extension of the overcivilized decorum we had long observed. A curse in marriage, that lockjawed decorum would prove to be a saving grace during the divorce.

In California, there are two grounds for divorce: incurable insanity and irreconcilable differences. I suppose that anyone in agreement with the Authors Guild poll which concluded that "the smartest thing a writer can do is find a lifelong partner with an independent income big enough for two" would tell me I was out of my mind to leave my marriage, to walk away from all I had, especially at the age of fifty. What more could I possibly have wanted anyway?

I wanted to become recognizable to myself again. I wanted to hear the sound of my own laughter again—and for my children to hear it, too. I wanted my children to understand that, deeply sorry though I am for the pain my decision to divorce brought them, I am even sorrier for the sad example of marriage we set before them. I wanted to be proud of myself for putting my well-being above being well-off.

I knew from the outset that getting divorced would mean leaving the Malibu house. That he would be the one to stay was never in question. The house was his, not ours. That was okay. I didn't want to live in Malibu anymore. I had had it with Malibu.

Besides, *home* would come with me. To reassure myself, all I had to do was remember an Easter years ago at Canyon de Chelly on the Navajo reservation. While the children slept—Lilly in a motel crib and William a bump in one of the room's two queen-size beds—I filled their Easter baskets by the light in the bathroom and tiptoed around, hiding colored eggs. Their favorite was the one in the wall-mounted coffeemaker. What I learned from this odd Easter of ours was that when it comes to a sense of home, it is not just a matter of where you are, it's knowing how to make it happen.

I began hitting the Sunday open houses with Lilly, house-looking with my real estate agent, scanning the real estate section in the paper, and braking at HOUSE FOR SALE signs. What I was looking for was not just a place to live but a place to make home: a house that felt *right*. I knew I would know it when I saw it. A "little charmer" with "loads of potential" would suit me fine as long as it had enough potential charm not to feel punitive. Punitive was unacceptable. After all, I had done nothing wrong. There was nothing tabloid about my reasons for seeking divorce.

In January, 1995, four months after our agreed-upon separation date, my husband and I were still living under the same roof and negotiating a settlement through our attorneys. In retrospect, it seems fitting that it took a natural disaster to serve as a catalyst. Fire had evicted Cory from her home. For me, evacuation came with the floods and mudslides of the so-called Hundred Year Rain of January, 1995.

Not only did the town of Malibu shut down but it was cut off from the rest of the world as well. The Pacific Coast Highway was closed. The bridge was out. Canyon roads were closed. Highway 101 to the north was closed. The insurance companies and FEMA descended on Malibu with their mobile field offices to process claims, Governor Pete Wilson performed the *de rigueur* helicopter flyover and on-site press conference, and President Clinton declared us a federal disaster area. It was the sort of major disaster that vindicates the belief that anyone who lives in Malibu is nuts.

Personally, I thought it was very nice of God—albeit a tad excessive—to have staged such devastation just to extricate me. Nor did I fail to appreciate the way Malibu's state of total collapse mirrored that of a failed marriage: bridges out; power lines down; communications cut.

On January 16, 1995, I moved to Santa Monica with only the bare essentials—my computer, some clothes, and the dog's bed and bowls. "SM Canyon furnished apartment; short-term ok," the ad in the paper said. This being L.A., it turned out that the apartment was the second floor of the two-story beach house William Randolph Hearst had built in 1928 for his longtime mistress, actress Marion Davies. It had hardwood floors, glass doorknobs, gleaming bathrooms, and the right number of bedrooms for the children and me. The kitchenette—an add-on during its renovation from a derelict flophouse—had a mini-refrigerator and no oven to speak of, but I thought everything about the place was terrific. Even the name of the street boded well: Entrada.

I was absurdly happy there. I felt so instantly at ease on Entrada that the gated isolation of my five-acre, oceanfront Malibu life—not to mention the 90.6 miles per day I had driven for eleven years to deliver my children to and from school—now seemed downright weird. The urban orchestra was music to my surf-deafened ears, and the quickstep pace of city life gave me the solace that others seek by going to the beach.

In that most uprooted and crazed of times, life seemed so unexpectedly grounded and sane. We were finally living where Domino's delivered, last-minute plans for movies could be made, and school was six car-minutes away. Best of all, though, was the leeway, the elbow room, in the way we lived there. We just made it up as we went along. Winged it. Instead of waiting for "the dinner hour," if we were famished at 5:00, we'd just go ahead and damn well *eat*.

I had a sense of having been catapulted onto a rising arc of exhilarating, burgeoning newness. I went for long walks with my dog Quita and discovered vine-festooned, old wooden staircases connecting the upper and lower parts of Santa Monica Canyon. I discovered the medieval monastic meditation practice called centering prayer. I rediscovered peanut butter on celery sticks. I discovered that when I wrote at the big Mexican desk in my bedroom the voice that came out of my writing was as changed—and unpredictable—as my new circumstances.

Meanwhile, I was keeping abreast of the real estate market so that I would be ready to come in with a purchase offer as soon as we reached a marital settlement. I kept a running list of candidates—definite maybes—but the one hundred and twenty-seventh house Lilly and I went to look at was, beyond a shadow of doubt, *it*. Not only did it have "curb appeal," it had pine floors, built-in bookcases, and a fenced yard for the dog. As if that weren't enough, its address was my son's birthdate, and it had just had a price reduction that put it within my squeaky-tight budget. Above all, it had the resonance of home at long last found. Somerset Maugham pinned it down perfectly.

"Sometimes," he wrote, "a man hits upon a place to which he mysteriously feels that he belongs. Here is the home he sought, and he will settle amid scenes that he has never seen before, among men he has never known, as though they were familiar to him from his birth. Here at last he finds rest."

Three months after moving into the Entrada apartment, my landlord—a screenwriter who lived downstairs with his wife and son—apologetically informed me that we would have to vacate the apartment the following month because they needed it for his aged father who would be arriving from Nova Scotia. The idea of having to find *temporary* temporary housing sent me into a tailspin—and cranked up the pressure to arrive at a marital settlement but quick.

Finally, with an eleventh-hour flurry of faxes, speaker-phone conferences, face-to-face meetings, and a courier revving his motorcycle, the signatures went on the settlement. Three hours later, my real estate agent presented my purchase offer, and, the following day, after accepting the sellers' counteroffer, I had bought a house—*the* house.

Between Martin Luther King Day when I left Malibu behind and Memorial Day when I was handed the key to my house, I had lived in the Entrada apartment, at two friends' places, and in two motels that would take dogs. At one point, my earthly possessions were scattered in six different locations. Everything for my inbetween life was contained in one duffel bag, one tote bag, and grocery bags from five different markets. The Hughes Market bag was my desk. The Gelson's bag had my real estate documents; the Von's bag, my divorce-related documents. The manuscript I was working on was in the Westward Ho bag, and my laundry was in the Vicente Foods bag.

ON THE HALLOWEEN that fell four nights after her house burned to the ground, Cory and I took our daughters trick-or-treating. As the girls trooped from house to house in the costumes they had gleefully assembled from fire-victim clothing donations, I thought about how homesick Cory must be, seeing the jack-o-lanterned houses with homeowners standing in their doorways with baskets of candy and robust cries of, "Well now! What have we here! Come in and let's get a look at you." Now that I am divorced, I know that when you are standing in the ashes of your house or your marriage, there *is* a wistful—sometimes even envious—sense of alienation from those whose houses or marriages are still intact: a matter of the haves versus the have-nots. It's an old story.

It was not until Bryony and Lilly were sorting and swapping their treats back at our house that I remembered the Halloween sixteen years ago when my husband and I had been having a drink at the brand-new Ritz Carlton in Chicago and had set the date for our move to Malibu. I also remembered how we had blamed Chicago for our unhappiness and thought—or hoped—that getting back to California would fix it.

Now I, too, have said, "Well, it's gone," and I, too, am rebuilding. Cory finished her house last spring, and she was right, it *is* much better this time—especially with the clerestory windows framing Boney Ridge.

I, too, plan to add more windows.

Splendor in the Mildew

JULIE SMITH

IT WAS CHRISTMAS and everyone was there—parents, of course, and grandparents, my aunt and uncle, all my cousins and siblings. Our grandmother had broken out the pickled peaches. She had also fried squash with onions and lots of pepper, concocted an eggplant casserole with crumbled-up saltines on top, and enlisted my mother to make her famous cornbread dressing.

The linen was white and immaculate, creased from months in a drawer, and the silver was polished to a dazzle, which is more than I can say for the manners of some of us under twelve. It was about three in the afternoon and this was lunch, though we called it dinner. We were so hungry we were hallucinating.

However, since Santa Claus *had* come, we were trying hard. I, for instance, had my hands in my lap to keep them from grabbing a turkey leg. Though on the brink of starvation, I was quite enjoying myself.

Southern Protestants have precious few rituals but Christmas dinner is one. In my family, we broke out the silver and china and crystal only twice a year, though Thanksgiving never seemed quite so grand—perhaps because more of the clan gathered on December 25th.

So I was soaking up white-bread culture, waiting almost patiently, while bowls were passed and plates were heaped.

"Julie," said my grandfather, "will you have some peas?"

To this day, I can remember how lovely and warm that made me feel; how cherished and cared for—that he would think of ten-year-old me, clear at the other end of the table, when there were so many others there. Carefully, so as not to spill any, I obliged and took some peas. Everyone laughed.

They knew what he really meant: Please pass the peas.

I don't know why, but southerners speak in code. Perhaps it's to confuse the imposters. True southerners are born with a gene that causes them to understand all manners, mores, and obscure phrases indigenous to the region and to know how to act accordingly.

I was not, and neither was my mother, though she's never forgiven me for failing to have it. Here's how I know she doesn't either: She told me the story, in tones usually reserved for funerals, of her first and second Shriners Balls.

She'd bought a lovely new dress for the first, only to find she was the only lady in a short frock. Having gotten the lay of the land, she showed up in a long gown for the second. This time, she lamented with tears in her eyes, they all wore cocktail dresses, knee-length or shorter.

In the South, mere embarrassment has a recovery time of about ten years. This was humiliation.

I doubt if she'll ever get over it.

I knew better than to ask why she simply didn't consult someone. I'd never in a million years have understood the answer.

She might not have the gene, but at least she is southern enough to cry over a fashion statement—and to cause such a tragedy in the first place. Drama, I've ascertained after long observation, is vastly important to the southerner, and must be created at every opportunity.

In her wonderful book, *Southern Ladies and Gentlemen*, Florence King explains about southern woman—their birthright, she maintains, is to cause trouble. She also sheds light on my mother's tears: "To a Southerner, it is faux pas, not sins, that matter in this world."

Best of all, she cracks the code of southern double-think—"a blasé acceptance of contradiction"—and I can only estimate the thousands of dollars in shrink bills her clear thinking has saved me.

I should say how I happened to read the book. After many years in California, I decided to go to Key West, Florida to work on my own book. A good friend gave me *Southern Ladies and Gentlemen* to take along, but I put it aside when I arrived.

I had a tiny yard, a postage stamp, really, but completely fenced and full of lush vegetation, including an avocado tree. One afternoon, dressed in the teeniest of bikinis, I was taking a break under my avocado tree, lying on my back and staring upward, enjoying the sinuous progress of a cat among the leaves. My neighbor shot the cat out of the tree. Revulsion rising in me like vomit, I fled into the house, hating the man, hating the town, hating the South. *Why in hell did I ever come back to this violent place?* I asked myself, more concerned with that question than with the greater problem of what to do. If I reported the man, he'd probably shoot me too. If I didn't he probably still would.

Swiveling frantically, as if looking for answers from the geckos in the corners, I saw Miss King's book on my shelf. I'll never know what latent instinct for self-preservation made me pick it up, but I did. I didn't even put on a T-shirt, just dug in and didn't put it down till I'd finished it, my near-naked body a feast for the bugs the geckos missed.

I love this particular passage, which applies to me in a way: "Yankees always make the mistake of going home the moment they realize they are going mad, which is why they have never understood the South. They do not grasp the simple fact that losing one's mind is the most important prerequisite for fitting in with Southerners. Sanity has never held any charms for us: in fact, we're against it."

A goosebump-producing notion.

Savannah, Georgia was my particular madhouse and I vowed to go "home" to Yankeeland the minute I reached the age of majority, but I got sidetracked and ended up in New Orleans. Thereby hangs a tale—in fact, this tale, but I'm going to tell it slow.

Miss King saved my sanity, or what was left of it, but her book nonetheless filled me with envy—she had the gene and I didn't. She wrote like the insider she is, and even when she mentioned the cruelty and violence that pervades the region it was with humor and affection.

I've come to the point that I can write about that myself, though not quite in the same way. But I find the joyous celebration of pettiness that is so institutionalized in Savannah—or was when I spent time there—almost as distressing.

My brother's wedding was so traumatizing I didn't return for fifteen years, though I was a grown woman at the time and should, in the words of a southern friend, have known better.

The trouble started when my mother got a call from my sister-in-law to be, who asked for me. Mother said later that "something told her" not to let us talk, but if she'd just handed over the phone, hurt feelings would almost certainly have been averted—I'm quite sure I'd simply have laughed, and Dianne would have had to too. All Mother could think, I'm sure, was that I was genetically unequipped to cope with the situation; she forgot that she was too. As a result of her inserting herself heroically to save the situation, five or six dramas were unleashed at once.

The first problem was my underwear. The wedding took place about 1969 or '70, I guess, at the height of bralessness, which I believed had swept the country, but which apparently hadn't yet hit Savannah. It seemed the entire Lady Jane Shop was simply abuzz because I'd tried on my bridesmaid's dress without a bra. That was bad, but it was going to be a lot worse if I didn't wear a bra at the wedding, lest my nipples show up in the pictures. I should mention here that the dresses were perfectly opaque and so shaped as not even to suggest a nipple, much less display one. However, nothing would do but an underwear inspection before the wedding, to make sure I didn't cheat.

Now all this would seem trivial—if not laughable—but for the fact that poor Dianne was in tears over the matter—or so my mother said. (Dianne and I have never spoken of it.) *Her* mother, I also heard, told my mother after the ceremony that "there's just never been anything like this in *our* family."

If we'd been dealing merely with the matter of the bra, no matter, no matter at all, But there was a second little problem in that Lady Jane Shop. It seemed the groom's sister had been accompanied by a hippie.

That was the part the ladies of the Lady Jane could really get their teeth into. My boyfriend Ron had been invited, cordially, in fact, though I'd warned all involved that he had long hair. "As long as it's neat," my parents had said, and I assured them it was kept safely corralled in a ponytail.

They also knew that Ron was Jewish. That was okay, that was just fine.

But what they'd never seen before was the coiffure then described as a Jewish natural. Ponytail or no, hair that curly was a scandal, pure and simple.

No one put it that way, of course. You don't *say* things like that. Even I knew that.

If I had any doubt the thing was a hair problem, it was dispelled by the man we heard whispering at the beach: "There goes one now. Look: hair up in a little bun. Idn't that sweet?" Did I say he was whispering? He made *quite* sure we heard it, after which, I expect, he went home and shot a cat out of a tree.

My mother was all for dis-inviting Ron to the wedding, which was fine with him, but my brother, who arrived from Georgia Tech in mid-drama, wouldn't hear of that, which stirred things up even better.

What else? All the extra beds had been given to non–family

members, and so some of the young people had volunteered to bunk on the floor in sleeping bags. Except that my mother decreed that, even though we offered to sack out at opposite ends of it, Ron and I weren't to sleep in the same room. Why? "Because my sister just wouldn't understand," she said.

When my aunt found out about it, naturally she told her baby sister not to be so silly, which upped the ante further still.

Later I whined about the whole event to my friend, Linda, from Forest, Mississippi, and she hadn't a sympathetic bone in her body. "Why didn't you *know?*" she said. "You *had* to know."

She has the gene.

I had a fifteen-year headache.

I didn't know, I really didn't, but what I knew then and what hasn't changed a bit is this: Savannah was not home. Not this place where the tiniest wrong move translated to a faux pas, which must then have tears shed over it. Where pettiness was a career choice, minding other people's business a religion.

Especially that.

Despite the risibility of nipples and curls, when I think back to those early years, my chest tightens and I feel once more the bleakness, the head-banging frustration of being on the outside looking in. Knowing I might as well have come from Jupiter or Pluto. To this day, when I read accounts of early emigrants or lonely travelers, I *know;* I feel what they feel.

But if I didn't belong in Savannah, then where? There was Somewhere Else, I knew it. There were places where you did what you wanted, even—imagine!—*wore* what you wanted, and no one said a word.

Something I thought a lot about was sex. I happened to know (because I'd been told) that in the South it was ugly and dirty if you weren't married, but if you were, it miraculously became "very beautiful."

I also happened to know (because I'd read it) that there were places where anyone could do it.

One of these places was no doubt "home," but which? Not New York. That was the place most of the books were about, but it seemed to have an attractive brittleness that, deep down, I knew wasn't right.

Wasn't warm.

I guess warmth was what I wanted. That and wine, men, and song. Giddy sophistication. Witty badinage. Not to mention the delicious anonymity of being someplace where no one knew whose little girl I was. It was just that I hadn't figured out about the warmth yet—except on some internal plane.

When I was a senior at the University of Mississippi, the subject of what to do next came up with two of my friends. I remember someone saying, "Let's go out to the coast," and how exotic that sounded. How right.

"The coast" was what we thought sophisticated people called California. That might have meant L.A., but it turned out we all had the same city in mind—Frisco, as we called it.

I was delirious with adventure. I was pretty sure that was it— the home I was looking for. Why, I have no idea. As it happened, if I'd had any glimmer of what was going on there, I'd have been sure I wanted it, but at the time I'd never heard of a "hippie."

However, the girl with the car backed out. My friend Ann and I, unwilling to forego the adventure, quickly regrouped and bought Greyhound bus tickets for the nearest interesting city.

New Orleans.

I can truthfully say that was the best eight dollars I ever spent, but that, of course, is with hindsight.

At the time it seemed merely an adventure, a pretty good adventure, but not the adventure I wanted. My plan was to get some newspaper experience (I'd majored in journalism), save enough money for plane fare, and then set out for what I thought of as the big league.

For eighty dollars, Ann and I rented a furnished apartment on the edge of the Garden District. The furniture was Naugahyde and fifties Danish, patrolled by about ten thousand guppy-sized roaches. But the place had fourteen-foot ceilings, a balcony on a Mardi Gras parade route, and floor-to-ceiling windows. As far as I was concerned, it was the acme of glamour, but the most colorful thing about it didn't even come to light until recently. In fact, the story may still be unfolding.

The story of our landlord, that is. Some years later he was arrested for the murder of his wife. He beat that rap, but only last year he was popped again, this time in a video poker scandal; it was alleged he was fronting for the mob.

Such a nice man. He got rid of those roaches for us.

Ann got a job at a restaurant supply company and I became a junior clerk at Shell Oil. We both quickly moved on, though not necessarily up. She got a teaching gig, and I cracked the mighty *Times-Picayune*, though only as a librarian. I made $35 a week, which was just enough to squeak by on for about a month. Much longer and I might have lost patience, but as it happened a reporter quit and I got her job. By plain luck, it was the best job on the paper—I became a feature writer for the Sunday magazine, which, so far as I was concerned, was a license to steal.

I wasn't yet twenty-one and I could go anywhere, do anything, and call it journalism. I wanted to go to Mardi Gras balls, so I asked to cover them. I wanted to make sense of something I knew well but didn't understand, so I did a story on bootlegging in Mississippi.

I met interesting people that year—my upstairs neighbor, the single mother (the first one I ever knew); the Frenchman down the street who had lots of time and even more women; Mike, who hung around Ann, but wore leopard briefs in public; and mysterious Jerry, who lived in the building where everyone knew there'd once been a grisly murder and who clearly had a secret. A closet mobster? Or merely a closet queen? I never found out.

And that was without leaving the block, which wasn't even in the French Quarter.

There were the people on the paper too, and friends of college friends, all of whom drank a lot, knew a lot about literature, and liked to stay up all night discussing it. Then around dawn, a brisk walk to the river and back home to a Bloody Mary for breakfast. I could never keep enough tomato juice in the house.

At night I went to blues clubs, interracial clubs (daring in those days), and a sailor's bar where I saw a bloody fight once—between a kid from Ole Miss and one from LSU, it turned out. Still, it was a fight.

It was easy to meet people and Life flowed. The streets were Parisian in their beauty, the food ambrosial. The men were courtly, the women wild as the wind, eccentricity the norm.

Looking back on it, life was a cabaret. Every day was Mardi Gras.

I took it all for granted.

Young men fell out of the sky, but I was fond of saying there was no one to date. "Everyone's either gay or married or both," I'd intone. What I meant was, the available men weren't from "Frisco."

One of the biggest hurricanes in the history of the city nearly leveled it one day. "It's boring here," I'd whine. What I meant was, the Haight-Ashbury was a few thousand miles away.

"It's just not . . . sophisticated," I'd complain. What I meant was, everyone had a southern accent.

I guess I just plain had a "Frisco" fixation—and my instincts, it turned out, were good.

The New Orleans of those days was both too wild and too stodgy for me. The wild part, the heart and soul of the city, probably frightened me a little. The other, stodgy part, represented proper southern decorum, which I'd had up to here. I wanted to make my own rules.

When I stepped off the plane in San Francisco, when I breathed that crisp air for the first time, I knew I was home.

This was the place I knew had to be *somewhere.*

I couldn't wait to get myself a pair of bells and a turtleneck, but first I had to get a job.

I managed to get hired at the San Francisco *Chronicle*, though the city editor was famous for sexism. For the time being, I was relegated to the section called "Women's World."

It was the winter before the Summer of Love—1967, I think, and surely as magical a place and time as Paris in the twenties. The first week I was there, I heard a man ask a woman dressed as a gypsy what the hippie movement was all about. "It's not a movement," she said. "It's a celebration."

Bad things happened that year. The Vietnam War raged on with no signs of abating. Martin Luther King was killed. But that woman's words were the hallmark of my first few years in what I no longer called "Frisco."

It was like being on another planet, one on which the atmosphere was a great deal more compatible. Not only could I wear whatever I wanted, the weirder the better. Not only did people here have sex, they felt free to talk about it. I didn't know a soul—which meant I was free to choose whom I'd know—and no one cared whose kid I was. I thought I was some kind of female Jack Kerouac.

I'd so very much disliked my hometown that I don't guess I'd have given the idea of "community" a millisecond, but I must have wanted it. In no time I was living in Berkeley, in what you might call a semi-commune, though it wasn't that at all, it was something a lot more practical. What it was, was the downstairs front apartment of a house with two other apartments in which all the other tenants were close—and sometimes even related.

At first I had various roommates, two or more at a time. But when it worked at its finest, it was just Ron and me, the same

Ron who made such a splash in Savannah. We had our best friends upstairs, my baby sister in back, and as the song said, two cats in the yard.

I still worked for the *Chronicle*, though now on general assignment, and pretty much thought I owned the town. But imagine my surprise when the kid sister got married and left, the neighbors broke up, and so did Ron and I. What kind of community is that?

Having thought "alternative life styles" were cultural changes rather than fads, I was shocked to learn that everyone else, in the end, pretty much preferred nuclear families.

The eighties changed the face of San Francisco. Everything I loved and understood, everything that fairly smacked me in the face that day I thought I had found home, didn't disappear, exactly—but it got a lot harder to find.

The relaxed quality was gone, that sense that anything was possible, all kinks would uncurl if one would only take a moment to admire the view. The feeling of warmth, I think, had dissipated.

But I didn't really notice at first. I briefly moved to Santa Barbara, just to try something different, and while I was there, I railed that it had no edge, no sense of zaniness, no exuberant, untameable center.

When I got back to San Francisco, I noticed that it hadn't got those things either. The realization came gradually, but its onset was greatly speeded, I think, by something that happened in Santa Barbara.

I began to write about New Orleans.

By this time I'd published a number of mystery novels set in San Francisco, I'd been told southern writers always wrote about the South, and I'd scoffed.

Not me. Not bloody likely. Since I didn't understand one thing about the South, I could hardly write about it.

Why this hadn't occurred to me many years earlier I can't possibly tell you—perhaps I should blame some bizarre form of writer's block—but it suddenly entered my head to create a detective character who also didn't have the southern gene, one quite sure she'd been spawned in some other world and dropped from her spacecraft to the mysterious Crescent City.

The book came alive in a way that none of the San Francisco tales ever had; I didn't know the dark side of my adopted home and I didn't want to know. But I sure as hell knew what went on inside a southern family. And due to my reportorial curiosity, I knew what a Mardi Gras ball looked like and where a few bodies were buried.

What I didn't know, I had to return to New Orleans to find out.

It had been a few years since I'd really spent time there. Yet things looked so familiar it was as if this were the place I'd grown up, instead of Savannah.

The city shrugged itself around me like a multihued cocoon, like the air of New Orleans itself, in summer near the river, when the humidity is so high, the atmosphere so nearly palpable, you feel you could turn round and round and wrap yourself in it, like Cleopatra in her rug. It has something of her quality, too, of beauty and mystery, the promise of erotic surprise when the rug is unwrapped.

And that is only the air.

A friend of mine, a musician who spends his life traveling, who has deplaned in every city in the country and probably in Europe as well, says that New Orleans is the only city you can smell the second you walk off the plane. He's right. What you get is an old smell, an earthy, musky smell that's somehow redolent with promise. It's there summer and winter. I expect it's mildew.

What is it that the mildew promises? I'm not entirely sure, and of course the mystery is part of the draw. But I think it evokes a feeling of decay, hence of age and history, layers of it—the Indians, the French, the Spanish, the English, the Acadians, the Africans. It is the old part that's important here—the age and the layering. Hundreds of years of tradition—flaunted.

That's a lot to get from a slight scent in the air and yet—I promise this—when you step off the plane, you are aware of something different, something exciting in the air, something visceral and vital and available. Indeed inevitable.

When people come to New Orleans they lose themselves. The quiet get loud, the uptight get rowdy, the sober get drunk, the cautious get reckless, the modest get naked (frequently in public), and nearly everyone gets laid. I'm not saying they know this is going to happen the minute they arrive, but sometimes the change is almost instantaneous. A friend reported coming for JazzFest—not even Mardi Gras—and as she walked through the airport, she and her friends spotted a herd of young men behind them, bearing down, trying to catch up. Suddenly, a maverick broke from the herd, ran straight at my friend, dove down between her legs, and lifted her to his shoulders. After that, she found the New Orleans experience rather like that of flying—you simply get comfortable and leave your fate in the hands of the pilot.

That whiff at the airport is so subtle you could miss it if you weren't paying attention, but the French Quarter (which happens to be my personal hangout) is such a carnival of redolence that once you've smelled it, your nose never forgets. I remember how it hit me when I first came back after years away—like gusts from a hurricane off the gulf, like long-lost memories come haunting.

Not all of it was nice: "Beer, piss, and vomit," a friend reminded me. Yes, all that, as familiar as the grillwork.

But also frying oysters and the river and perfume mixed with sweat, jasmine and tea olive, pheromones. And that mildew, of course. That oldness.

And once again, the promise. Of something. Something more. Ripples under the surface, aching passions, and passions having nothing to do with sex.

In San Francisco, where I first marched in the streets and heard the Grateful Dead in the park, people are currently into vegetables and working out and working hard. Socializing online. Corner offices and BMWs. Going to bed exhausted and early.

In New Orleans, the Mardi Gras Indians stay up sewing. These Indians are not tribes of Native Americans, but "gangs" of black men, most poor, some not married, living only for Carnival, who spend the year making feather and embroidery costumes for Mardi Gras. They shop. They spend giant chunks of their salaries. They sew. They design. On the front of each costume are several embroidered pictures, one beneath the other, that tell a story. The costumes can be worn only once and, since Indians parade in their own neighborhoods, are rarely seen by tourists or even by white natives. They are frequently museum quality.

Now that's passion.

Perhaps the corner-office crowd and the Indians are apples and oranges—I don't mean to compare them. I mean that the hard drivers are people who deliberately constrict their lives, making them bland and, BMWs aside, spartan and mingy. The Indians are people who inspire with their passion and their art and their commitment, who make you believe the Twentieth Century could be more than cyber-space and raw carrots.

But they are admittedly archetypes. What of the regular folk? Ah, now. Here we have the nitty-gritty—the utterly mad populace is what keeps writers writing. People say that Ignatius Reilly, hero of *A Confederacy of Dunces*, is a unique creation, but I beg to differ. A brilliant *character*, but perhaps not a creation at all. Ignatius was probably the author's next-door neighbor. Everybody in New Orleans should get a book written about them.

Last winter I stayed on a stretch of St. Louis Street that has the distinction of possessing the worst bars in the French Quarter. My friend who lives at one end of the block gets up at 5 A.M. to write, just as the drag queens are calling it a night. They wave as she sips coffee on her deck. By noon, they're up again, wearing trousers, wigs off, real hair in ponytails under bald spots. Her writing done, she chats with them as they water their plants or pop out for a carton of milk.

Then there's young Cassie at the other end of the block. She's in college now, but she used to dash out on her way to school only to be sent back in by the hookers sitting on the steps: "Young lady, get back in that house and get your sweater. It's freezing out here."

And there's Max the Mime at the other side of the Quarter. When he goes off his meds, the neighbors coax him back to the hospital, but sometimes it takes a few days. When he's acting out, we know it clear over in my neighborhood. "Watch out for him," people say. "He's a little shaky these days." No one knows his last name.

What I love is that Max and the hookers and the queens are not something *other*, something strange out *there*, but part of the texture of the community. It's a small space here, just a few blocks, and somehow or other we find ways of getting along.

I find these stories get me a little teary, regretful for what we've lost. Somehow, middle-class America got the idea it ought to live in sanitized ghettos because if the kids met a whore, it would be catastrophic. Rich America went further—to gated communities where, if the *adults* met a person of color, it would cause heart failure.

Call me weird, but I kind of like the idea of people taking care of each other. Actually, it goes a lot farther than that. I'm sick to death of the anonymity I thought would be so freeing.

Where I live in California, I'd be so happy to know the neighbors, I wouldn't care if they were jewel thieves, let alone hookers. I've lived at the same modest address for three years, and I have yet to have more than a moment of conversation with any of my neighbors. I say "hi," they say "hi"; I say "How are you?," they say nothing. They are not unkind, merely distant. Mark next door once gave me a jump when my battery died, and Louise, on the other side, comes calling when her cats are missing. Once, I used her phone when mine went dead. Other than that, none of us has been in the other's house.

My friend Ken, who lives in the French Quarter, says the reason everyone there is so nice to each other is that they're all dying to get in each other's houses. He may have something there—it's a house-obsessed culture.

Be that as it may, there's certainly a strong sense of that community I'm missing so much. And maybe it's all the stronger because it has developed against such great odds. When you get down to it, there's no bigger collection of cranks, rebels, and nonconformists in the world than the population of Louisiana. One of my novels, a book called *The Axeman's Jazz*, is set against the background of Twelve Step programs—not AA, but the others so popular in this time of "creating community" rather than getting to know the neighbors. Some of these are Al-Anon, Coda (Codependents Anonymous), Sex and Love Anonymous, Overeaters Anonymous, even Shoppers Anonymous. Having attended meetings in California, I know that one of the primary rules is that there must be no crosstalk—so that people will feel free to say anything they want without fear of being judged, contradicted, or argued with.

When I went to my first Coda meeting in New Orleans, a man got up and said he didn't really think much of Coda, after which he elaborated.

The proper answer, I knew from experience, was, "Thank you for sharing." Having expressed his appreciation, the person running the meeting was supposed to call on someone else, who'd be free to speak on any topic except his opinion of the preceding "share."

However, this chairman not only failed to thank the speaker, he failed to call on *anyone*, and evidently he forgot the crosstalk rule as well. Instead, he rebutted the speaker, which ignited those who agreed with the first man, who then spoke up themselves.

"Pretty soon," I told a friend after the meeting, "There was pretty much of a free-for-all going on in there."

"Honey," he said, "you should see the Louisiana legislature."

Isn't that the truth. Cranks, rebels and nonconformists. My kind of people.

I'm not quite sure why I didn't see it all those years ago. Perhaps I was wary because I expected all southerners to behave like Savannahians.

My brother Steve, who has visited New Orleans only once or twice, said something smart about why they don't: "It's the difference between a Catholic culture and a southern Baptist culture. The Catholics have this built-in notion of absolution."

We were brought up Methodist, my brother and I, so I haven't any idea what Catholic dogma actually holds. But I've certainly observed that people in New Orleans behave as if they think it's fine to sin up a storm on Mardi Gras, so long as they behave like saints during Lent.

On reflection, it seems as if many similar cultures—including the one that coined the phrase "joie de vivre"—are Catholic as well. Mediterranean cultures, Caribbean cultures; cultures where fiestas abound and carnivals are routinely concocted; where people stay up all night, usually to dance; where ambient pheromones tug at your vitals. (Those with a touch of paganism, like Brazil and Cuba, are the sexiest and have the best music.)

There is something in the human soul that craves ritual and pageantry, theater and glamour, foolery and festivity. A Protestant culture offers none of the above, not even, in most cases, so simple a pleasure as incense.

I think I can see now that, failing a Mardi Gras, most southerners, taught from birth the virtue of living a vanilla life, must make do with impromptu drama, cobbled together from available materials. They learn from infancy to turn a pair of mismatched socks into a Tennessee Williams one-act.

An edgy event like a wedding—characters in place, emotions raw—is a perfect focus for whomping up grand opera. And the merest scrap of scandal—even so fragile, so thin and gossamer a thing as a drunken party-kiss—can be lovingly transformed into the Ashland Shakespeare Festival.

This is why embarrassment must be accompanied by tears and hand-wringing, misunderstandings so carefully coddled—some days there are just no good movies playing.

It's enough to make you flee three thousand miles to Frisco.

In *Beach Music,* Pat Conroy has a character say something I would have found ominous ten years ago: "You'll be back soon. The South's got a lot wrong with it. But it's permanent press and it doesn't wash out."

These days I don't find that terrifying and, furthermore, even think it might be true. Maybe you can go home again. Maybe it's possible to be southern, even if home isn't the town you grew up in.

So I'm going.

It's Thursday, and this is the last thing I have to write before getting on with my packing. I'm moving back Saturday, to the heart of the French Quarter. I can't wait, and would have gone tomorrow, but it's Friday the thirteenth. I don't want anything to mess this up.

when i go home

lucille clifton

i go to where my mother is,
alive again and humming
in a room
warm with the scent of dough
rising under damp towels,
and i walk
linoleum again, hard against
the splintered floorboards
that she held
together with her song.
i hear and smell and almost taste
the tremors of that house
and i am home, i have gone home
wherever i might find myself,
home
where the memory is.

New Jersey, 1963

DANI SHAPIRO

THEY COME IN the night, setting fire to our front lawn, cars careening across our soft summer grass, tires digging dark grooves which will grow muddy and dank in the August heat. Their methods change with the seasons: In autumn, they toss raw eggs at the white columns of our house. In winter, they leave TV dinners filled with dog shit steaming in the snow outside our front door. In summer, the cars come screeching down the street, gaining momentum until they fly across our front lawn, ruining the sprinkler system my parents so proudly installed when they bought their piece of the American suburban dream.

I am asleep in my bed, in my pink-and-orange ruffled room with its shelves of dolls from foreign countries: Spanish dolls wearing layers of brightly colored skirts, wooden Russian dolls, tiny bowling pins of color which open up, revealing smaller and smaller versions of themselves inside. Downstairs, my parents are talking in hushed tones. Perhaps they are sitting in the living room, peering from behind the heavy brocade curtains at the arc of headlights flying across their lawn, as improbable as a shooting star. Maybe my mother calls the police, maybe not. They are used to this by now; they know the police do nothing.

Next to my parents, there is a glass case filled with ancient Judaica: blown glass from Jerusalem, antique silver wine goblets, parchment so old it crumbles to the touch. An intercom lets them hear me rustling in my bed. They look at each other, worry etched in their faces. They blamed themselves, they blame one another, they blame history and the accident of geography that brought them to this neighborhood. Outside, there is a lone shout in the night—*Dirty Jews!*—and my father holds his head in his hands, fragile as an artifact.

Later that night, my mother checks on me. Her heels make soft thuds on the shag carpet of my room. Her breath is sweet and warm as she bends down and places a finger under my nose to make sure I'm still breathing. There is a mobile fluttering above my head and lithographs by Miró and Ben Shahn on the walls. The Ben Shahn has words on it, too, words I don't yet understand: *Who is God?*

I GREW UP in a house protected by three different kinds of alarm systems: A steady red light outside the front and back doors switched on by a small circular key. A motion detector in specific, supposedly crime-prone rooms, activated by currents in the air. And carefully placed "panic buttons"—one in my parents' bedroom and another in the kitchen. When pushed in unison, they set off an ear-splitting siren in the house and an alert to the local police of a crime in progress. As a child, I often wondered what would happen if, just for the hell of it, I pushed those buttons. Maybe, I thought, those buttons would make a bad situation worse.

We had alarm magnets on every window and alarm pads scattered throughout the house beneath the wall-to-wall carpeting like land mines. The inner doors all had push-button locks, and some of the telephones had a unique feature—a little plastic hinge which, if someone elsewhere in the house picked up an extension, would prevent them from listening in.

The key word was *protection*. I don't know if this quest to seal us off from the rest of the world began before or after the violence and the screamed epithets in the night. But I have my hunches; my parents were both fearful people who believed that it was possible to control life, to keep the bogeyman away, to buy safety.

It was, I suppose, a piece of bad luck that my parents bought a house in a neighborhood where Jews weren't welcome. They were hardly kids when they married—well into their thirties and each divorced. Their decision to choose this particular house, this particular neighborhood, was a well-considered one. No doubt, they wasted hours debating the merits of the city versus the suburbs, New Jersey versus Connecticut. They wanted a home they could settle into, within commuting distance of the city and walking distance of a synagogue. My father, a born and bred Manhattanite, loved the idea of life in the suburbs.

I imagine them now, laying eyes on the Georgian colonial for the first time: the red brick walls and white pillars, the flagstone walk winding up from the cobblestone street. A wrought-iron light hangs above the front door. They have driven from the city in my father's baby-blue Chrysler, more boat than car, and they have brought my father's parents with them to see the house. I am an infant, bundled in my grandfather's arms. It is early spring; there are still icy patches on the ground, and my father steadies his father, holds on to his mother's elbow as they make their way around the back of the house, past two red brick lightposts which remind my mother of something she once saw in London. There are new trees in the backyard—a shady elm, a young oak—and my parents squeeze their clasped hands, imagining their family growing in this house, imagining these trees a few decades from now. In their mind's eye, the rooms are already being filled—they can see the teal velvet couch, the Eames chairs, the Ben Shahn lithograph in my room. My grandfather gives a nod of approval. *Now this is balebatish,* he says, this man whose own father was an immigrant and who now lives in a grand apartment on Central Park West. This is proper and beautiful.

WHEN I CLOSE my eyes and try to breathe Hillside, New Jersey back into my senses, I return to a place of immense contradiction: I smell the forsythia and the putrid smoke of nearby oil refineries, I hear the chirping of bluebirds in the backyard along with the roar of jets taking off from nearby Newark Airport. Hillside was less a town than an enclave. There was no village, no Main Street, no general store. When people referred to "the city" they were talking about New York City. Though Manhattan was only half an hour away, to many of our neighbors it might as well have been halfway across the country. They saw it as a dangerous place—a place where anything could happen. Whenever my parents and I drove through the Lincoln Tunnel, I kept my eyes peeled for the tiled line in the tunnel wall indicating the border between New Jersey and New York, and felt an almost electrical *ping* shoot up my spine when we crossed that line and entered Manhattan, the tunnel spitting us out onto Ninth Avenue, into a world which seemed rich with possibility. The city, for me, usually meant a treat: tickets to *The Nutcracker* at Lincoln Center, a visit to my grandmother's apartment on Central Park West, overlooking the steeples of The Dakota. A turkey, tongue, coleslaw, and Russian dressing sandwich at Fine & Schapiro on Seventy-second Street, where the old waitresses would treat my father like a boy, urging him to eat more, chucking him under the chin.

But inevitably, we would head home. I would sit in the backseat and watch the Manhattan skyline disappear around the bend, and a familiar heaviness would descend as we passed back over the tiled border to the jagged, graffiti-covered cliffs of Jersey City, the newly built Newark Airport, the neon Budweiser eagle slowly flapping its wings over the Anheuser-Busch plant.

✳   ✳   ✳

I'M HARD-PRESSED here, pushing, searching for something positive and uplifting to write about the place where I grew up. After all, it is my own internal landscape, the place where my stories began, and thinking about it raises a moral question: Would I trade my own painful childhood for a happier one and not possess this material as a writer? Those years of childhood isolation are what have shaped my voice. There is no doubt in my mind that those years made me a writer, but they could just as easily have made me psychotic.

We had a hard time in Hillside. It was just one of those towns, a piece of bad luck, the wrong place to live. We were surrounded by families who were all more like each other than we were like them. Worst of all, we were Orthodox Jews. In a neighborhood which didn't take kindly to Jewish families to begin with, my parents arrived with their foreign customs, such as a wooden *succah*—a glorified shack— which we erected in the backyard each autumn to celebrate the old harvest days with shafts of wheat and bitter lemons. We had mezuzahs on all the doors, and we didn't drive on the Sabbath. We were kosher, in every sense of the word. Each Saturday morning, my father would don a dark suit and yarmulke and walk the mile or so to synagogue, past the houses of those who had thrown eggs and set fire to his lawn.

If asked, my father would have defined himself first and foremost as a Jew. Even before he was a husband, a father, a Wall Street businessman, he was an observant Jew. The traditions of orthodoxy were his roots, the bedrock of the family he came from, and though he was probably conflicted at times, he never rebelled, never ran away. For a while, he and my mother agreed to raise me Orthodox. Until I was thirteen, I went to a yeshiva in a nearby town, where I became fluent in Hebrew and learned to climb around in the intellectual branches of the Talmud. But while my classmates went home to neighborhoods and communities where there were other Orthodox Jewish families, in my mother's chocolate-brown Eldorado I reentered a neighborhood where it was a bad thing, an odd thing, to be a Jew.

It was the beginning of my sense of not-belonging; an invisible wall had gone up between me and the rest of the world, and before I knew it, I was banging against it, trying to get out.

In those days, we had live-in housekeepers, though now, as a grown woman, I don't understand why. I was an only child, and my mother didn't work outside the house. What did she do all day? The house was spotless. These housekeepers, who never lasted more than a year or two, were from faraway islands: Jamaica, Trinidad, Martinique, Antigua. They wore white uniforms during the day, and at night they retreated to a small room in the basement, near the laundry room, where it was implicitly understood I should not bother them. I now think of this room, with its small window which overlooked the inside of the metal grate in the backyard, and remember sneaking in and seeing Bibles, crosses, pictures of Jesus Christ.

My mother fired one housekeeper for asking her where her horns were. When my mother asked her what she meant, the housekeeper said she had been told Jews had horns. She was gone the next day. The others, they had a hard time getting the hang of our strict dietary laws and religious customs. The kitchen had two sinks, two dishwashers. Milk and meat were kept strictly separate. And this isn't counting Passover, with its whole other set of dishes and the traditional, ritualistic banishing of all breadcrumbs throughout the house with a flashlight and a feather.

GOING HOME. GOING *back home. Going home to visit my parents.* These are words my grown friends still utter, friends well into their thirties and forties with families and children of their own. I tried to stop thinking of 885 Revere Drive as home when I first left it to go to college, sixteen years ago. I was in the midst of a fairly violent rebellion against my parents, and I hated everything the house and neighborhood had come to stand for: the bourgeois suburbia of private tennis courts, heated swimming pools, new Cadillacs, prized sons who went to medical schools, and the prized daughters who married them. Though more Jewish families moved into the neighborhood over the years and the overt anti-Semitism faded into something more subtle than burning lawns, it was a place that never felt like home. I was furious at my parents for digging their heels in and staying in a neighborhood where we were second-class citizens, for not seeing the writing on the wall back when I was an infant. Why hadn't they packed up and moved back into the city? There, I imagined, we would have been one among many families just like us, a single cell in a larger organism. I longed for community. And of course I was rebelling against Orthodoxy itself: while my classmates were sneaking around smoking pot during high school, I thought God would strike me dead for eating bacon or driving on the Sabbath. When real rebellion finally did strike, it did so with the force of a small tornado. It didn't let up until I was well into my twenties.

I FELT LIKE a wanderer, rootless, in need of a home. I tried to make a home for myself wherever I went, even in my college dorm room, where I hung a floral sheet over the window and kept lighted, scented candles on my nightstand. I chose a college which was listed in a guide to colleges as a "haven for neurotic upper-middle-class artsy types who don't know where they fit in." I fit right in. Then, at nineteen, I married for the first time—*not* a medical student—and went about the business of playing house while still in college, picking out fresh flowers each week at an outdoor market on Columbus Avenue, giving dinner parties, planting trees in huge terra-cotta pots. I decided I was a grown woman, that I could skip certain developmental steps (like late adolescence) as if skipping over Boardwalk in a game of Monopoly.

Even though I stayed away from Revere Drive and tried to forge a life of my own, I always knew it was there, a house I had lived in so long that I could have found my way from attic to kitchen blindfolded. I still knew just how many steps it took to get up the front walk, how many stairs separated the basement from the first floor. I still heard the milkbox clanking with fresh bottles every Tuesday morning and saw the gardener trimming the forsythia hedges on alternate Thursdays. I knew where to find my own initials, which I had carved deeply into an attic beam to ensure they would always be there. But most importantly, I knew I could go there if I were sick, tired, in need of care—and that my old room was there for me any time I wanted it, with its pink shag carpeting and the Ben Shahn lithograph on the wall.

By twenty, I was divorced. A twenty-year-old divorcée is, or should be, an oxymoron. I felt too old to go back home and have my mother take care of me, and I was too embarrassed to return to dorm life, so I rented a cottage at the end of a long dirt road not far from college. Each night I'd stay awake into the early morning hours with my golden retriever, listening to the creaks of the cottage, the wind howling through the trees. The cottage was on the property of a sculptor, a woman whose work took the form of huge plaster, metal, and concrete boulders that littered the fields around the house. If I peered out my window in the middle of the night, by the light of the moon those boulders looked like droppings from some nasty prehistoric creature—a grown-up version of the shadow on the wall, the monster in the closet.

I was accomplishing one part of my objective—putting distance between me and home—but my quest was beginning to have the unfortunate side effect of making me feel even more rootless than before. While I was in the throes of my rebellion, swimming against the current, something stronger than me was beginning to pull me back.

I OFTEN GIVE my creative writing students this exercise: Write about a house from the point of view of a character who has just lost her child in a war; then describe the same house from the point of view of a character who has just fallen in love.

This exercise stumps them. When they return to class after a week of struggling, they are often frustrated, filled with questions:

How do the actual physical properties of a place change, they wonder, depending on point of view? A wastebasket is a wastebasket, an oven is an oven.

The key to creating a sense of place lies with the narrator, I tell them. The details, in and of themselves, are not important. They are a reflection of the inner life of the teller of the story. And as we discuss the meaning of metaphor, I am drawn back to a moment in my own life, a moment in which I am a grown woman, sitting in my car outside my parents' house.

I am twenty-three, and my father has just died in a car crash, an accident which very nearly also took my mother's life. She is in the hospital, her legs shattered into eighty pieces. It is unclear whether she will walk again, whether she will recover from the immensity of this physical and emotional blow. After a lifetime spent protecting themselves from the world, my parents have had their lives busted wide open on a New Jersey highway.

Six months earlier, my parents had finally moved from the house at 885 Revere Drive. They were looking for a calmer, more aesthetically pleasing life for their later years, and a house in a more rural part of New Jersey was supposed to do the trick. I did not come home to help my parents move. When my mother called to ask what I wanted her to do with my wooden Russian dolls, the white Formica dresser with its orange knobs, the poster I kept on my bedroom wall—*If you have to get out of town, get in front of the crowd and make it look like a parade*—I told her she could throw it all away. I believed I had no sentimental attachment to the stuff of my childhood. It never occurred to me that my parents, both in their sixties at this point, might need my help moving out. Nor did I go see their new home. I was angry with them for moving because it made me realize what I had long known, that we could have moved many years earlier, perhaps to a more welcoming community.

So there I am, days after my father's death, sitting in my car. My mother has asked me to go to their house—the one I have never visited—to pick up the mail, throw out any spoiled food, check the pipes to make sure nothing is frozen. She gives me directions to the house, and I drive there early one winter afternoon.

I pull up to a newish, pale brick house on a hill, more bland than I had imagined. There is snow on the ground, and the driveway is unnegotiable. On my car radio I am listening to a Brahms piano concerto. I am alone, adrift, twenty-three. My lips and nose are chapped from two solid weeks of tears.

I park the car and make my way around to the back of the house, my boots leaving deep imprints on the snow covering the driveway. My breath is a cloud in front of me. My mother has told me to let myself in through the garage, and I do so, pressing the familiar alarm code, fiddling with strange, new keys. As the garage door slowly rises, I notice my father's green rubber galoshes on the floor, his tweed cap, hanging on a hook.

Later that day, after spending the afternoon wafting through my parents' new house and sorting through mail addressed to a dead man, I lock up, turn on the various alarm systems, and begin to drive back to the city. But my car has a mind of its own, and as we reach exit 14 on the Jersey Turnpike, I find myself signaling left, getting on the exit ramp, and driving down the icy streets until I am somehow parked in front of 885 Revere Drive.

THE MOST OBVIOUS Freudian interpretation of a dream about a house is that the house symbolizes the unconscious—the deepest part of the self. I stare at the white columns of the house in which I spent the first eighteen years of my life, the front lawn blanketed with snow, the second-floor window where my bedroom used to be. There are lights glowing inside. This house contains my secrets—secrets which may never be fully excavated on an analyst's couch or in the unconscious metaphors of my fiction. I contemplate knocking on the door, ringing the bell which may or may not still chime eight times, and introducing myself to the stranger who answers. *I lived here once,* I will say, and this fact will connect us, the way siblings separated at birth are connected by the realization that they share a parent. The house is my mother, a womb for my dreams, the place where a door to a hidden room might finally creak open, a wealth of dark jewels tumbling out.

I gaze at the second-floor bedroom window and remember a night when I was sixteen and my neighborhood friend, Allison, and I decided to sneak out of the house and go to a party across the street. It was a party we were strictly forbidden to attend, given by the sons of the neighbors my parents had always suspected were the culprits behind the violence years earlier.

This time it is a balmy night in early spring. My parents are out, and my cousin Sylvia is babysitting. Along with three alarm systems and babysitters for sixteen-year-olds, my parents believed in the additional preventative measure of a folding chain-link ladder which was kept on the top shelf of the closet in my second-floor bedroom.

Allison and I, dressed in our best light-blue corduroys, Docksiders, and LaCoste alligator shirts, drag the ladder from its storage place and hook it over the sill of my window, peering down to the flagstone patio below. It looks like a long way down. We lower the ladder, careful not to let it clang against the side of the house, particularly not against the shutters of the living room where Sylvia sits on the teal couch, listening to *La Traviata* on an enormous stereo system with two globelike speakers.

Across the lawn, rock n' roll is drifting our way. The neighborhood boys are considerably older than Allison and me, old enough to have driver's licenses and kegs of beer. Their friends' Volkswagen beetles and ten-year-old Volvos are parked all the way down the street and around the corner. It is so glamorous to me. I pat my pants pocket, making sure I have my soft pack of Marlboro Reds, hoist myself over the window ledge, and start to straddle the window— when Sylvia's head pokes out the front door.

When my parents got home that night, Sylvia handed us over

like two collared dogs. I was grounded for a couple of days; Allison wasn't allowed to accompany me to summer camp because, according to her parents, I was a "bad influence."

LATER THAT SUMMER, I wound up making out with one of those sons. I knew that he and his parents probably still called us dirty Jews behind our backs, that they had tried to burn us out of the neighborhood when I was a child. He invited me into his house, up to his room, where he still lived with his parents at the age of twenty-eight. I felt like a secret agent; I had snuck behind enemy lines. I knew I was doing the *very worst thing* I could possibly do, which was exactly why I was doing it. I was very blonde and blue-eyed, and had been fielding comments—compliments!—about how much I looked like a shiksa, a non-Jewish woman. I wondered, as he kissed me and I felt his full beard scratch my lips, my cheeks, why I was good enough for him to kiss but not good enough to live nearby. I let him put his hands on my breasts. I kept my eyes open the whole time, watching his desire grow, feeling him get hard against my thigh as we rolled around on his single bed beneath the football pennants he had won a decade earlier. His eyes were a cold, icy blue.

AS I SIT in my car with the motor idling, I stare hard at the front lawn of 885 Revere Drive until the snow begins to shift, an avalanche of memory. I see a girl and her mother walking hand-in-hand through the snow, dragging a sled behind them. I see a blonde child in a white snowsuit, building a snowman with a carrot for a nose and Oreo cookies for eyes. I squint and imagine my father pulling into the driveway in his ancient Citroën, his galoshes on his feet and his tweed cap covering his bald head.

I light a cigarette—a few years later I will quit—and walk around the side of the house. The pool, which my parents installed after my father's back surgery so he could do laps—is covered by a dark green tarp, and a small wooden bird-feeder in the shape of a house hangs from the lowest bare branch of the elm near the kitchen window. A wood-paneled station wagon is parked in the driveway, and I dully remember my parents telling me that the new owners have several kids.

I wonder if the house is cursed—whether in the proportion of the rooms, the angle of the roof, the rise of the chimney, there is an unwritten code which will bring any family who lives here unhappiness. At twenty-three, I am confused as my future students will some day be confused—I am bestowing power on the inanimate, giving objects independent meaning of their own. My father is dead, my mother is in traction, and I am a baby-divorcée who smokes too much and has no idea what to do with her life. This house, with its red-brick facade and flagstone patio, is the container of a new family's joys and sorrows. But the darkness it holds for me remains carved into the beams of its attic, just like the initials I left behind.

Living on Top

MARCIE HERSHMAN

I LIVE IN a two-family house. I bought it in 1978 after my
landlady died, because two years before, when I was twenty-five
and came out to my parents, my mother looked up amid her shock
and tears and said something extremely practical but at that delicate
moment odd: *You should buy a two-family house, so you'll have something to
count on.*

She must have sensed for some time that I was not going to
marry any of the boyfriends with whom I'd once walked arm in arm,
bringing them home on triumphant visits from college; must have
understood as men's names cropped up on my lips less frequently and
a willful, stubborn silence took over my part in what always had been
such light and animated conversations between us that she'd need to
find a good way to stop worrying. After all, she had always wanted
a secure future for me, her first child and only daughter, whom she
still and in her deepest heart loved.

It was as if my mother had heard my unguarded voice traveling
up through the walls, though she probably couldn't say she'd even
been listening for it, nor that she'd kept herself busy in order to filter
out the sounds of any more unwanted secrets. But in that moment in

my Boston apartment, when candor and emotion burst free, she found that unbidden she already had prepared a reply. Her abrupt suggestion about my buying real estate—and of all things a two-family house— was almost as much of a surprise to all of us right then and there as the *at-last!* open acknowledgment of my true sexuality.

The basis for her suggestion was pragmatic, rooted in economics. I don't know when it was that I first decided to become a writer; I seem always to have wanted to be one. My parents had acted pleased, lending their encouragement throughout my schooling—through elementary school, junior and senior high, and college—until it became clear with the final graduation that I was determined to actually live out what I'd been learning. This, despite their warnings! The children of Eastern European Jewish immigrants, both my parents had grown up during the Great Depression. My father in particular had felt the complex personal and societal tensions brought on by economic insecurity. He had worked hard to be a man with his own business. And eventually he became successful; my three younger brothers and I grew up in a traditional family in a big, new single-family house in a green suburb outside of Cleveland.

It was a home built on nearly every kind of security. Surely we wanted for nothing that seemed very important. We four children had bikes, toys, books, good public schools, wild-enough backyard fields to explore, a neighborhood full of friends. Aunts, uncles, and cousins lived a few doors away. Often one or another of our grandparents' cars sat parked in the circular driveway as they came by for Friday night's Sabbath dinner, lox and bagels on Sunday. They were vibrant in spirit, and our grandmother especially was a great storyteller. In the tales of her own childhood back in Europe in the "old country," she passed on to us an intimate sense of the other, lost part of the family. When she leaned back from a story—done, we'd hear as if in the silence and afterbeat only a hint of the wider, sadder history that was also our heritage. Old-country stuff, but was it ours, too? The quick spark of fear this ignited, the adults usually calmed with a hug, a wry shrug-of-the-shoulders joke, a kiss on the forehead. It—all of it—was far away from this house; here everything was good and familiar. At night, we kids lay abed and the muted voices of the grown-ups filtered up the stairs. The sound of their stories, no longer distinguishable but for a suddenly rising phrase or two—*I gave him what for, let me tell you! So then what happened? You have got to be kidding!*—continued to the faint percussion of forks against plates. We fell asleep to the murmurs, still half-listening.

When, twenty-two and living in Boston, I graduated from college with the conviction that writing would not be a hobby but a vocation, this first home seemed to fall even farther away. Unhappily my parents stayed back in that distance. As I took on low-paying, temporary, part-time secretarial jobs, taught once-a-week fiction classes in adult continuing-education programs, reviewed books—freelance and sporadically—for various publications, their apprehension increased. It was a clear announcement they wanted, that it was no longer worth it to me to take on such unreliable, financially tentative jobs, just to have the time to write. Or, equally as good—no, better—they hoped to learn I'd gotten engaged.

Meanwhile, I liked how things were going in the inexpensive Brookline apartment I'd rented with two other young women. In the quiet, glass-walled back porch surrounded by overgrown bushes, I sat each day at an electric typewriter to work on my first book. Like most first novels, mine was semi-autobiographical. The plot relied on personal details from the author's own life—details that took the place of more sophisticated and less neatly compliant fictional creations. On that garden-level sun porch, it was so bright. It was so easy to work there. I felt myself amazingly free, radically daring, unencumbered. The words just seemed to flow and, of course, I was happy; I wanted to keep on with this one book, forever. Though I didn't quite understand it then, what I actually was doing was getting the sound of my own self-involvement out of the way, so I could hear the more intricate, wider stories that had always been whispering to me, quietly, insistently, from somewhere under the surface.

The pages that stacked up by the windows in those first years out of college were filled with the pert dialogue and bright attributes of a thinly plotted, happily glowing coming-out story. Done, polished only once and quickly, it wouldn't find a publisher. The real writing, like the life, would take shape over a longer stretch elsewhere, in other, less glassy rooms.

IN BOSTON TWO-FAMILIES are common enough structures. They're part of streets both grand and modest. They rise with gingerbread trim and painted-lady colors from behind privet hedges on quietly preserved Victorian cul-de-sacs, and stoop after stoop they line the curbs in those neighborhoods cut into single blocks by traffic. Wherever someone decided to build toward the practical. Perhaps the idea was to maintain relative proximity: one part of an extended family lives "up" while other relatives live "down." Perhaps the money made from renting out one unit was to go toward paying off the full mortgage. In any case, seldom are two-families dream houses; they're not romantic or extravagant or sited off in the distance. Rather, they offer solutions.

When, stirred by my mother's outburst of two years previous, I became practical and bought the real estate solution to the challenges of being a writer and a lesbian, I found my long-term home. It's a place I never imagined I'd choose. After all, I too had dreamed of my perfect house, an abode light, airy, quiet, standing nearly alone above a curved Cape Cod shore. Instead, I took out a twenty-five-year mortgage on a two-family that won't ever feel completely private or be within my singular control.

Architecturally, the house makes sense. It's solidly built, circa 1920, and makes good use of what space there is. Stained slate gray, shingle-sided, with a neatly green postage-stamp yard, front and back wooden porches, a driveway—but no garage—and the lowest taxable square footage of any house on a nice neighborly street, Number 46-48 demands little for itself in the way of attention. Inside, too, it is intelligently—that is, modestly—designed.

As landlady, I live in the same top-floor unit I first rented for a year as a tenant. During the daylight, this positions me up near the very front of the structure, sitting inches away from the north wall, in a room quite small and irregularly shaped. The study's walls are painted a delicate pale yellow and the widest holds floor-to-ceiling bookshelves. I sit facing the shelves, a computer screen aglow on my cherry wood desk, the windowsill close enough to knock my elbow whenever I lean a bit too much to the right. If my fingers are working at the keyboard, they're beyond a passerby's vision; if I'm lucky and concentrating, they're beyond mine, too. This is the profile dimmed, slatted by blinds, head bent and still as a statue, seen by the neighbors. The writer motionless above, framed for the street, no more than an image.

I rarely utter a word. But what comes toward me then is another matter. It's not the sounds floating through the open window which have the power to disturb; they're usually a mix of the too direct and too transitory: children happily reciting at the top of their lungs the unvarying rules of Red Rover, a car radio wailing the last chorus of "Gimme Your Lovin'"—and the bass notes give way in the squeal of tires (the corner of Washington has come up again, too quickly). None of that. Instead, think of what shivers and slides through a place supposed to be solid. The thud that travels, translated in a faint aftershock. The echo caught in the long walled-in mumble. The power to unsettle comes from being reminded of lives getting lived below the level of what one can see, except in the most tangential way. Lives to which one is in some manner connected.

"I'm home during the day," I recall stammering the first time I tried to rent out the ground-floor apartment. "I need it to be somewhat quiet then. I'm a writer."

The two prospective tenants nodded, not much interested. Instead of asking me what, if anything, I wrote, they were trying to peer beyond me and into the living room where I'd just flicked on a light.

"Does that come off?" the stouter of the two women asked, her chin jutting.

"Come off?"

"Would you let us scrape the wallpaper and paint the walls?" She was clearly more experienced at renting houses than I was at owning them.

"Oh, sure," I said. "I guess."

"You'd pay for all the materials, of course? The steamer and paint and brushes? Because we're supplying the labor, and any real benefit accrues to you and your house, really." She was a law student. Her friend, who'd written down on the rental application that the two of them had met as children attending the same temple Sunday school, smiled placidly and then said, "I have a cat. Declawed." She waited. "Well, is that okay with you?"

Not having given the issue of pets any thought, I muttered something noncommittal.

They glanced at each other. A moment later, with my awkward approval, they walked on alone through the rest of the five hardwood-floored rooms that were clean but smelled empty. I remembered how Mrs. Kelly, my lace-curtain Irish landlady, used to invite me down here for tea; she, elderly, in failing health, and I, young and focused on work, were the only ones home in the neighborhood most afternoons. Different as we seemed to be, we'd sit and talk, sip a little tea, and, refreshed, be ready again to return to our separate lives. In the weeks following her funeral, her daughters had the task of coming by to move out her furnishings. From my desk I heard weighted, erratically paced footsteps breaking into the long stillness below. It seemed they kept retracing the same narrow route through the hall, through the rooms, traveling incessantly back and forth, back and forth. One morning that rhythm ended, and the low roaming rumble of the vacuum took over. Then the space below sounded endless, unbroken by any obstacles. It was being swept clean; in the daughters' devotion, even the dust was taken away.

So that's why it surprised me to see, gently wedged against one of the French doors to the living room, a large, perfectly smooth gray rock, the size of a outstretched hand. A river stone, set back down in a spot where it wasn't quite necessary, for what wind was going to angle in through the windows and sway a pair of doors set so deeply inside? It wasn't there to be practical; it was to hold open some memory: a sweet spring day, perhaps, or a shared landscape, entire, or someone who, laughing, agreed to take it in and transplant it.

"We have a question," one of the women called out, irritated.

The two prospective tenants were conferring in the back of the house. As I hurried into the hall, their voices rang through the emptiness with real vibrancy. They were in the larger of the unit's two bedrooms, the one directly beneath my own. I couldn't help hearing the words: *drab, too dark, shaded by trees, close quarters.*

The law student, said, looking up, "We'd like to take it."

"Oh?"

"Yes. But only if you'll allow the cat, without asking us for an extra security deposit. And if we can strip the wallpaper and repaint certain rooms."

In my hand was the application they'd filled out. Besides providing references, they'd also initialed the line stating they understood the rent to be $485 a month. What they probably didn't know is that without that amount, I couldn't pay the mortgage or live on top without taking in roommates. Four hundred and eighty-five dollars a month, added to what I earned from two adjunct teaching jobs and weekly book reviewing, would also allow me to keep working at the one job I truly needed. I was then at the very start of a project that I hoped would end up as a real, published novel. It was my third attempt to write such a book. This try concerned a love relationship as it changed in tenor and gender over four separate centuries and in four different cultures. I wanted this book's completion to prove the pivot, sending me off, finally—done with my lengthy, demanding apprenticeship.

Hoping to look businesslike, I flipped to the second page of the tenant's personal information sheet. Some quick movement caught my eye: the long wands of the lilac bushes, waving against the window. Their tight purple blooms were just about to open. I remembered how in the previous spring my nights and early mornings were filled with a scent subtly intoxicating. Without meaning to, I glanced up at the ceiling. The old hand-skimmed plaster was smooth, except for a few faint hairline cracks. Who knew what sounds and sudden quick shifts of weight might travel between upstairs and down? Mrs. Kelly had lived so quietly and, ill, she couldn't pay much attention to the rest of the world.

"Listen"—I tried to take them both in—"Joan, Nadine. Here's what you have to know, besides the fact that I write at home during the day. I'm seeing someone."

"But we don't—"

I held up a palm and rushed on. "See, I have a lover and she comes over, and stays over, often. If this is going to be a problem for you in any way, my being lesbian, then this isn't going to work. Because, see, this is my home. I want to feel comfortable, even if I'm only walking in the front door and I pass you sitting out on the porch. I suppose the best way to put it is that there's one skin on the house—we share walls."

The pages shook in my unsteady hand. In the moment of silence that burst between the three of us, I let my breath go. I was exhilarated. I'd done it: said what I needed in my new role. I'd claimed my home. Now it was up to them to say whether it was here they wanted to live or, in fact, no, their place most likely lay elsewhere.

I saw before me the bare unconscious paralysis that overtakes the features of those who have just heard a piece of news they didn't expect, yet about which they don't want to seem to be shocked. Two faces, each wiped of emotion. Instant immobility. The truth, the final but delayed message, doesn't necessarily have to end up being disapproval, though that is usually how it looks when you're the one waiting. But might simply mean this: *Time to switch gears.*

I said, "Well?"

"No problem here," the law student said, cheerily.

"Fine with me," said the cat-owner, after a moment.

I decided to trust them. They also had to trust me. All of us hoped to prove more than this moment of a fill-in-the-blank type of information and wrong assumptions.

BY 1987, MOST of my apprenticeships seemed to be coming to an end. A year earlier, I'd met the individual who in the most profound ways made me feel I'd come home; Rebecca and I were living together in the upstairs unit. Already, three very different households of tenants had moved in, lived in, and moved out from the first-floor apartment; and now two women—a couple also, like us, and friendly and quiet— lived downstairs. I'd become more competent as a landlady—or, to put it in cheeky but politically correct terms: I was a *land-woman.* I'd completed that third long manuscript and had found an agent in New York eager to send it to editors. It felt as though I'd just moved into the life I'd always been planning. I looked around; I liked where I was. A secure place, finally. And that's why, that spring, I accepted my brother's invitation to travel to the country whose name had echoed in the middle of the night in our Cleveland home, that name a silent insistence inside the darkened rooms, a slide along the quiet stairwells.

With my brother Robert, I went to Germany. I hadn't wanted ever to go, given all our grandparents had endured: parents, brothers, sisters, nieces, nephews lost in the huge events and intimately complicated private stories of what we now call the Holocaust. I didn't want to see any of the sights touted in the glossy brochures: the "Romantic Road" or castles on the Rhine. But Robert was going to shoot a short documentary on the World War II anti-Nazi student group the White Rose, and more than anything else, I wanted to travel with my brother. It's a great gift, you know, for siblings to travel past their childhoods as adults who enjoy one another.

I had no other goal than that, to be with Robert as he went about his work. After all, I was free and breezy for the first time in years. I had a neighborhood and a home to return to, a love I could trust, a future to my career—for I left Boston thinking I'd written the novel that soon would get published as my "first."

On the surface, the trip took only two weeks of time, but in truth in Germany with my brother beside me I entered the land that had filled the nights and our hearts with emptiness in our spacious, safe childhood home. In Munich the silence was full of voices still calling out for attention, just as the city's restored buildings duplicated almost exactly a physical landscape that almost fifty years before had been bombed to rubble. The stealthy slip of footsteps, the massed cries of triumph, the single entreaty, the sharp report of guns—these sounds don't ever quite dissolve; they don't fall into nothingness. The people I met in the streets looked pleasant. They moved around Munich the way I did Boston: going from grocers to cleaners, pausing to chat or to extend invitations. Would I now—? Wouldn't I like to come inside with them, visit inside their homes?

But of course what happened is that by entering these homes, I came to more fully and finally enter my own. Back in Boston, in the two-family, in the separate unit that was set right atop another's, something had changed. My days in the small, irregularly shaped study overlooking the street were shaken by a sense of strange disquiet—not caused by individuals, for Rebecca and I were happy, and downstairs the tenants were sending up only the usual noises: a phrase caught aloud out of all the humming silence, a clinking of dishes, the scrape of chairs or perhaps of a table. But the careful structure I'd relied on for so long felt as if it were shifting. I couldn't shut out the signals, not as I once might have. Instead, I had to turn my attention down to the very base of where I lived, deeper down, past all the layers. A shifting in the foundation: that is what was happening. I was living on top again; but as if detached, I heard traveling up toward me messages I hadn't wanted to take in and claim as part of my own life: the pauses within my grandmother's stories; the shadow slipping inside the light suburban joy; and endlessly the cries I both feared to hear and did not hear at all, anyway, in Munich.

The distant home, the one boarded up, the one that belonged to one's parents; the one not dreamed of nor sought; the one always separate and yet below and connected, the one always on top and yet part of; the one different, the one not quite alone; the one beyond the self, opening...

IN MY FRONT-WINDOWED study over the course of three years I wrote about what happened inside ordinary German—Aryan—homes, in the brick rowhouses and small buildings which lined the streets of an imaginary Bavarian town during 1939-43, the years that had forever silenced more than half of our family. *Tales of the Master Race*—my fourth attempt at a book-length manuscript—became my first published novel. One Sunday night, just after the book's release, I climbed the stairs to the top story, flipped on the light switch in the dining room, and found in that first flash after darkness the house was filled with relatives and friends. In whatever room I walked people were smiling. Without my overhearing a thing from all the plans, the whispers and secrets, Rebecca had done it, surprised me in a new way again, with a full house. One that could hold celebration as well as silence, solitude as well as connection. Modest. Pragmatic. Just as I'd dreamed. A two-family, indeed.

The Lake

MEG PEI

I'M A WANDERER. Over the past decade since graduating from college, I have moved a dozen times. This is by choice, a personal vagabondage, a prodigal quest; my universe is portable and able to be packed within a week's notice. I'm the sort who merits pencil and never the permanence of ink in address books and who when answering the telephone is often greeted with the words: "What? You're still there?"

But despite my transience I do have a home, or hopes of having one, as symbolized by the sugar bowl in my kitchen. It's very kitschy. Shaped like a strawberry, bright red with little indentations where seeds would be, the top lifts off and is crowned by a stubby green stem. I found it when a friend of mine was boxing up items for charity and offered me first pick; upon seeing the sugar bowl I gasped and clutched it to my breast like it was a Faberge egg.

"Oh, do you want that tomato?" my friend asked.

"It's a strawberry!" I shot back, still cradling it, overwhelmed by a true spiritual joy which tangible items, particularly crockery, rarely effect in me. The strawberry was an exact duplicate of the sugar bowl my mother had had in our lake cottage when I was a child. How many summer mornings had I padded into the kitchen, only to see that bowl upon the table, so bright within a square of mountain sun. I had not known there was another like it in the world, and somehow in finding a replica I began to imagine that "the Lake" as we always called it, long since sold, could be reclaimed as well. I continue to harbor that dream along with the sugar in my own bowl, for in all my wandering I have never found a place more special than the Lake and no place I feel so surely to be home.

Tyler Lake is located in northeastern Pennsylvania in a town called Harford, population 250. It's the rockier corner of the state, once teeming with coal and factories, now unable to boast much industry of any kind. My mother's family came from the area, having emigrated from Ireland to work in the mines, but I had never known about my mother's family and so when in 1972 I was hustled into the car and driven from Long Island, New York to that hardscrabble region I was confused. I was seven and without comprehension of such matters. The only relatives I knew of were my father's kin, a bunch of Italian characters always chorusing over my existence and stuffing my pinched little face with delicious food. It was explained, however, that we had bought a cottage in Pennsylvania and from now on we were going to spend our summers there. My parents were both teachers and had summer vacations just as I did. I became even more confused. I could not understand why we needed another house and, if we had so much money to spare, then why hadn't we bought a color television so I wouldn't have to watch cartoons in black and white? My protests were ignored. I endured the trip, lying in a sickly heap in the backseat and displaying no enthusiasm whatsoever.

I was not a strong child. From birth I had been forever suffering with some form of illness—colic, pneumonia, ear infections, flus— and by the age of seven I had developed a premature invalid cynicism. What did it matter where I was, I thought: I would spend half my time in bed with a fever. My world consisted of thermometers, antibiotics, noxious syrups, chicken broth, and Jell-O; my world was behind the window screen, watching other kids play on the street. The only fate awaiting me in Pennsylvania, I suspected, was another screen to press my nose against and a new strain of germs; if anything significant was to be found there it would be a doctor who knew how to give a good fast shot and didn't have clammy hands.

We arrived. My parents got out of the car and rushed toward their new purchase while I stayed put, using a book to shield my eyes from the sun until a man came and rapped on the window.

"Hey there, chicken," he said, as he coaxed me out of the car and puffed on his pipe.

This was Floyd. Floyd and his wife Anabel owned a neighboring cottage and would serve as native guides to our strange new rural world. Both in their seventies, full of piss, vinegar, honey, and much salt of the earth, they had spent nearly a half-century together and seen and suffered many things. As my mother often said, had she ever needed to cross the country in a covered wagon, she would have wanted Anabel by her side. Anabel had a sharp face, a sharper voice, and dressed in an unconscious uniform of trousers and smock shirts oddly similar to those of Communist China. Floyd, though equally hawkish and lean, was a shade more reticent and curiously gentle at times. He could fix anything—no machine ever stumped him—and had the thrilling talent of being able to stick his finger into a live socket without fear of electrocution. I often suspected that like a great shaman, Floyd became one with what he healed. When I first met him I said nothing, but with unusual trust I immediately felt I had found a kindred spirit and allowed him to carry me to the house. Evidently he did not think I was sturdy enough to walk.

And so the first summer began. The cottage itself was in need of renovation; if it had had a nickname it would have been Sutton's Folly, in homage to the man who built it. He had put together a house of scraps. The linoleum differed not only from room to room but also from square foot to square foot, and every wall was a different color. The floors slanted, the doors were a bit askew, but all in all it held together and after we had swept out a million or so dead flies, we managed to settle in. In the first few weeks my parents were busy painting and cleaning and so to keep out of their way I began to hesitantly explore the parameters of my new turf. There was our cottage, surrounded by a small plot of land; there was a dirt road I was not yet allowed to wander along; and there was a large lake I was not yet allowed to stick even so much as one toe into. On an incline near the house, however, I discovered a bench built between two beech trees, and spending time reading on this bench was approved by both my parents. For ten years this was to be my favorite nonaquatic spot at the Lake: my shady idyll. Overhead leaves rustled and branches groaned, while waves lapped gently toward the lake's inlet. The ground was littered with beech nuts, small spade-shaped burrs with pale green centers. The bench was just wide and long enough for me to sit on, with my back propped against a tree while I pored over countless books. The first summer all I did was read and absorb, since the elements were a bit too overpowering for me then. The weather in the mountains seemed very strange—hot during the day yet cold at night—while the sun seemed twice as intense, blazing down from a cloudless sky. But I had not been sick once, and though I was still watching the activities of others at least it was not from behind a screen. I was outside, and when I left my bed in the morning I did not return to it until I went to sleep. To me such freedom was a miracle, to be savored privately on my bench along with the peculiar taste of beech nuts.

From then on a pattern formed and with each passing summer I became healthier and more able. I was being built up along with the cottage, which now sported all kinds of fascinating details: glass hurricane lamps, a striped couch, Peter Max cookware (bright, enameled, cosmic yet functional, the frying pan was crimson with a psychedelic egg painted in the center), and of course the strawberry sugar bowl.

Life in general seemed more vivid and colorful at the Lake. While for nine months of the year we lived in safe suburbia in a house much like everyone else's, at the cottage life was a challenge. Only lake water flowed from the faucets, so in order to take baths a huge laundry kettle had to be boiled upon the stove and then poured into the clawfoot tub; for drinking water we had to fill empty plastic milk gallons from a nearby spring. This was my job, as I was small enough to scale the slimy rocks to where the spring gushed out of a pipe, and I took this responsibility quite seriously, forcing myself to fill as many jugs as I could, fingers and bare legs freezing as the coldest purest water I had ever known splashed all over me in a great cataract. I was charged with energy. At the Lake I would tap springs, walk two miles to the general store, boil water for dishes, pick wild blueberries for breakfast, and hang clothes on the line, whereas back on Long Island my mother was lucky if I cleaned my room. But Long Island was tiresome and limited; it inspired me to do nothing. There was no poetry or character. No hummingbirds, no dragonflies, no dirt roads or twisting pikes. You had expressways. You had malls. You had crowded beaches and stagnant nights. Even the screen door there was boring—aluminum, it shut with a hostile bang—while the screen door at the Lake was old and wooden and squeaked invitingly. Each summer I grew more alive and enthused, shooting up like the corn in the nearby fields and developing as tough as a stalk, but then everything came crashing down around Labor Day. I was Persephone with a shortened season, forced to endure the hell of New York suburbia two-thirds of the year. How my heart sank when we crossed the George Washington Bridge, my father throwing a handful of change into the toll basket like he was tossing clods of earth on a grave. My grave. Summer was finished. It was back to the Underworld again.

Because the Lake was an isolated spot with a transitory summer population, friends my age were not often available. I had no brothers and sisters and was used to solitude, but still I took to hanging around Anabel and Floyd, following them from place to place, watching Anabel cook or clean or recane a chair or Floyd fix a broken pump.

Everything they did enthralled me. I loved Anabel because she had the straightforward habit of talking to children as if they were adults, and Floyd was close to mythical in my eyes. First of all, he tolerated me as no other human being aside from my grandfather was able to, allowing me to yammer away like a set of chattering teeth without once telling me to shut up. He even resembled my grandfather, keen-eyed, sinewy and quiet, forever puffing on a pipe. We fished. We sorted out nuts and bolts. We painted the outhouse. One time I emerged from the lake after swimming and Floyd calmly motioned for me to come over. I had five or six leeches on my legs, but rather than being horrified I watched in amazement as he cut each one off with a knife.

"You have to get the head," he explained. "Otherwise they're still in ya."

The man was a demigod. And so when my grandfather made the trip down from Buffalo one summer to visit, I was beside myself. I had Floyd and my grandfather together; I was torn, my allegiance in a frenzy. I was so distracted by their mutual presence that I cannot recall whether they got along or not, but I'm sure they did, both having been working men and alike in temperament. It was even revealed that they had been neighbors at one time in Scranton. Floyd's family had owned the house whose yard adjoined my grandfather's family's yard, although despite many years of proximity the two had never met. My grandfather's family had been Catholic and Floyd's Protestant, and in those days that was reason enough to keep mothers from chatting over the back fence. But whether they had met or not the relationship seemed apropos to me and made me feel that Floyd and my grandfather were somehow parallel souls. My grandfather also spotted a leech on me once, removing it with a glowing cigar tip instead of a knife, but still offering the same wisdom:

"Make sure to get the head," he advised. "Otherwise they're still in ya."

My first comrade of my own age was a boy named Campbell.

He was from Alabama and I'm not quite sure why his family had traveled so far north to rent a cottage among us Yankees, but he and I met and we were joined at the hip after five minutes. Campbell was on the pallid and frail side, whereas I, veteran of three mountain seasons, was close to indestructible. I was his scout, his Pocahontas, able to pick up newts and caterpillars, bait a hook, row a boat without tiring. He could not swim and I tormented him to learn, describing myself just a few years earlier, how I had floundered miserably about in a blue-checkered life jacket, but now I could swim from shore to shore. I was not boasting, I simply felt that if I could do it, anyone could. My confidence soon got the better of me, however. Once when walking by the eddy across from the lake, we noticed a swarm of insects ahead. Wisely, Campbell expressed concern about going further, but I said they were just flies and forged on. I stepped right into a swarm of yellow jackets. I ran screaming, they followed; finally my father braved the stinging tornado, grabbed me, and got me out of their path. He attempted to pull my shirt off and let loose whatever had flown up it, but I began slapping him in resistance because I did not want Campbell to see my naked chest. (A ridiculous display of modesty, since at that age it was no different than Campbell's.) When the hysteria subsided I sat holding a cold beer to the side of my head for lack of an ice pack while my mother calculated that I had been stung close to forty times—even on the eyelid. The next day my body was covered with strange bruises and I looked like a walking blister, but otherwise I felt fine. I was up with the sun, hunting through the encyclopedia hoping to find out whether wasps died when they stung. They did, I discovered, and thus vindicated I went back outside, eager to tell Campbell of my triumph.

There were darker lessons to learn at the Lake as well. When our cat chose my room as the place to have her kittens I saw actual proof of the agony of birth, and while it had all been described to me by my mother in our facts-of-life chat, I had often suspected her of exaggerating. Apparently she knew what she was talking about. It was not pretty, and I hoped that by the time I was of childbearing age there'd be a better method. In my constant keeping of other "pets"—toads, fireflies, field mice—unhappily I discovered Death. I left a small and adorable brown toad in a Currier & Ives tin full of water on the back porch overnight, and in the morning my father called me to the porch so that I could see the toad's body and how it had been ripped open by a bat. He was not being sadistic; he merely wanted me to know that because I had taken that creature out of its element, it had been left defenseless. I stopped keeping pets after that and I also stopped fishing. I did not like the taste of fish, and even if you threw them back in the water oftentimes the hook had mangled their mouths badly or had torn down into their throats. Nature was cruel enough, I decided. It did not need my help.

Having found such a wonderland at the Lake and having given such exciting accounts of the place to my New York friends, I soon had them fighting over who could come and stay with me as my summer guest. Their enthusiasm, however, tended to evaporate after a day or two. They grew bored and homesick. They wanted to watch something other than Andy Hardy movies on television. (We only picked up one channel clearly and it was the public broadcasting affiliate, which seemed to have peculiar taste in what was public and educational.) I recall my first visitor, my best friend from elementary school, who though she had begun smoking at ten and would have fit in well with Fagin's gang, was nonetheless horrified at the sight of a daddy-longlegs spider. She was also appalled at the lack of hot shower facilities. My New York cousins reacted similarly.

"Jeez, how long can you just do nothing?" one of them complained. They were jaded and unadventurous, and in a way I felt sorry for them. They got no pleasure out of simple things like swimming all day and then eating dinner outside on the redwood table with a view of the lake in all its twilight glory. Taking a walk along the dirt road, listening to a chorus of crickets and doves, toasting marshmallows on sticks—even the drive to buy ice cream on a road with more hills and twists than a rollercoaster brought no thrill. And this wasn't any Good Humor or Baskin Robbins franchise, this was Country Ice Cream: fresh strawberries on the sundaes and real butterscotch topping, not a goo of chemicals and artificial flavors. If you could not find some spark of joy in that first chomp through the brittle chocolate shell of a Brown Bonnet or in the last exquisitely soggy bite of a waffle cone, then you were one sad kid. Perhaps I myself was unsophisticated, but I truly enjoyed evenings at the Lake, despite the lack of television; having been dragged out of the water after a moonlight swim, I would sit shivering and waterlogged and drink hot cocoa while my mother read or embroidered and my father listened to the radio. My father, though 200 miles away from the urban fracas, still liked to tune in New York news stations, rationalizing that he just wanted to be sure the place hadn't "blown up." In truth, however, like most New Yorkers my father was an information junkie and in a land without twenty-four-hour broadcasts of murder and traffic jams he became anxious. The calm was menacing. During the late seventies' Citizen's Band radio craze he might tune in that slice of life as well, Pennsylvania with its interstates being a trucker's natural turf. I seem to remember the handle "Horny Beaver" being very popular; we even ate once at a truckstop, a thrilling experience as our waitress wore tangerine stretch pants and I found a drowned fly in the "Eye-talian" salad dressing. We were called Eye-talian too, incidentally, even though my mother's family was as "white" as the rest of the native population. There was a persistent rumor that my father was in the Mafia, because he had an Italian last name and hailed from New York. Rural folks liked to stereotype city slickers as fast as urbanites liked to stereotype hicks, it seemed, but we did not discourage the gossip. As mobsters, we were treated with an edgy respect, *The Godfather* still being popular around that time. No one trespassed on our property, nor was the cottage vandalized—evidently for fear that Al Capone (or Pacino) might show up toting a violin case. Even a fairly coveted item among locals remained on our porch one winter without being stolen: a big sack of cement mix, sleep-with-the-fishes size.

Two events at the Lake did pique the interest of cousins and friends, however: the annual Fair and a celebration called Old Harford Days. The Fair was a local extravaganza, complete with amusement park–type rides, agricultural competitions, and live entertainment, generally in the form of polka or country bands with names like Stankey and the Coalminers. There were hogs the size of Volkswagens and squash the size of baseball bats, cheeses shaped like the state of Pennsylvania as well as a bovine beauty contest. There were carnival games you could never win and even a fortune teller's booth, my destiny being that I would "marry a Greek or a Jew," a strange prophecy yet to be proven right or wrong. My cousins loved to go to the Fair and make fun of the exhibits, as if the Feast of San Gennaro in Manhattan's Little Italy were any less comic or absurd, while my friends preferred Old Harford Days. During Old Harford Days people dressed in costumes from the late 1800s, when the town was founded, and set up booths and displays. Life in all its old-fangled glory was celebrated, butter churned, ice cream cranked, candles dipped, and horseshoes pounded. This was entertaining and instructive, but what my friends and I tended to be more interested in was the fact that Boys were there. We were beginning to find all boys very fascinating, particularly farm boys, who seemed more straightforward and engaging than their suburban counterparts. These males saw animals mating on a daily basis; they themselves started mating young and if you were willing to join them, you were more than welcome. My friends and I did not partake, though we enjoyed mulling over the prospect, just as we enjoyed the sight of guys our age, tan and lean and wearing overalls and nothing else. My first good glimpse of the male anatomy occurred at the Lake—not from a farm boy, unfortunately, but from another New Yorker. A cop from Queens had bought the cottage next to ours and while I was swimming his sons felt the need to stand on the dock and flash their wares. I was not impressed. Much ado about nothing, I thought. My first kiss also occurred at the Lake, in the woods on a day so hot it was close to tropical. The kiss was from a boy several years older than I, and it was not a sweet and tender initiation but rather an explosion of intensity I could not comprehend. The boy was dark, always scowling, and had a glorious nose like a blade; I was utterly infatuated with him but after receiving the kiss I staggered back a few paces and then ran. It had been too overwhelming, like the sun that day too potent, too much light and heat at once. But I still recall this memory with amazing clarity—the patch of moss I was standing on, a blue jay's sudden shriek—as if the whole episode was, at that bright and blinding moment, seared into my brain.

After that summer, things changed. My parents made another purchase, a farm with a house and numerous acres about ten miles from the Lake. And while this was the beginning of a new era for my father, who loved land and privacy and who had never cared much for swimming and fishing or the society of neighboring cottages, it marked the end of something for me. I sensed correctly that we would not be able to maintain three houses and that the Lake would soon be sold. I was very resistant to the Farm at first. How dry and isolated it seemed, with nothing but flat fields and a mucky beaver pond and a skinny creek. I pined and languished, and eventually my parents agreed to let me stay at the Lake by myself. I was sixteen and had never spent a night alone; I woke in a state of exhilaration, running outside and looking at the sun glinting on the water like Vespucci contemplating the New World. I was an adult now. I had conquered.

Another feat of independence came when I drove my parents from the Farm to the Lake. I had just learned to drive and my mother expressed apprehension about letting me behind the wheel, but my father was oddly calm and insisted I could do it. In hindsight I can share my mother's concern, as it was no beginner's track. There was Route 11, a fast pike racing beneath the golden span of the Nicholson Bridge; then several blind-curved, steep-hilled roads; then, finally, the dirt path leading to the Lake, narrow and bordered by ditches. At first my hands were clammy and I nearly pulled over, afraid I might confuse the brake with the accelerator and kill both my parents and myself, but then I picked up speed and confidence. I remembered the hundreds of trips my father had made over those roads and I imagined his skill rising up in me with each passing mile. By the time we reached Harford and a tractor allowed me to pass, and I honked and waved at the farmer just as my father always did, I knew I had arrived. Ironically, I have never driven since then. I have always lived, carless, in cities and never needed a license, but still I know I can drive very well simply because I completed that course.

When the Lake was sold shortly after I turned twenty-one, I cried. I understood that it had become more burden than blessing for my parents, I knew I personally could not take it over, but when I heard the news I sat in my Chicago apartment, looked at photos of the cottage and the water and the town, and slowly let the tears ooze. It was very therapeutic. I contemplated Sutton's Folly, before and after. I smiled at a picture of my grandfather and me fishing, a picture of Campbell, my mother, and I sitting at the redwood table, my father in a straw hat painting the house. The glimmerglass perfection of the Lake at dusk; Anabel in a rowboat; Floyd smoking his pipe, his hawkish stare fixed elsewhere, far beyond the camera. Floyd had passed away the year before, and his last words were strange yet somehow apt: "There's plenty of room in the cellar," he had said, and I hope there was. I then laid two photos side by side and studied these without nostalgia or longing but with gratitude: one of myself down by the beech trees, aged seven, pale and hunched over *Little Women,* and another, taken two summers later, of me holding a deer skull I had found, laughing fiercely like it was some exquisite plunder. They seemed almost photos of two different children, so dramatic was the contrast. I had built up more than resistance to germs at the Lake, I realized. I had built a spirit, and I had found a true home, a place where I had felt both safe and strong. As an adult any time I have trouble sleeping I imagine myself floating on an inner tube in the

lake, drifting peacefully, or I pretend to be lying in my cottage bedroom, happily exhausted, breathing in the purest of air. When I wake
I will go outside in my pajamas and sit on the stoop and share my
toast with a chipmunk or a bold wren; I am eager but never hurried
or nervous, and I find pleasure in the tiniest of things.

Success, to me, will be achieved on the day I buy my own lake
cottage and set the strawberry sugar bowl upon a table in a square of
mountain sun. It may be in Wisconsin, it may be in upstate New
York or New Jersey or even the very same cottage in Pennsylvania—
the specific place is not important but the ideal is—just a simple
four-room shack with a creaking screen door and no hot water. I'd
like to have a balance of rural and urban in my life, and if I have any
children I'd like to watch them sprout up in body and spirit and
enjoy the challenge of nature just as I did. Every summer I become a
bit more determined. I catch a whiff of pine trees or pipe smoke; I
buy blueberries or sweet corn at the Farmer's Market; I take long
walks after thunderstorms, when even a city gives off a curiously
cleansed and earthy odor. This past summer I was sitting next to a
man I work with, whose dark scowling features had confused me for
weeks—they reminded me of someone, but I was not sure who. It
was as he was staring out the window of the thirty-sixth floor of a
skyscraper that I made the connection, particularly because his gaze
was fixed on the view of Lake Michigan. How nice it looked out
there, he said, how blue and calm; how he'd love to be on a sail-
boat or fishing instead of trapped in this tower. I stared at him
staring at the lake and then I had a sudden flash; I recalled standing
on a patch of moss beneath a bright hot sun and hearing the shriek
of a blue jay.

"What's wrong?" he demanded. "You look strange. What do you
have, vertigo?"

While I gave no answer I did nod, having succumbed to a bit
of light-headedness at that moment, a dizzy spiral of memory—a
swoon even—but one which led, as always, to a very solid place.

The Shelter of the Alphabet: Home

CAROLE MASO

NEWPORT, RHODE ISLAND

THIS IS THE place I will be conceived. In joy and love, with awe and fear—some fear. This is the place I will be made—next to water. And the longing for water shall never leave me. What are my parents, two kids from Paterson, New Jersey doing here? That's my father, over there, stepping off a navy destroyer. It's 1955 and he's stationed here, and my mother has come to be near him. They love the song the water sings and the sailing songs. Later my mother will tell me that they read books aloud to one another and I like to imagine they read Yeats, and Melville, and maybe *Sonnets to the Portuguese* and other such conception texts. I like to imagine that language conjured me and the sea and these two people crazy for each other. Photos from this time reveal them to be so young: my mother golden blonde, with eyes the color of the sea. She is sitting next to a window, looking out—the window like the eye, transparent, suggestive, dazzling. And my father, a stringbean, a stick figure, though an ecstatic one, in a white sailor's suit. The pants with nobody in them, as we children will call him later.

I cannot from this distance hear their sighs or prayers, but I can imagine them. They are desirous, delirious, blindingly in love. But looking at these photos now, more closely, I see that something belies the surface joy. Of course. They have already had two miscarriages. I am wanted almost too much. Their devotion to the unknown future, their longing, is nearly palpable. After their lovemaking, in those first moments after my conception, there is absolute stillness, and prayers to the Virgin; they are wishing I might stick; they are hoping I might cling like a barnacle. My mother lies by the oceanside, lulled in blue, unmoving, my father's dreaming head resting on her breast—my small fin forming. Ocean child. Fin, small flipper. My mother says her rosary to the mysterious, silent Mary who smiles her wan smile. Great sorrow and great joy already live in me: sandwiched as I will be, on one side by two silky siblings who could not hold, and on the other side by a brother with a hole in his heart. But I am all health, I am all hope: I am miraculous, I am beloved from the start—and they make hope my home, my domain. I am desire and ocean, song and songs the blood sings. And they call me Carole, of course: song of joy. I am feared for and wanted beyond all reason. I live in their watery blue world of worry and desire, with the ghost images of the bodies that did not take.

Home is my mother's breath and blood. Home is my mother's voluptuous body and the darkness—the miracle of it and the ocean that cradled us. And their hope.

There must have been an element of ferocity...

There must have been an element of ferocity to have produced such a fierce child. To have made me at once so fierce and so mild.

PATERSON, NEW JERSEY

PATERSON IS ONE of the great American poems, and it is a place, and it is the place where I was born and lived for a time. From the beginning home to me is a poem. I am born in a modernist masterpiece by William Carlos Williams. And in fact as I am being born he is completing Book Five of that opus, the book of the triumph of the imagination. Mysteriously he is handing this to me as I now begin to breathe. I am not surprised; it seems like destiny to me. And in the times of my illness, I will in fact believe I am the chosen one, handed this directly from him who wrote not for love or fame or because he wanted to say something, but to keep his sanity.

"It's a strange courage you give me, ancient star."

And yes, I am a daughter of Williams, who combined poetry, fiction, fact, criticism, bits of this and that in his work. A strange brew. I am his daughter as you, even if you know nothing of my work except this essay, will see. He has sent me on this charmed path.

"Rigor of beauty is the quest."

And then there is Allen Ginsberg, the other native of Paterson I grew up with. I adored his great heart and hunger, his music and outrage and audacity. His fallibility. How, as a teenager, I howled his Howl.

I feel thankful to have had these two as my literary fathers. It feels like a much more fortunate literary inheritance than my southern friends who have Faulkner to contend with. Williams, that troubled iconoclast, seems to me a far more benevolent, happy influence simply in terms of what he allows. Somehow Faulkner continues to look best far from home on the Latin American writers. I, as a North American, am grateful not to have to wear his necklace of crowns and thorns.

Home is my father playing the trumpet—the music drifting. In Paterson. My grandfather's house has a stained-glass window and when my grandmother weeps, sick of this life, sick of the burden of simply being herself, there is the stained glass to focus on. My Grandpa Frank on the other side of town—with his Armenia and his wife, who will not live long—worked in the silk mills. Later, he will be beaten nearly to death with the pipe he began to keep under his bed for protection. Paterson, by then, having turned against us.

But not against me, not then.

Cadence was the block I lived on. Language my home. Charmed one, I was born into a poem.

ERSKINE LAKE

HOME WAS A blue lake in summer then and a man in a boat who followed us as we swam its length and a woman who taught us all the names of the wild flowers and they were our parents. I don't know how it happened and so quickly, but suddenly there are five of us children. There is not one quiet place. And I learn to build a place of silence and serenity and space in some newly discovered zone of my brain. A place where I might not only live, but flourish. Without it, there is no interior life, without it I sense I am going to die. Imagination was my home, my salvation then. The blue lake. The space in me.

And my mother, too, is a consolation through the chaos, constucting a safe universe, a world of love and stability in which to experiment, play; a place of confidence where in those long summers before school started she handed me the secret key. As we sat next to the water, she taught me that glittering, miraculous handful of charms—the alphabet. The child draws the letter A and makes a home under its roof. She learns of the shade a T might cast. The light coming off K. The shelter of the letter M.

And my mother reads to me. All kinds of wondrous things: Wordsworth and Blake and Jarrell and Poe as I fall into a dream next to the lake's pale oval. A B C D...

VASSAR COLLEGE

HERE I MEET my triumverate of women, the women who will be always true, always rigorous, demanding, loving, always urging me to the next place, always meeting me at least part of the way.

Helen. During our courtship in that Hudson Valley we pick apples. I recite Frost's "After Apple Picking" to her so that words and the apples become interchangeable—round, heavy, luscious, carrying sensual meaning: the apples, the language, and my strange love for this woman I have only just met. Everything becomes entangled; the apples falling, and the falling in love, and the delicious surrender to it all. Everything round and gorgeous and falling: home.

We in the nearly twenty years since that day have created a place—a familiar place, on which for the most part we can agree: home. A continuity. A kind of home is in her arms, in her enormous intelligence, in her flexibility, in her passion—and we are, despite everything, despite danger and madness and sorrow and addiction, safe. A little safe.

How did she know so long ago what it was I would need? We would need? How has she done it—continually been willing to reinvent, the world and our lives, so that we might not only continue, but thrive?

And at Vassar there is Miss Page, my beloved teacher, my most trusted ally, my support, my role model. Everything about her awed and terrified me—a brilliance, an intelligence as I have never seen, a sensitivity, a discretion, an extraordinary intuition. And six feet tall! She was everything. Miss Page, who allowed me my first chance to write, to try, even though I had been rejected from the creative writing senior central course where one wrote a creative thesis. And for many years I will be rejected over and over from almost everything—but not by Barbara Page and not by Helen. And not by my mother. What can they see that I can't? That no one else can?

Miss Page introduces me to the third woman—Virginia Woolf. We read her together in class. I begin to write. Both for the first time. And I am left permanently changed.

On almost any page of those luminous beautiful novels I can find peace, challenge, the shock of recognition, company. One could live here, in lines like this, happily, for a long time. And I have done just that. In *To the Lighthouse, Mrs. Dalloway, Between the Acts, The Waves.*

And in fact I feel more at home there than just about any-where. And it is for the most part home enough to dispel the ter-rible house that mental illness builds, for the first time really during the time I am at Vassar—a place that will become so demanding and after a time so familiar that I do not have a choice but to live there. And chanting sentences is the only way to feel better finally. And writing sentences, making shapes, is the only way to feel bet-ter. Sustaining, miraculous language, that all these years keeps illness at bay. Dear Virginia Woolf. Dear Barbara, dear Helen. Dear fifty pages toward a novel I write as a senior in order to graduate. Maybe I will be saved.

72 CARMINE STREET

WHERE WE RAN the ten blocks breathlessly because back then you got the *Village Voice* classifieds the night before and ran to each possibility and hoped somehow amid the crowds of people all wanting the same thing, you would somehow luck out and find a home in it all.

We did find one. We have kept it now since 1978. We will never give up these two rooms and when I think of home as a place, this is the place I think of. Two miniscule rooms I share with you and our two cats on the edge of Soho in the West Village of Man-hattan. I love you, though it doesn't always seem so obvious, and I love unreasonably these two altogether unremarkable little rooms. The place I have witnessed in every kind of light, at every time of day, and in every season. A place of so many intimacies, and revelations, and heartbreaks. Sometimes for breaks from writing I will talk to Mr. Angelo, our ancient, Greek superintendent, in the street; or bring my clothes to the Rastafarian tailor; or pray for whatever seems dire and impossible at Our Lady of Pompeii. In fact, we have grown up here together. The Minetta Tavern, the Van Dam Theater, the Bleecker Street Cinema, all the things that were once ours—now gone. I feel the accumulated memories of being long in a place—or at least having that place as a base. Here we bought the Christmas tree that year, here I kissed another, here is where we sweated under lights, dancing. Here, the corner where we wept, and here—all this—a place so resonant. If memories take up space and possess color, these streets are black by now from the overlapping of so many accumulated events. Here I lay down in the snow for hours, unable to imagine a way to go on.

How many times did we walk those same streets "dead drunk," and for once a phrase seems to fit, seems to make some sort of sense, "dead drunk," limping toward home? In all the sorrow and regret and frustration we could not express any other way back then.

But somehow we have survived. Survived the deaths and acquisition of cats, the thousand disappointments, all the drunkenness, all that we did to each other that was unforgivable and that we have somehow forgiven. All the good and bad news—and the devastating news—deaths of friends. This is where the calls come. This is where life seems unlivable and I get under the covers for days and days.

And you launch me again, sending me off on the next necessary thing I must do in order to write, to keep writing, in order to survive. You set me off for the first time in what will be many, to do what I must do—and it doesn't finally somehow destroy us (though it sometimes comes close), but strengthens us in our love for each other and allows us to go on and change and grow and grow up. Much of the time we live off your student loans or a credit card or a meager salary or nothing. I go to my first artists' colony. It is the first time I am given months of uninterrupted time. When Yaddo says no, when MacDowell says no, when there is nothing, nowhere to go, there is Cummington, a community of the arts where artists are not guests but residents, a place that offers space and solitude in an excessively beautiful countryside. I stay for months and months on end.

NEW YORK CITY

SUDDENLY GARY IS dying. The new virus. Thus begins our long season of suffering. Of renunciation. Of fear. Of sorrow. Of good-bye.

And I am back in the apartment. And my first book is finally published. Without compromise. And with that, I am satisfied.

And then the phone call in the middle of the night: the first of October 1986.

PROVINCETOWN, MASSACHUSETTS

I AM BACK at the ocean, pale zygote, after a long separation. Back in silence to my one dreamy cell of being. Another new home. Provincetown in winter. The off season. I am given a small studio at the Fine Arts Work Center. I have brought my few familiar things, my portable Virgin Mary, my pocket Sappho. I paint everything white. In this home at the end of the world—surrounded by water, desolate, beautiful—I enter my long period of mourning. Home of grief and water. Home of sorrow. Having for months counted T-cells, having learned the incredible shadow a T is capable of casting, I try to heal. I walk the streets, the dunes, the beaches. I go to the bars and St. Mary's of the Harbor.

If home is physical sanctuary, comfort, recognition, bliss, then home for me is Provincetown. Much of my earthly longing goes there. I ache for the place. It's a primal longing, a sexual one. It is the place I am most drawn to in the world. And irresistibly, and a little against my will, I keep returning there. I am a Pisces after all.

I have lived now almost ten years without fear. Fear was a home and then it was not. Sadness was a home and then it was not anymore. And what could be worse? AIDS. I think of the urgency in me that Gary's death created. A monstrous acceleration, a new conviction to living, working—loving with a new recklessness, abandon, urgent, urgent. Gary who taught me to do everything, to be everything, to want, to have, to try everything—to not be afraid anymore.

VENCE, FRANCE

TO KEEP LIVING. To keep writing, to not tire. I get an NEA and decide to leave the country and live cheaply for a long time on the money. I choose an artists' colony in France called the Michael Karolyi Foundation.

It is perhaps the oddest and most strangely lovely time in my life. I am at once utterly at home and completely alone.

> What do I remember
> that was shaped
> as this thing is shaped?
> *William Carlos Williams*

Stepping off the plane I am shocked to find that I remember this place, though I have never been here before. I remember clearly being a child, walking through a forest of small oaks, carrying a metal box of cinders to keep warm, with a woman who is my mother. She is not my Paterson mother, but another mother. I remember the war. There are terrible things, there are wondrous things outside the reach of my recollection, my consciousness, that are suddenly set into motion here. I, as a result, acquire a false sense of security, of belonging, of fluency. I am born for a second time into a different and distant home—a home from long ago. And I am filled with longing and unfinished things and I feel unspeakable pain and sorrow at this intimation of a home which perhaps never existed, and which I have been separated from, severed from until now. And what else eludes me, slips away? What else goes unremembered? I am bereft. A home I have been separated from and have forgotten and yet has haunted me. I have written about it from the start . . . France.

I think of all the things that are outside the range of our memories or imaginations or intelligence or talent—it's the place I suspect which is our true home. If we could get there we would finally feel okay. But we can't. We are all homeless, groping, roaming in the darkness, aware of only a fraction of it.

But I am delighted and in great awe over the resonances I can perceive and the repetitions. At the Karolyi Foundation in the form of two extraordinary women, Judith Karolyi and Zenka Bartek, the reiteration again comes of who I am and why I live. I am reminded again of what I must do. It comes through with great force and clarity. They press me on, they press me further. I have stepped off the plane and into the care of these two women, lovers, both in their seventies, who offer me, like guardians at the doors of the psyche, fearlessness, diabolic and sometimes harsh judgments, support, and after a while unconditional love. And they watch me unravel, as I will in the next months, and they will stand by and they will watch out for me, protect me, wait for me—as I too wait. Until I can take the vow again—having gone a long way off.

And in the New York I inhabited and left in 1988, my publishing house closes and Helen, tired of all the separations, tired of all my antics, goes off with another woman, and I become lost. Almost irretrievably. I had left her again. Because I had to. But she was tired, bitter, lonely. Fed up finally.

I had left her behind, again—because I could not write—write, that is, on my own terms, without concern for the marketplace, without selling out in small but grave ways: writing for magazines, or teaching prematurely, or making unconscious decisions that might make the work more sexy, more accessible—but for all the wrong reasons. It seemed crucial not to derail myself now, not to subvert myself, not to give in. But she is less and less capable of understanding all this, or caring.

I was too afraid of not allowing my talent, my potential to go where it needed to go.

I begin, as I often have, a long series of affairs. Because the body all along has been a kind of home to me. But I am sad, and deranged, and so far away. And I miss New York, and I miss her, but there's no place for me there, and no way I can afford to continue writing.

And I write what happens down because it is the only way I know to survive. I write it all down, and eventually even it takes on the glow of the imagination, freeing itself from the known world. And I give it in the end a title of dislocation, my novel of France. I call it *The American Woman in the Chinese Hat.* I return to New York; I return to France. At some point Helen and I are reunited. I go back to France a third time. I am writing a wild, visionary thing, *The Bay of Angels*—but my precious time doesn't last, can't last.

AMERICA 1995

THIS COUNTRY IS not a home to me. I am tired of the America that has increasingly come to mean selfishness and avarice and cruelty and meanness of spirit. I have had it for good this time with the Republicans. I am disgusted by an America that loathes difference, otherness. An America indifferent to beauty. A country hostile to art and to its artists—and to all that makes life worth living in the first place. Ruskin wrote, "Great nations write their deeds in art." But America more and more ceases to be great, to aspire to greatness. We are lost, violently blinded, bankrupt. The children are hungry, the elderly are frightened, the mentally ill wander the streets. Whose family values are these? If it were not for the handful of people I love too much, I would have found a way out of here by now.

I am leaving out many of my moves at this stage, many changes of address; I tire. Other temporary residencies: Park Slope; Washington, D.C.; Normal, Illinois. In four years, I will teach in four schools; I despair. I am tired of roaming, exhausted, depleted. About to give up.

HOUSE

IT IS A quiet September evening when the phone rings, and as in a movie or a dream the world changes in an instant. Various people on the unreal speaker phone saying "fiction," "prize," "fellowship." It's the Lannan Foundation, audacious angels from Los Angeles. "Fifty thousand dollars." Impossible. Awards like this one, when they come, arrive like blizzards of love, seemingly out of nowhere, a kind of grace. Such gifts open a whole new realm of imagining. They give the recipient an audacity of purpose, alter previous self-conceptions, make the impossible suddenly possible again: house.

That I found the house with ease surprised no one; it was, of course waiting for me—an 1860 white colonial, in the enchanted, beguiling Hudson Valley. It had everything: a pond, a smokehouse, a bank of lilies; it was not hard to recognize, nor was the ghost of the woman who greeted me when I opened the door. Her joie de vivre, her intelligence, her wit, a spirit present through the presence of possessions. A Chinese scroll, a clay bird, a chaise longue, and in the closet Christmas ornaments, a kitty-litter box. A dulcimer, a violin in an unopened violin case—the house had been filled with music . . . Schubert on the record player.

I leave her there in winter and begin the long ordeal of securing a mortgage. The mortgage broker wonders with some exasperation who will give me a loan as he examines my "unorthodox employment history," my living from one grant to the next, a visiting professorship here or there—and me like a child holding my one golden egg with pride. "It doesn't look very good," he says, as snow continues to fall. I dream of lilacs and mountains and Chinese scrolls and snow all jumbled up. I cling to these things in sleep: the body of a violin shaped like a small insistent woman or the rowboat's shape next to the pond. Having let in the possibility of house, I cannot bear to be houseless again—and without her. But all winter I cannot see it; there's too much snow and the house seems suddenly to disappear as fast as it appeared. But Elizabeth is fierce: "Don't be silly," she whispers, "it's yours now. You deserve it." And she passes me a ring of shining keys. She's handing them to me because it's the end of her time here—and the beginning of mine.

I'd like to sit with her for a minute, safe within the sanctuary of our study, the lilacs like an ocean in the distance, and just talk, the way you can with those you genuinely admire but don't really know. I would like to whisper my fears to her, tell her I dread the impending publication of *The American Woman in the Chinese Hat.* Tell her I fear the person I was when I wrote it, and know, on any day waking, I might be again. Almost everyone else is less patient with this sort of thing. They just want you to get on with it—enjoy your successes, don't worry so much about the past. But she's more understanding. This time around at any rate. I am afraid of the person I was then, so resigned, so desirous of death. I'd tell her. And I imagine she'd say, "I, too, was afraid at times."

She is like the women, starting with my mother, I have tried to keep up with my whole life. You must run breathless just to sit next to them. They prod. They urge. "Look closer, be braver," they say.

Everything of hers is gone now: the dulcimer, the bells, the music she loved preserved on vinyl—all the books. It's okay; she'll grace these halls a long time, I know.

We'll sit until the light is gone. She'll ask if I've found the asparagus patch yet, seen the mockingbird who lives near the mailbox.

She'll wonder how my new work is going. She's stretched out on the chaise longue, her hand keeping time to some irresistible music. Her beautiful voice drifts through this precious house. She closes her eyes—says she's so happy about the prize—pats my hand, this drowsy angel, already two years dead on the first day we meet—whom I love.

PROVIDENCE, RHODE ISLAND

THAT NEARLY PERFECT lilac-infused existence I am forced to miss. To in some way already give up.

I am returned to the state of my making. Back to the state of my conception, the very idea of me. Returned to the place of my invention. Home of water and watery memory and pull. I am a little at home. I have come to direct the Creative Writing Program at Brown University. It is perhaps the job that will best allow me to continue doing the writing I need to do. I will only have to teach a little; there will be time enough to continue writing.

HOME

I AM A wandering soul—but not an aimless one. I've learned well how to listen and I've gone wherever my work told me to go. Wherever my work took me, insistent, I went. I have been forced, in order to continue writing on my own terms, to leave over and over again. I who live everywhere and nowhere have built a home of language. I have been forced to create a home of my own making. A home of music and desire. I can at this point make a home wherever I go. I open my large artist's notebook, I pick up a pen, I turn on the radio; I dream of you—the best, the most mysterious one, the most remote and beautiful aspects of self.

The necessity to find ways to continue, without for the most part the luxury of financial reward, has made it imperative to imagine a home that might be moveable. It has had to be okay to live outside familiarity, outside comfort, outside anything that seems mine. All along I have found it necessary to live with a home that can be conjured within.

Home might be a studio in a loft in Tribeca, a room in Provincetown, an office in Normal, Illinois. Home is anywhere my mind catches fire, my body. Where language trembles and burns.

I am at work now on several projects—a book of rage called *Defiance,* a book of desire: *The Erotic Etudes.* And *The Bay of Angels,* of course. The continued exploration of the possibilities of language is the only real life I know, the only place I've lived truly, fully, all these years. I have spent fifteen years of devotion at the altar of the impossible. I've spent fifteen years building my unshakable home of language and love. The place of longing and failure (for who could succeed?) where I live madly, recklessly, without concern for the product, or the consequences, or the future. My house of yearning and mystery and awe. A place of grace. My mother praying for a child to be born, to come to term, and another mother singing French songs—and the war. And in the étude I've just finished—a woman on a bridge, dressed in white, dipping her hands into the sacred Ganges; it is and is not me. One lives in awe, next to the silence and the strangeness as the lost or hidden or forgotten fragments, aspects of self and world, only glimpsed at—are sensed, if only a little. In the challenge, I am at home. In concentration I feel at ease—pure pleasure, pure joy, as I have never experienced in any other way.

After a week of interviews, readings, anxieties, stresses of all sorts—no time to write—I finally can get back a little to some work on *Defiance.* Having been away, disoriented, without anchor, and coming back, I write the line, "Who will mind my savage goat and pole dog?" and this arrangement of words makes me feel more calm, more relieved, more at home than I have felt in some time. Why? Why does this sentence have such an effect over me? It is because a sentence like that completely embodies in language all of my anxiety and frustration and uncertainty and rage—it is an awkward sentence, strange, off-balance, precarious. Darkly imagined, it seems to break off from the body of the rest of the text it is a part of, to assume an eerie and haunting independence. A splintered, troubling thing. It so captures my emotional state *in language* that I am no longer so alone, marooned in it: the emotional state is approximated through the physicality of language, mirrored, and as a result becomes company, something present, something palpable.... The language construct is no longer *about* an emotional state for me, but has become one, and in that way I am no longer utterly isolated in it and without a viable structure. Home is any ordinary, gorgeous sentence that is doing its work.

Home for me is in the syntax, in the syllables. In the syncopations and in the silences. A movement in the mind, the eye, the mouth. Home is the luminous imagination. India haunting me after the Satyatjit Ray retrospective. Home is in Sappho's fragments, in imagining what was there before the papyrus tore. The imagination providing a foundation, a roof, and windows that let you see forever.

The glowing imagination. The place in the distance, amidst the maelstrom of the blizzard toward which "poets will walk without thinking, as if walking home," as Tsvetaeva has said. That place, distant, mysterious, ever fleeting, changing and shifting, but glimmering in the distance *is* home as far as I'm concerned.

Home is that drugged, seductive other state—creation not so unlike the dark, sexual descent. Now a house burns on the page. Now I am in flames. This is the aim of my erotic études: to explore those relationships between language and desire, my sacred, twinned notions of home. In this alternate place, this other reality, outside, apart from one's other life (having moved again, having left, been displaced, been hurt, been diminished and forced to operate in a world so unlike one's real world). A state so deeply meditative, so deeply sexual, so like music. Home is still the music drifting. My parents whispering. The precious alphabet she taught me. And her lovely body. Home is the bodies of women: safe. And all the songs they sang—and sing.

One afternoon while I am dreaming *Defiance*, I finally realize, I know, yes, the little girl Bernadette and Kennedy, her older brother, will go fishing—that is it—and somehow it all falls into its proper balance: austere, mysterious, impossibly simple and elegant. Yes, that is it. And I am completely elated and then serene. As happy as I have ever been. Who would not choose to live there?

When I write sentences I am at home. When I make shapes. When I do not, I am damned, doomed, homeless; I know this well—restless, roaming; the actual places I've lived become unrecognizable, and I too, monstrous, am unrecognizable to myself. In the gloating, enormous strangeness and solitude of the real world, where I am so often inconsolable, marooned, utterly dizzied—all I need do is to pick up a pen and begin to write—safe in the shelter of the alphabet, and I am taken home. Back into the blinding waves, the topaz light, the fire. Or far off into the enthralling, voluptuous dark.

Displaced Person

ROSELLEN BROWN

The writer operates at a peculiar crossroads where time and place and eternity somehow meet. His problem is to find that location.

—FLANNERY O'CONNOR

WHEN PEOPLE ASK me where I come from I tell them nowhere. Someone introducing me at a reading recently told the audience that I grew up in Philadelphia, which was a fair enough assumption, based on the information on some book jacket or vita that I was born in Philadelphia—this is Pennsylvania, not Mississippi—but he was entirely wrong: I lived in Philadelphia for ten weeks. At the end of ten years of not much belonging there, my parents, who were New Yorkers, were obviously waiting with their bags packed for me to be born, so that we could take off to what turned out to be a series of other places in which they also never felt at home.

Our vagabondage was not particularly exciting. We weren't natural gypsies who chose the next town over the hill because it looked inviting; nor was my father a circuit-riding preacher or a military man, as many are quick to suggest. He was following a job or two to this or that unlikely outpost and was indifferent to the charm or charmlessness of our living arrangements. These days, "quality of life," as it's quaintly called, is being ranked in yearly studies that inform us which cities we should seek out, which we should make a wide berth around. (Choose Austin, Texas but not Beaumont; Palo Alto, California but not Compton. Some news: Go for beauty, class, and amenities; eschew poverty and the industrial wasteland.)

But that was not always the most salient concept. My father went to work as a typist for a railroad company at thirteen, having had a few desultory months of business school, and my mother, though she also missed out on high school, worked hard at transcending the tenements in which she grew up as a Russian immigrant. They started their family during the Depression. (My oldest brother was born in 1930.) I assumed that for them, dutiful and loving parents, once having ascertained that we lived, as the ads say, near schools and shopping, a good job was a lot more potent an attraction than a graceful skyline or a dozen lakes scattered across the horizon. As for family, in that kind of vertical move family is necessarily left behind; or if it does not disappear, it hangs on the way my grandmother did, barnacle-like, once her own household had dispersed, moving as we moved for want of anyone else to live with or anywhere else to go.

In any event, until I was a teenager the longest I lived in any one place was four years, which I spent in a town in Westchester County outside of New York City. Now, we all know that "where you come from," where you grew up, is a matter for the imagination—for anyone's imagination, not only a writer's. The dates on a questionnaire don't begin to approach the significant center of one's experience. That town I lived in from ages five through nine was called Mount Vernon. It was a short and to me wondrous commuter-train ride to Manhattan that we made on many a Thursday night (when the department stores stayed open late) or Saturday afternoon for shopping or a concert. But when people say to me, "You grew up in New York," I have to demur. From time to time I borrowed its vigor and its cultural endowments, but the city (by which people mean Manhattan, whether they realize it or not) wasn't mine. I was not that kind of New Yorker. (Similarly, my husband, who grew up in a part of Brooklyn called East New York, says he had a village childhood; as alien as any visitor from another coast or continent, the only time he ever set foot in Manhattan was for an occasional holiday foray to Radio City Music Hall.)

Although reason tells me that every year of those four that I lived in Mount Vernon consisted of the requisite four seasons, and even though I can recall plenty of winter and summer scenes if I try, still for whatever entirely subterranean reason, when I remember what I think of as the central years of my childhood—the others trickled away a year or two at a time in places that left no particular residue— it is always fall and I am kicking up noisy leathery leaves in a particular stretch of woods within sight of the solid-stone castle-like bridges that cross the old winding highways of Westchester County. I don't know why this is the abiding image I have taken from the full years of my childhood. Nothing special happened there, either ecstatic or traumatic, I have no whole picture that tells me whether I played there once or twice or a hundred times, and I don't remember who I played with. I must have felt some heart-centered, solitary, sensual delight, some essence of childhood freedom otherwise denied me, in that place. I remember that certain grim sunlight that precedes winter-in-earnest, and the kind of temperature in which you keep your jacket open because it's not quite cold, but yet your ears hurt with the hinted beginning of serious weather.

But this is very nearly all. The rest of my memories from childhood, I should say, though they are numerous, are not continuous. They yield less than they ought to of pattern and ritual and of rich pictures of neighbors in their characteristic places, of townspeople whose behavior became, after years, predictable to a concentrating child, whose family laughs about this one or that, or shakes its collective head in disapproval at the dinner table. I did not have the repetition of year-in, year-out expectation that comes of belonging in a community. The only advantage to this kind of random childhood, I ought to say, is that when I want to date something in my mind I can think, ah yes, it must have been 1948 when that happened because that was the year, the only year, we lived in Los Angeles. There is a backdrop for the memories and it is always recognizable because it changes so distinctly with each move. So, while those who have lived in a single place may see a blur of years, I have them all too neatly separated and captioned, like photographs, according to city and setting.

It goes without saying that I missed a great deal in our peripatetic life. Though my parents were wonderfully adequate to the tasks of parenthood, this is the only detail of nurturing they didn't bother to provide, and I think they suffered considerable loneliness themselves for the lack of a single place we could call home. (Even Flannery O'Connor's character was luckier than we, who came "not even from a place, just from near a place.") Mainly, I think, the bit of geography on which you grow up, with which you identify yourself before you even think about such things—the world to which you first belong— acts in your life much the way your parents do: it becomes that immutable *fact* in your existence which, when you come to conscious- ness, you either embrace or resist. You are defined by it, your vision made by it, though no one ever asked your opinion of the matter; and so eventually you will either love your hometown, your neigh- borhood, your house, or you will struggle against it, you will dream of the bus station or the college admission that will set you free, or the simple year of majority after which no one can force you to stay and continue your childhood past the time when it is seemly to be "Sue Anne's girl" or "Junior" to your father, or the ex–football star or prom queen. Or you will love and hate it in unpredictable alter- nation.

Edgar Z. Friedenberg in *The Vanishing Adolescent,* a good book pop- ular in the early sixties, talked about the problems of adolescents who grow up without resistance from their permissive parents, without boundaries against which to hone themselves, to sharpen and define their differences: to discover who they are not and, consequently, who they are or may want to become. I think that, lacking a hometown to spurn, I lacked a starting point from which to move away, toward which I might one day have decided to move back, in a sweet reconciling return.

And, parenthetically, I should say that I began writing as an antidote to the loneliness of exile. I can, of course, place the memory against a particular backdrop: it was in the lee of yet another move, from one coast to another, that I found myself at nine bereft of friends. I would go off to school clutching to my—nonexistent—bosom a secretarial notebook in which I wrote stories of perfect girls who possessed perfect horses, and *they* kept me company. (D. H. Lawrence really did have it right about girls and their stallions, but he extended the age for that bit of displaced erotic fantasy far too long into adulthood: nine to eleven is just about right.) Thus, telling myself stories, I looked busy while all the old friends stood around in comfortable groups to which I had no invitation, and in my notebook—out of words—I made new friends far more dazzling than those who were merely real.

But let me not sound too forlorn: we live with our biographies, whatever they may bring, and in my case it is starting nowhere, having no sense of place, that has been my bedrock reality. I have scraped up against *that* to make my world on the page. My prevailing subject has turned out to be exile; turned out to be place, which, unpossessed or forfeited—the obverse of home—can be just as obsessive a preoccupation.

So, as it's happened, I have immersed myself in a rather unwieldy number of borrowed terrains in my writing: four, so far; or maybe three and a fraction, since Houston, my current home, makes only a cameo appearance at the end of my most recent novel, *Before and After.*

The first time I left my teenage home, which was a characterless though not entirely unattractive part of Queens, New York, called Forest Hills—very few people who live outside of New York or occasionally visit Manhattan realize the astounding aesthetic bleakness that prevails for most New Yorkers at home, the darkness of ancient apartments and the industrial clutter of the boroughs—when I left that home to which physical memories have trouble sticking as if it were too smooth a surface, it was for New England. There I discovered that there were places with a visible history, with an indigenous feel to them, characteristic textures, colors, climate, and that people in small towns took an intimate interest in each other's affairs. Without having partaken of the pleasures of the rich or the impacted intimacies of the poor, I had the middle-class New Yorker's anomie with relation to our neighbors: we went unimpeded, on our street, by much curiosity or concern. Good and bad in equal parts, this freedom again left a void I hadn't even known I possessed. Once I got a glimpse through a crack in the door, I longed for the life of the New Englander, to be lived under an afghan on a high antique four-poster bed in the imagined company of Emily Dickinson, who had lived hers that way. This was an ideal of quaint specificity I wished for but couldn't have.

After New England I lived in San Francisco, which was a different sort of picturesque, an ideal that I loved but didn't want—it seemed to me a diet of lotus and civic self-congratulation.

I came to Mississippi in 1965 half-mature at best, as a grown-up in any case whose childhood book was closed on many empty pages, and that is where I learned that if one could not be born again a native of a place, it was at least possible to bring to it the cultivated virtues of curiosity and freshness of vision—of entranced concentration—so that no one need ever be thoroughly barred from writing about *anything* if one found it interesting enough. "Write about what you know," we writing teachers are reputed to tell our students, but I don't necessarily tell them that at all because I agree with the critic Denis Donohue that "many events casually called experiences are merely happenings. The test of an experience is that it alters the structure of our feeling; if it doesn't, it has been merely a circumstance, it hasn't entered our lives in any radical sense." And, of course, the converse is just as true: a writer who finds him or herself profoundly affected by a circumstance or by a place can by a kind of exaggeratedly focused attention render that scene. It has become an experience in Donohue's terms; it has counted on the pulses, it has taken its place in the circuitry of the brain. But (no sense denying it) with a difference.

It would have taken nerve I didn't have to write about Mississippi as if I were a native. Probably because I don't much value those pallid experiences of mine, the skills I have are different from those of someone writing from memory: I am not so much a historian as a sociologist crossed with an anthropologist, both of whom are passionate outsiders, and an inventor, or perhaps an intuiter, rather than a preserver. The question of perspective always looms for a writer— who speaks, and with what authority? The care with which one chooses that distance at which the narrator will plant his or her feet is exaggerated when the writer is, like me, a newcomer, a native of nowhere; Flannery O'Connor might say, a displaced person. Writers can be carpetbaggers if they're not careful, or colonialists, if you will, immodestly appropriating that which is not theirs. Sometimes they ought to dare if they can pull it off. But if they can't, such appropriation ends up looking like a moral failing, like lying or the crime of theft: petty larceny.

THE FIRST THING I wrote about Mississippi was a poem. It was the summer of 1964. The poem was called "Landing in Jackson" and it begins my first book, *Some Deaths in the Delta*.

> I wear my fear like wool against the skin,
> walking from corner to corner of this graceless city,
> squinting down doorways, warily at faces.
> For a familiar token I take the sky,
> stretched taut between the tent-poles of my sight—

that northern sky that bore me up for hours,
then set me down in this ungentle place.

What shame may be here keeps its uneven heartbeat
under the breast-pocket, the clean white hanky;
if any danger passes, it keeps its eyes
turned in like something hidden in the palm.
I sniff from corner to corner, guilelessly,
skulking for welcome.

This is, of course, a poem about being a stranger in a strange land. Since an experience can be something you create for yourself without benefit of the occurrence, the real event may be the least important ingredient. Which is to say, I wrote the poem on my back porch in Brookline Village, Massachusetts, in terrified anticipation, before I'd ever set foot in Jackson, Mississippi. (I should add that since life is more complex than I knew at the time, it has since turned out that working-class Irish Brookline Village, Massachusetts, to judge by the behavior of similar Boston neighborhoods, probably harbored—covertly—as viciously racist a climate as anyone might find on the continent. Only its particular history and the publicly civil behavior of its leaders had kept that ugliness sufficiently surreptitious in 1964 so that I really thought I had to go someplace else, by airplane—some mysteriously evil city surrounded by alien woods, in a different time zone—to find racial brutality and the indignities of segregation.)

Eventually I was to write more than half a book of poems about Mississippi, not didactic but, I would say, elegiac and often angry. Even though one can fudge a thousand details in poetry—this is how, later, I dared to write in the voice of a New Hampshire woman—I was sufficiently daunted by what I still thought of as the other-ness of the South that I wrote as an outsider. Thinking of Jackson again, the self-appointed "crossroads of the South," I saw myself accosted by a woman amidst the "alien corn":

> Blonde as the grass in January,
> walking with legs padlocked above the knee,
> she asked, sweet as a lime,
> what country was I from.

The bitterness of the poem, which was distinctly a product of its period in history, was unyieldingly hostile to white Mississippi, a population for which I—who had come south as an advocate of black rights, to teach in a black college—was not about to feel sympathy. What an extraordinary sense of double displacement for a northern white woman—I was a girl, really—to belong neither to the dominant population nor, of course, (I couldn't kid myself) to the world of my black friends.

After a collection of stories, *Street Games*, which is set on one hypothetical block in Brooklyn inhabited by characters white, black, and Puerto Rican, of all classes, the (actual) place to which we return after our years in the South, I revisited Mississippi in a brief section of my first novel because it was still a potent symbol of social malaise, and a simpler one than any state or city in the north.

"After the first exile there is no other," says one of my characters in *The Autobiography of My Mother*. Some people, I was learning, perhaps from studying myself, are at home only in continuous displacement. In that novel I make alienation an overt theme. The mother in the book is a civil-liberties lawyer named Gerda Stein who is forcibly removed from her native Alsace at an early age, bearing nothing intact except her convoluted Germanic syntax. Although the book takes place in New York, Gerda does something uncharacteristically passionate, even heroic, during a brief sojourn in Mississippi where she is arguing for school integration. But she dismisses the act as not particularly courageous:

It was the act of an outsider with whom the consequences would never catch up. Having been cut free of my past the one, the first time, I was cast into a lifetime of freedom. One accepts such freedom of movement like a doom, a taste of certain death, do you understand that? I was not easily to be hurt or frightened. Perhaps that is all that is necessary for mere humans, not saints, not martyrs, to act. . . . [I] had come from nowhere, in whose accents I persistently spoke, and would soon return to nowhere. Mine was a privileged freedom which compensated—at such times—for my rootlessness. So you see, even the Lone Ranger could afford momentary lapses into heroism. They did not truly cost him so much, surely not so much as children believe, for he habitually vanished, did he not, into some canyon, some purple sunrise, leaving only his silver bullet behind.

Should he not merely have been called The Exile?

In another place she says impatiently of her law partner,

I can better comprehend the life of a hoarse-throated, one-legged, blind, garlic-scented, God-fearing Malaysian who has lived in any twelve cities of the world than, say, that of my partner, Jack Tenney, who was born in Washington Heights and has merely rolled downhill a few miles to the nearest viable neighborhood, barring Harlem, to live in a building which must be nearly identical to the first; and so, except for a short lifeless sojourn to the barracks of Fort Dix twenty years ago, he has moved gently through his life yet to be truly surprised, I would wager, or truly inconvenienced.

Snug Jack.

This is, I suppose, my own very personal sense of the paradox of mobility: Gerda's perpetually angry acknowledgment of her dislocation, with its concomitant freedom from hometown constraints, is the best and the worst one can expect. For certain purposes, we displaced persons have special powers; for others, no power at all.

Though Gerda may speak more explicitly about her exile, none of my four novels deals with characters at home where they began. *Tender Mercies* marries a hometown New Hampshire boy to the daughter of a Cambridge professor; when she is crippled in a boating accident, it is not only her body from which she is alienated, but she and her husband must grapple with the differences in their origins that have made their marriage, and their smalltown life, an uneasy one.

And the novel that followed *Tender Mercies* turns right around and returns me most pointedly to Mississippi, some of it at the inflamed high point of civil-rights activity, most of it fifteen years later— 1979—in a Jackson much changed, its racial mores (inconsistently) assimilated and less lethal, blander, its general profile less "southern," more American, all of that for better and for worse. Again, it's written from what I like to call the *Gulliver perspective:* the stranger can comment on what he (in this case she) sees without bias. (Since there is no neutrality, of course, I should amend that: with the biases of the observer who has grown up on other sights.) Henry James in Europe had such a vantage point, or Paul Scott in India. Southerners do not often resort to it unless they, like Elizabeth Spencer, say, go to Italy.

My novel concerns a white husband and wife, Teddy and Jessie Carll, who are staying on in Jackson many years after the high season of their civil rights heroism. By now, so long after the exhilaration of that time, Jessie, who is one of those New Yorkers who came south for what she called the second Civil War, is looking with a somewhat jaundiced eye at the world of her Mississippi-born husband. Teddy, a renegade in his family, has fought hard for his moral autonomy, has alienated himself wholly from his childhood. When Jessie considers

Teddy, she does so as a newcomer to his world, both attracted and repelled by so much that comes to her too late to be taken into her imaginative sympathy. I'd like her sense of the place to be illuminating to northerner and southerner alike: to show another New Yorker, say, what she might have seen and felt had she been in Jessie's place (for Jessie is a stand-in for any other alien's experience) and I'd like the southern reader to apprehend what it all must look and feel like to someone who's dropped in, Gulliver-like, from across the sea, or in this case, the Mason-Dixon line.

Because one's obsessions will surface wholly unbidden, I doubled the alienation factor. Without exactly realizing what I was doing as I chose the plot to pull the load of social observation, I forced the Carlls, by the accidental death of Teddy's sister and brother-in-law, to take into their house in an integrated neighborhood in Jackson their niece and nephew, who have grown up in affluent Birmingham in an emphatically segregationist household. These children are southerners but they are, not to mince words, little bigots, and rich ones to boot, come to live in a commitedly ascetic (and, to them, a morally bizarre) household. Their world and the world of their aunt and uncle and cousins are 180 degrees—360 degrees—different, because ideology and its local manifestation, habit, can make rackingly different worlds out of the same point in space. No one in *Civil Wars* is living with the same sense of place as anyone else, even when they stand with shoulders touching. I give young Helen, who is thirteen and one of the orphans-come-to-town, her own diary through which to show us what it feels like to be turned out of every comfort of home; her way of dealing with this tragic disorientation, finally, is to take refuge in her own unchanging solace, a good southern solution, I think:

> No home there,
> No home here,

No home anywhere
But Jesus.

In my most recent novel, *Before and After*, I discovered I'd done it again. I've taken a New York family and moved them to a new locale, their dream place, that same New Hampshire town where *Tender Mercies* is set (named, with the self-delighting power one has as a novelist to rearrange the world, for one of my daughters' first grade teachers, a woman named Anne Hyland). In this story, the outsiders think they've bridged at least some of the gaps between themselves and their neighbors, but there's always an uncomfortable sense of being on borrowed turf, some of it abetted by their privilege: she's a pediatrician, he's a sculptor who has also, therefore, been a house husband. These professions present a large challenge to the gender habits of a town like Hyland, and when the worst possible thing that can happen does befall—the permanent dividing line between Before and After—when their teenage son is accused of murdering his "townie" girlfriend, of course all their marginalities rise up like a set of bars between the Reisers and the village they had perhaps foolishly hoped they belonged to. At the end of the book, in need of a "city of refuge" like the ones in the Bible to which inadvertent murderers can escape to live without fear of reprisal, they fly off to Houston, which is as far from their bucolic Hyland as anything could be. I chose it because, as Ben, the father, says with resignation, his wife now works in a hospital the size of the entire town they've left behind. So much for the dream of intimacy and rural grace.

Intimate or not, Texas is at least one of the few parts of the country that still has any real distinctiveness left (though of course it is fast being leveled). But both the South and New England are good candidates for an adopted home that could exist nowhere but where it is. I know that, because of the time we spent in Mississippi, it was the southernness of Houston that pulled me to it, not the westernness: the heavy-laden feel of the air, and the hanging moss. It was the familiar long-missed look of the chipped-paint shacks leaning exhaustedly against each other like nothing in the North; the live oaks and the modest bungalows with no foundation, the smalltown shops with their metal awnings only half an hour from the Astrodome. It was the bayous and the violent late-afternoon summer showers that drew me to Texas, not its oil money and Houston's beautiful brittle glass skyline.

FINALLY, I HAVE to say a few words about my own favorite among my books, because I have learned from it, once and for all, that because of the imagination's relation to one's own psychic history, there's about as much chance of escaping the old obsessions as the man had in the O'Hara story when Death made that appointment with him in Samarra. What a paradox, I find myself thinking as I proceed from one address to the next, that my location will always be the lack of location (though not, I hope, the dead letter office of undeliverable messages!).

In 1977 I published a book of poems in the shape of a novel—it had a single speaking character surrounded by family and town; it had a sort of plot—called *Cora Fry*. Since I hadn't lived in New Hampshire that long when I wrote it, this was a rather presumptuous ventriloqual act in which I speak as a country woman born and persevering right down the road from where she began. In a crisis, she flees to Boston for a brief time and comes gratefully home again, with a clearer sense of the virtues and drawbacks of intimacy and anonymity. I wrote about Cora, it was clear to me, as an antidote to my preoccupation with not-belonging: she knows as little about exile as I know about living on native ground, and I got to live in her skin for at least a little while and to ponder the implications.

Seventeen years later I found myself still pondering, curious about what kinds of turns Cora's life might have taken while I moved on into a different climate and time zone. That is how the sequel, *Cora Fry's Pillow Book*, came about. And it's astounding to me but I've made even Cora (who swore she'd never move because her little town of Oxford is "bred in my flesh...like a fingerprint. A watermark") into a victim of my old habit of displacement: Trying to be attentive to the devastating recession that plagued New Hampshire a few years back, I got Fry laid off from his factory job and—after much torment and resistance—when there seemed no other recourse but to find him some work a good long distance away, I've torn Cora out of her nest and sent her packing. Ah Cora, I thought when I realized my handwriting was on the wall, poor Cora, I've had to make her truly mine by taking away the place she loves, the old house she's put her stamp on, the shelves of canning jars, the memories of generations. I wonder if I was jealous of her for having something I didn't have or if I simply lack the inventiveness to end a story any other way.

THERE IS A part of me that believes that every writer comes upon, or is made by, a distancing element. I don't think any writer has ever in fact been fully at home anywhere or he/she would sell insurance or decorate cakes for a living, or sit and rock and chew. Family politics and village politics, class and racial and religious and sexual politics wrench us out of complacency into clarifying insight, and if they don't do it, then there is always the suspicion, glimpsed early by the sensitive, that even the most peaceful home or village will one day perish, and so will the people in it. That's enough to modulate and darken the most self-satisfied of melodies.

Still I find myself envying those who have known a community, loved or despised it but *known* it—a place to start out from. Even those who have had to abandon their homes, I think, can take some comfort in imagining their lost ideal (though I say that on no authority: for all I know, this is the keenest pain of all).

About ten years ago I visited the then–Soviet Union, and there I met a number of Refuseniks, vivid, courageous people desperate to change *their* addresses and leave the oppressive country of their birth.

It was wrenching to hear them speak of their desperation to emigrate, their willingness to become the proverbial wandering Jews, to give up familiarity, comfort, language, profession, their own particular histories, in return for freedom from harassment. But when I returned to Houston and watched a few of the "successful" emigrés making their painful adjustments, I suppose I must have felt, yes, this I can understand. Their nostalgia might be for an actual place and mine, apparently, for some faceless Eden I never knew, but yes, I thought, as my Gerda said years before I had so many poignant examples: *After the first exile, there is no other.*

EMIGRÉ (*Houston*)

Here you get yourself a car.
It takes you to town, it takes you home
at your own good time
and no one else's.
You have a house standing separate,
and a garage like a belly on the house.
Here's what you do at the end of the day: you ride up
fast to the house, put the wheels
between two little margins of short-haired grass.
(You have to keep it short).
You point your finger at your house
and slow as a drawbridge the wide door yawns
up, up, showing your cans of paint,
your dog-eared valises to the world.
You inch into the dark, gently.
For a while you get to sit, then,
peaceful, like the cut-off motor cooling down.
Your hedge-clipper dangles on the wall, open-mouthed,
your exercise bike sits at the back
like a patient horse in its clean stall.

In Leningrad this is the hour
when they hang suspended in the Metro,
shoulder to shoulder to elbow to groin.
Nobody's feet at five o'clock
ever touch ground. When the full train lurches,
no one has room among so many friends and strangers,
not even an inch, to fall down.

On the Continental Shelf

JANE SHAPIRO

WHEN WE GOT rich, in 1952, our parents built a house on an East Coast barrier island, set behind low dunes, facing the Atlantic. My father—like his father—was a real estate developer on this twenty-mile spit of sand; finally he was making money of his own, and now we could step into the lavish life he had been intending all along. By the 1980s, my father had died and my mother moved away; my brothers were far from any home, one in a mental hospital, the other just gone; the house was empty, the greenhouse flattened, the vegetable beds and cutting garden a thicket of weeds, the pool filled to its pear-shaped edge with sand.

ON MARTIN LUTHER King Day, 1992, I'm down on the island, standing on the lawn in a twenty-degree breeze, talking with Moody, whose wrecking company is tearing down our house. I'm videotaping. Moody and I stand side by side as companionably as if we knew and liked each other, in the roar of machinery and freezing sea air, and watch his Komatsu claw taking bites out of the roof. The garden wall has already been crashed through; beyond it, on the dune, where summer people build their houses, pilings have been sunk for new vacation places.

Moody says the guy working the claw is starving. He has no money at all. Moody had to give him a hundred dollars this week so he could eat. He looks at me slyly, red-eyed and porky and scary. I look, to him, as always: rich girl. Should I offer him fifty dollars to pass on to the claw driver? I don't like Moody and I don't trust him, and I don't know whether the guy needs money or not, so although I'm afraid it may be true, I don't pull out my wallet. I shoot some more tape.

Watching the house come down, I'm as lonely as I've ever been. Even Moody's company is better than none. After a while I say, "The claw works so gracefully."

Moody: "I hate Japs so bad. I can't even look at a Jap without spitting. But when it comes to paying $50,000, $60,000 less..." So he broke down and bought the Komatsu, which never needs fixing.

Growing up, I don't think I knew Moody, I tell him—can't remember him. He says he missed ten years' worth of local people because he was away. But people down here don't go away—"Where were you?" Creepy grin: *"Oh, law school."* So now that he's been released—paroled, or served out his sentence—he and I are standing here on my family's former lawn, catching up.

"You have slaves?" Moody inquires pleasantly.

What?

"You had *slaves,* I'm saying. *Then.*"

"What do you mean? Did people work in the house? Yes."

"You have butlers and maids and chauffeurs and stuff?"

I laugh. I say, "Not butlers."

He tells me he once hired James Boyd, a really nice young guy, a childhood friend of my sister Juliet's. "Boyd worked for me after he was *your chauffeur.* So I already know you had chauffeurs."

I say, "James worked on a crew. He probably drove the car six times, if that."

Moody, sweetly: "Chauffeur."

The claw grinds forward, maneuvered like a cutting horse, and bites off a corner; a piece of wall smashes, sending up clouds of Sheetrock and asbestos dust. The new owner is standing around looking quietly thrilled. The land is zoned for seventeen houses; showing tasteful restraint, he's planning to build only seven, set around a cul-de-sac, and another three for himself and his family on the dune. He crosses the lawn to shake my hand. "I'm sorry," he says, and I shoot some tape of him backing away, apologetically smiling. Moody says, "Looked like there was slave quarters in the house."

Shut up, Moody. I try to laugh.

"We saw 'em."

"That's ridiculous. There was just a little apartment in the back of the house. My grandfather lived there for a while."

"Slave quarters."

I turn my back and watch through the camera.

"I wanta be rich enough," Moody is saying, "to afford a slave." One of his men walks over and Moody tells him in greeting: "Yeah! That's what I want! My own personal slave."

I THINK EVERYBODY in my family recalls with gratitude, as they should, all the people who worked in our house—who not only kept the place running but who brought, just by their presence, news of the outside into that sequestered life. Ruthie, a large patient Swedish woman, with us all our lives as cook, housekeeper, and surrogate grandmother, was one of the kindest people I've known. She took care of everybody—I recall her straining cream for my mother's morning coffee before she sent up the tray; and, in winter, warming my mother's hands between her own. Because of Ruthie, we were accompanied. By loving the children she cared for, she seemed to keep us alive; without her, we would've certainly perished.

But Moody's remarks were not wholly surprising. Although our family had been rooted in this community since my grandfather's arrival in the 1920s, knew everybody here and were known by them, and loved the island and many of the people, at the same time our money and books and mobility and Jewishness separated us profoundly from this place that was our home. We were both like and unlike; mainly we lived in solitude and fantasy inside a house like a tiny, self-contained world, then at intervals traveled away.

As children, we would occasionally be wakened by traffic noise and open our eyes to find ourselves in New York City—we'd been carried there in the night; now we would stay a couple of weeks. I recall with something akin to homesickness the hotel suites, their tall windows with heavy draperies and city light slanting in.

During the winter, dead season, when it's too cold to sink pilings and there are no vacationers shopping for beach houses, our parents would cast around for something to do. Then we'd sail to Europe for two-month stays. We traveled so often and so luxuriously as children that hotels feel completely homelike, and I still do most of my weeping in restaurants between courses, comfortable on the banquette. Nina, the youngest of my four siblings, was raised by our beloved Ruthie and loved her deeply; when she heard years later that Ruthie had died, Nina was so bereft that she immediately flew to Majorca, checked into a hotel, and dialed room service—she needed to grieve in a correct setting. So in our case, as long as you can afford the hotel bill, you can go home again.

Or home can be in your car! We all drive, in my family—when nervous or troubled, we get on the road. Distances don't discourage us; we like spending days and nights with the highway unfolding and semis nudging us along. In this way, my family are unlike most other easterners—we have more in common with people who live in, say, the Dakotas. Of course we can be taciturn that way, too. (Growing up, we didn't need to speak with each other for days and often just passed in the hall. I remember having silent breakfasts with my sister Juliet and my brother Daniel before school. Ruthie wouldn't have arrived yet for the day, and our parents were sleeping. We'd stand in the kitchen not talking, and I'd have a cigarette, Juliet a Coke, Daniel some wedges of cake, and then we'd walk to meet the bus.)

My brother Daniel's final break with his family—in retrospect, of course, long in coming—almost seemed to begin on a random road trip. When Daniel and our other brother, David, were young, they rode their motorcycles side by side across the country and straight back, smoking hash in the desert and staying high until New York. Fifteen years ago they wanted to repeat the trip and decided instead to drive two of their cars, a Lotus and a custom-edition Porsche, down to Florida. When they reached Daytona, they drove at wild speed the eighteen miles along the hard-packed shore from Ponce de Leon Inlet to Ormond Beach, then started north again. On the way back, somewhere in South Carolina, in a confused way they got to quarreling, and they parted angrily and, as it turned out, finally: Because Daniel was on the point of disappearing then, he and David, who had always been close, never patched things up. When I visited him recently in the mental hospital where he now lives, David said, "I would still like to reconcile." But Daniel has been gone so long and we don't know where. Nevertheless, David said he does not regret that Daytona trip: "On the way down, it was one of the best drives we ever took."

When I drive long distances myself, some people I've lost come back to me. When I see a man hitchhiking—or sometimes just a boy standing near the road—I always think it's Daniel. Sometimes I half-see the man, don't immediately register him, but tears come to my eyes. Still, like everybody in my family, I'm genuinely soothed on the road—not happy, necessarily, but calm. We drive to outrun anxiety, or grief. We're out looking for a place we once knew.

IN 1926, OUR Latvian immigrant grandfather, summering at the shore, took a drive and found a barrier island approximately a million years old but still rather undeveloped; envisioned the resort he would build; and bought up some expanses of sand, cheap. This place became truly a home—this sandbar. Not the family, but the place itself, its dunes and grasses and jetties, the changeable sky over the ocean, shifting winds, silvery waves breaking.

"The history of sandbars," my mother used to go around saying, "is that they return to the mainland."

I looked into this, and it's true. The continental shelf, that flat, relatively shallow undersea plateau edging the world's shores, has been, over centuries, alternately submerged and exposed—20,000 years ago, in the time of the glaciers, it was dry land. For more time than Mom has imagined, and long before Columbus's cartographer drew, on ox-hide, a new map of the world—showing North America as one with Asia because Europeans hadn't found the Pacific yet—all this time, our little sandbar has been almost imperceptibly waning.

"Our little sandbar"—actually, this isn't quite right: Elie de Beaumont, the father of barrier-island research, proposed in 1845 that such islands are, as you'd assume, built up from bars. But now it seems that instead of sand just accreting on a bar to create an island, an already extant ridge finds itself surrounded by rising water, ending up stranded, or, conversely, exposed as the water level drops. If you include their submarine time, the North American barrier islands, Pleistocene-epoch creations, are literally a million years old. None of this would've cheered Mom any.

My mother never learned to swim. I don't remember her even walking from the house to the gazebo on the dune, though when we were small and still living crammed into a garden apartment, she trudged with us to the beach, only out of duty. To prevent our slipping away and instantly sinking to our deaths beneath the waves, she'd draw, with her toe, a big cage in the sand, and we'd spend the afternoon inside this cage. Years later, she sat often alongside the pool, preoccupied, doubtless imagining a 600-mile-an-hour tsunami, pondering the slow separation of continents, expecting a seaquake.

Recently I told my mother I've been reading about islands. "The configuration of the continental shelves is not permanent," I told her. Mom: "You bet."

NOW A FRONT-END loader is getting under sections of the walls, jamming them up and ripping them out; Moody's flatbeds are hauling away the pieces. When the machines pause, you can hear the ocean, waves breaking in still air. One end of the house is gone, exposing the basement: The playroom, still holding its pool table and oak shuffleboard. The storage rooms, holding shelves of waxed paper and bottles of ketchup that never got used up; and all our wooden skis and leather boots—in a heap, just as Dad dumped them on the rug the day he bought them thirty-eight years ago; and gallon bottles of ginger-ale syrup, stocked in the 1950s for the soda fountain. The walk-in refrigerator room, inside which we once found our cousin Arlene in her organza dress during a dancing party, drunk and cheerful, lying among watermelons and bottles of seltzer, getting cooled off.

My bedroom, where I hid myself, is gone. In Princeton, in the little suburban house that after twenty-five years continues to become my home, I have the Nakashima furniture from that childhood room, and I've always felt as though the stuff got pulled out of a burning building. So I've been somehow cheerfully anticipating this demolition. It's an old, perverse, sanguine fantasy of mine: the family home burns to charred foundation, and I'm strong enough to drag my Nakashimas clear and take them wherever I decide I'm going.

HERE'S AN ASTOUNDING thing that happened: while I was watching the house disappear, I saw my brother Daniel ride by on a bicycle. Because it was deep winter, of course 90 percent of the people were gone from the island and the boats were out of water and the streetlights turned off—still, my brother pedaled past. Eleven years before, not long after his and David's Daytona ride, Daniel stopped speaking to everybody in our family, changed his name, and moved away. I had last seen him on the beach, the first week of July 1981; I was still waiting and hoping I would get to talk to him again. Now here he was.

I was astonished: he has a bike! Then I got my bearings: they're razing his childhood home and *of course* he has come to see, anybody might own a bike, and he's just riding by. After he passed, I ran to my car and followed, cruising slowly down the ocean road, blocks behind—staying far enough back to be hidden, not to alarm him, though of course he wouldn't, after eleven years, know my car. The day still clear, just space and winter sky and the churning sound of the waves, the road empty, a broad avenue lined with blank-faced, closed-up summer houses; me driving, and blocks ahead, my brother pedaling.

Three miles down, Daniel made a left. I followed but lost him. I circled the block and wrote down the plate numbers of a Chevy with nicked robin's-egg-blue paint parked alongside a small house with asbestos shingles: this had to be Daniel's. I didn't feel my excitement—I was busy, preoccupied, entranced. I thought about how, if I didn't find him now, I'd come back, walk to the shingled house, and knock, and my brother, eleven years older, would open the door.

Then he appeared on his bike. I called, *Dan!* and he circled and rode over. Under his helmet the lower part of his face looked like David's—I thought, that's perfect: Daniel turns out to look more like his brother than I recalled, or has grown more like him all these years they've been apart.

He circled to my car and lifted the helmet. His upper face showed, and the Dan-like face disappeared. He said, I don't know you.

He wasn't my brother. He was just some guy who had heard me wrong when I called; he heard me say John. You guessed my name, he said now, in an angry, familiar tone.

I didn't like this man—I was repelled by him, who looked so unlike the way he should—but I didn't want him to leave. Over my shoulder I could feel the house, where I began to dream that my brother might be peeking out a window or inside the kitchen microwaving a snack. I insisted the man was wrong, that I definitely knew him from someplace, a bar maybe, Nino's, or the Clam Shack; I asked how long he'd lived on the island; he said ten years. But he had seen me tailing him, he thought I was crazy, and he kept saying I had guessed his name.

Why would somebody do something like that? I demanded— both of us pissed off: Why would I bother to try to guess your name? We squabbled awhile longer. I couldn't bear to say to this stranger: I hoped you were my brother.

When I got back, the holly trees and white pines still stood and the driveway still curved up to them. The house was gone. The embarrassed smiling new owner was gone, and Moody was gone, and my aversion to them suddenly flooded into my chest like water. The house had lasted forty years. It had taken eight hours to tear it down and cart it away. The last wall had fallen while I was driving, following my brother, just on the point of surprising him and saying hello.

AS I WRITE this, it's been almost fifteen years since I've actually seen my brother Daniel. I ran into him on the beach above our house. We sat side by side on a little scarp, watching rip currents, and the sound of breaking waves kept swallowing his voice. I would move slightly closer in order to hear him, and he would slightly, economically move away, and in that fashion we traveled, during our last conversation, quite a distance down the beach.

But driving carefully down the island that winter day in 1992, of course I wasn't tailing the adult, faraway Daniel of our last meeting. I was looking for the small sunny boy, charmed and charming, who once followed David everywhere, walking in his footsteps.

FOR MUCH OF 1995, my mother and I were O. J. watchers. When the jury broke for lunch, we could take showers and run out to buy food.

Early March, 1995, Mom calls from Boston: "Notice anything about the trial?"

"What?"

"Who does the defense attorney Robert Shapiro look like?"

"I don't know, who? Uncle Morris?"

"And who else?"

"I don't know."

"Your father."

"He looks like Dad?"

"Exactly. He looks exactly like him! I thought, My God, he's back."

Mom is so inventive and lonely she sees Dad, thirty years dead, wandering onto the screen. "I'm not sure he looks like Dad," I say. I tell her he certainly looks like the son of Russian Jews, maybe Latvian ones; maybe his family came from Dad's family's section of Riga! He is a Shapiro, after all, so it's plausible he's from another branch of our family.

Mom: "There is no other branch. I know all the branches."

I say maybe Robert Shapiro, famous defense lawyer out there in California, who now, as I hold the phone and watch the screen with the Mute button on, is indeed beginning to look weirdly like my late father—maybe Robert Shapiro is from a branch of the Shapiro family my mother *doesn't* know.

We're stubborn, Mom and I, especially in pursuit of lost worlds. She says, *"There are no other branches."*

"Are you sure?"

"Am I *sure?* I'm *absolutely* sure." Mom says that Robert Shapiro possesses not only Dad's looks (except for the eyebrows) but also Dad's special complicated intelligence and his wily toughness and his tenacity and his hidden temper and his almost courtly manner and his predilection for making deals and his air of being utterly certain of getting his way while simultaneously having all the time in the world. Mom says it's clear that Robert Shapiro is not much older than I, even though he "appears" older, and that my father spent some time without her in California in the early 1940s, and that the net effect is: Robert Shapiro is my half-brother.

What a wonderful idea—it's nuts, but it's wonderful. I love it. My interest in the trial had been flagging; now I'll watch for weeks more. I say, "Okay, if he's my half-brother—and I'm not denying it's technically possible—"

"He *is.*"

I chuckle helplessly, sort of quietly losing hold. But, you know, she's got me. Mom and I are engaged in a shared reclamation project; all of a sudden, and secretly, I'm utterly committed to it. We've been in exile! Now Dad will return, bringing with him the gardens, the gazebo and the library, the Model Ts and As and the '32 Packard touring car, the golden retrievers and the Siamese cats, and our house-keepers Beverly and Lona and precious Ruthie, and Tecla the seam-stress and Mrs. Hansen the laundress, and my young healthy brothers and sisters, and all his nerve and dynamism and wonderful money-making ability along with the entire little deeply insular world these qualities created.

I say, as if playfully, "Ma, if Robert Shapiro is my half-brother, what about this: Why would his mother have given him Dad's name but never contacted Dad, and never bothered us at all, and never asked for any money?"

"That's a problem," Mom admits.

Late at night I suddenly think, Of course! Robert Shapiro's mother *did* contact Dad, and Dad set up a trust fund and supported Robert Shapiro and his mother for decades, and we never found out! I figure this out while lying on my back in the dark, in the precise moment of falling asleep, that moment when, slipping away, you might hear some lost person calling to you.

WEEKS LATER, AT Mom's 78th birthday dinner, she tells me she phoned the courthouse in Paterson, New Jersey, Robert Shapiro's birthplace, to get the official story about his parentage. "They won't tell you," she says. "You have to be a family member."

I laugh. "Ma, you *are* a family member! Go to the Paterson courthouse and tell them you're Robert Shapiro's father's widow."

This story has staying power—it's still almost real to us. Possibly to her it *is* real, and to me it's been *as if real* from the first moment I heard it. When I was a child, my mother introduced me to a magical world that lives in me still: anything can happen. If you have a videotape of a house being taken down, run it backwards. If you lose a brother or a son, or two, and can never find them again no matter how carefully you look—well, then, you grow another one. He's Robert Shapiro, my new brother; he was born in New Jersey and lives in the television set, and he already has our name. Any day now, egged on by me, Mom will journey to the Paterson courthouse and—the way in 1923 my father carried his own week-old brother home from the hospital in a wicker basket—bring Robert Shapiro home.

THE LAST WEEK before the demolition, long after my family and I had taken our things from the house, and before the firemen would wreck the house in a training exercise, I drove down with my friends Kitsi and Ron, perhaps to acquire a few final souvenirs. Not a few— I suddenly wanted as many as I could get. Ron, a cabinetmaker and builder, removed the curved banisters and the enormous, useless copper hood over the stove and the round mirrors from the powder room and stacked them in the truck. Kitsi cut armfuls of firethorn and holly and unscrewed the house numbers off the doorframe. I selected cups and plates for my sister Juliet in California, who had explicitly wanted nothing. I took mismatched flatware and chipped bowls and ugly ashtrays and knives that had long since been sharpened down to splinters. Then I wanted to take the hardwood doors. Ron and I had a long discussion about this; the doors were oversized and wouldn't fit anywhere in any house I am ever likely to own; still, I had to be talked out of them.

For the first time in decades, the house was open and filled with light and visitors walking through. Wind blew in from the ocean. Some local people were bouncing on the diving board, browsing in the library for books, stripping the fireplaces of their marble facings, prying slabs of slate out of the patios. When I was ten years old, while the house was being built, it had been like this, wide open and full of people collaborating on the project; now it was another festive communal scene, all of us working together to take away anything that would move.

WHEN WE FIRST moved in, my brothers and sisters took the house for granted. But I was my mother's child, excited about turning rich. I loved the place inordinately. Watching it be razed, I saw through the eyepiece of my Camcorder that I'm still in love with it.

But this was the most surprising thing: once the house was torn down, my life started. I was fifty years old and of course hadn't expected the demolition to have the effect, so late, of freeing me from anything. But it did. In a curious, hidden way, I had been struggling for decades to cultivate an interest in my own passage through the world outside those walls. Long after my younger sisters had turned to their adult lives, I still thought of that claustral, frantically lonely, cold, sad, luxurious childhood place with true fascination—all these years later, I couldn't take my eyes off it. Then, when the house was actually gone, my own life became, for the first time, more real than any remembered or imagined alternative. I began to feel at home in the world.

*　*　*

ALL ALONG THE beautiful North Atlantic coast, the beaches typically lose sand in the winter and regain it the following summer. But, for instance, between 1839 and 1871 alone, the land line of our island lost more than 500 feet to the sea. Recently I sold some oceanfront building lots whose amazingly steep appreciation in value had actually been started by the great storm of 1938; on the tax map two years earlier, the lots were still six blocks inland.

The 1944 storm blasted in, swept away the boardwalk, and occasioned the snapping of many wonderful photographs of citizens riding through the streets in boats. In the storm of 1962, the ocean cut through the island in two places, meeting the bay, and three hundred houses were washed out to sea; our old friend Don Kidman tried to drive a truck through the rushing water to evacuate some people and he was drowned.

My family still continue to enjoy explicitly unstable, vulnerable places. My sister Juliet lives in Monterey (hard by the submarine Monterey Canyon, which has roughly the depth and configuration of the Grand Canyon, only beneath the sea); recently the drought there gave way to extreme floods that temporarily separated the peninsula from the rest of the world, and occasionally Juliet has watched an earthquake shiver across her tile floor. My sister Nina owns an oceanfront place on the Outer Banks, about as old and fragile a strip of pulverized quartz and feldspar as exists. I summer on Cape Cod, a crooked finger of sand created by a glacier, whose ordinary beaches are partly amethyst, sapphire, topaz, and tourmaline—a place that is, geologically speaking, as temporary as the island where we grew up, just another little pile of junk sticking out of the Atlantic for a while. A seashore naturalist said in the 1960s: "Barrier beaches are only ephemeral stages along a shifting scrimmage line at the edge of the sea. They exist in a dynamic equilibrium and the forces that formed the island will eventually destroy it." In the New Jersey State Geologist's annual report of 1885, this conclusion had already been reached about the volatility of the edges of the islands: "that loss is absolute and gain but relative." Any student of beach erosion could've told us all along: our situation was not unique but utterly ordinary. All our young lives in our home on the continental margin, we were in the process of losing it.

Knowing Your Place

SYLVIA WATANABE

BEFORE SETTLING IN Grand Rapids, my husband and I spent life out of graduate school on freeways, in U-Haul trucks, pursuing tenure at 55 mph. We traveled back and forth along I-80 from California to New York, to California, to Michigan, jettisoning ballast along the way. The boxes of old Christmas cards were the first to go, along with the deep freeze that could hold five hundred pounds of meat. Next went the barbells, king-size sofa bed, a mutual interest in geology (complete with rock collection), and *The History of Western Civilization* by Will and Ariel Durant. Somewhere in Wyoming I abandoned my fear of driving in the dark. On our second pass through California, I stopped putting rice out for the family ghosts. Bill, my husband, was reassuring. "They'll just go to Honolulu," he said. "They still know the way to your mother's house."

I HAVE COME to think of home as where I am not. As a place I've just left, or a place where I have not yet arrived. There are others too—perfect strangers—who have apparently given these matters some thought. I usually meet these people when I am walking down a street somewhere. "Chink!" they yell from their cars, as they speed past, "Why don't you go home!"

I WAS BORN and raised in Hawaii, on an island maybe eighty miles around. There was no such thing there as a perfect stranger. If people yelled at you from their cars, they were liable to get the epithets right. And if you talked to anyone long enough, you would probably discover that their cousin Albert was related to your uncle Mitsuo's brother-in-law's wife.

It would have been impossible not to form those kinds of ties in a landscape where everything—the weather, the fact you were surrounded by water, the distance to anywhere—conspired to make you stay put. But none of what made leaving so difficult prevented the outside—including an enormous variety of exotic plant and animal, and human life—from moving in. My Japanese grandparents, who were Confucian Buddhists on my mother's side and Confucian Presbyterians on my father's, were among the "exotics" who put their roots down in the Islands and never considered anywhere else home again.

BACK IN JAPAN, my mother's mother said, everyone occupied a place that was already decided. She said, "I came to Hawaii to make my own place." She was first made to understand, however, that there was *no* respectable place for an unmarried, non-Christian Japanese female who didn't speak English except employment as a domestic, then marriage. Only after the births of five children, the death of a son, and widowhood—once more single, but forever respectable— could she finally make a place for herself as head of her family and keeper of the rituals binding us to whatever had come before Hawaii. It was she who taught my mother, then me, that the dead are hungry and must be fed—that home was where they could find their way to us.

MY FATHER'S PARENTS were a different story. "They were missionaries," he says—as if that explains everything about them. They were educated in Japan by American Presbyterians who persuaded them to go to Hawaii and attempt to convert the Japanese workers on the sugar plantations. When my grandparents emigrated it was not so much with the hope of making a place for themselves, but with the confidence that wherever they went, their place in the Lord was already secure. "Thy Kingdom Come," my grandfather wrote in a letter to one of his teachers. "All Christians must realize that it is their responsibility to Christianize the world."

This belief wasn't shaken when he and my grandmother were informed soon after arriving that the church was unwilling to provide long-term support for their "subsidiary efforts." In present-day academic parlance, they were not tenure track. When support ran out, they didn't complain; the Lord would provide. They looked for other ways to secure a living. Grandmother held classes in American cookery and English conversation. Grandfather worked, at various times, as an insurance salesman, a bookkeeper, and a postman. They moved from one island to another before finally being called by one of the plantation communities on Maui to establish a Japanese language school. My grandparents regarded it as intrinsic to their teaching efforts to "instill" in their students "American ways of thinking, ways of doing, ways of worshipping, as well as the spirit of Democracy." How could they know then that manifest destiny had nothing to do with them?

"We came because they called us," my grandfather said later. "Perhaps they could not get anyone else who knew both English and Japanese—though our English was not the best. Most of the community were from poor farming families back in Japan, and they could hardly read and write in Japanese. So we taught the children. The parents always had something to translate—immigration papers, bank papers, personal letters. One way or another, I guess you could say, we spread the Word."

IN SOME FAMILIES there are lawyers, architects, or investment bankers; in my father's there are missionaries. Before his parents there was his mother's mother who labored for years among the Ainu in northern Japan. More recently his youngest sister converted to Mormonism and went off on a mission to Okinawa. My husband believes that we are carrying on the family tradition. "What else would you call what we've been doing since graduate school?" he asks, and then points out that, as adjunct writing instructors, we too spread the word, go where we're called, and labor under the necessary misapprehension that a higher power will provide.

BILL IS THE first to receive the call to a tenurable position. We are living in Hayward, California, and the English department with tenure is in Allendale, Michigan. It is true that we have always talked of settling on the West Coast, where family is near, but tenure means health insurance, the end to camping out in a chancy job market, and maybe someday a house of our own. While I am apprehensive about my own lack of a position, something is bound to open up. And when Bill suggests that I use the breather to write full-time, who am I to resist? He being the higher power who will provide.

AFTER MANY BAD adventures in moving, we decide that this time we will get it right. We will not hold a garage sale. We will not scour the dumpsters of all the local liquor stores for cardboard boxes. We will not mail our belongings ahead by Greyhound and the USPS to the houses of relatives all over the state. We will not hire a fifty-foot moving van to drive ourselves, even if it *is* the only truck left at U-Haul. We will not attempt to drive the entire distance in just two days. We will *not* start packing the night before.

Many weeks before we are scheduled to leave, Bill goes from room to room, measuring things. He measures the bookcases, the queen-size bed, the dining set, the dressers, and the computer work stations and writes all the figures down on a yellow pad. He opens cupboards and drawers and, after looking inside and doing more calculations, scribbles more figures. When he is finished, he makes a sweeping gesture that takes in the entire apartment and announces, "We can break most of this stuff down and fit it into a five-by-ten trailer."

"What about that?" I ask, indicating the suddenly enormous-looking, foam-padded sofa.

"We'll leave it," he says.

"What about the mattress on the bed?" I ask.

"We'll get a new one; you always said that one was lumpy."

"What about all the kitchen stuff? What about our clothes? What about the books?" I am beginning to feel depressed.

"Ah, the books." Bill looks thoughtful. "Well, maybe we'll need a six-by-twelve and a car top carrier. And," he adds, as gently as possible, "We'll have to cut down on the load—way down."

Out of curiosity and desperation, I begin calling moving companies. The three questions these places always ask are: How big is the load? How much does it weigh? Do you live upstairs?

The last is the only question I can answer with certainty—at least until the third call I make.

"Do you live upstairs?" the man at the other end of the line asks.

"No," I explain, "We live downstairs, on the ground floor."

He says, "How many flights up did you say that was?"

"One," I reply. "Downstairs."

"But you still have to go up those stairs in order to get out of the apartment, don't you?" he points out.

I can't disagree with the logic of that.

"Well then, you live up one flight," the man says.

So, down is up. What can I say to the other two questions? The load is big, it is enormous, it weighs on us.

One night we are sitting in front of the TV, drinking beers and watching the NBA playoffs, when Bill suddenly sits up, stricken. "I forgot to measure the television," he says. We have also forgotten the teak stereo cabinets, the record collection, the cassette tapes, the tape deck, the speakers, and all the rest of the sound equipment— not to mention the box of baseball bats in the storage cage and the bicycle he took apart to ship here by Greyhound and never put back together again.

Whenever we are at the mall we spend a lot of time at the electronics counter in Macy's. There we wistfully handle the two-inch televisions, the portable CD players, the notebook computers, and the micro–cassette recorders you can carry in your pocket. Bill says, "Just think how easy it would be to move if we could miniaturize."

MY GRANDFATHER LIKED to describe how he and my grandmother arrived in the Islands with all their belongings in a single trunk. Although he himself had always been fond of a well-made suit, they were embarking on a new life in which it would be necessary to put aside such worldly tastes. And of course, he would add almost as an afterthought, they could not expect the church to pay their moving expenses.

The tenured missionaries sent to the Islands by the American Board of Commissioners for Foreign Missions had all of their expenses covered. Their move from Boston to Honolulu is described by Michener in the novel *Hawaii*. For years I worked in the education department of the museum run by their descendants, and my job was nothing more than to research, catalog, and make up stories about all the items in the many trunks that came over from Boston. It is quite literally true—not to mention metaphorically significant—that among the things these missionaries brought with them were the disassembled pieces of a two-story, woodframe, New England–style house. As they themselves recognized, they were not mere purveyors of a spiritual doctrine, they were instruments in the grand (some might even say

Faustian) endeavor of transplanting an entire material culture. Judging from the present state of "development" in the Islands, the success of this endeavor has surely surpassed even their wildest dreams.

BUT WHEN IT is not possible either to dismantle and move your entire apartment building or to pare five roomsful of possessions down to a single trunk and the clothes on your backs, the question remains: What do you take with you and what do you leave behind?

This is the time to face up to the fact that you probably don't need a drawer full of harmonicas. That you will not learn Russian, or take tap-dancing lessons, or pick up the alto sax. That you will never manage another recreational baseball team or put together the ten-speed you took apart and whose headgear you can no longer find. This is the time to realize that you will never again wear the size two black bolero jacket that you can't remove from its drycleaning bag without instantly attracting every white cat hair in the apartment. This is the time to part with the collection of ceramic bunnies that your cousin in Germany continues to send you every Christmas, as well as the dusty box, unopened from the time it was stored in your parents' basement, containing every piece of homework from elementary school.

Then there are the things that you would like to discard but cannot, the things you never desired to collect but that have accrued nonetheless. These are the memories: the swastika on the carport wall. The dog excrement smeared on the front stoop. The young white men in the pickup pursuing you down the street as you walked home from work. These are the words: Gook. Nip. Dink. Flip. Slope. Slant. Slant eyes. Rice eyes. Dogeater. Yellowskin. Yellow housenigger. Chink. Jap. These are the questions: What's your nationality? What kind of a name is that? Where is it from? I mean, where are *you* from? Well then, where are your parents from? Is *he* your husband? No, I mean where are you *really* from?

✻   ✻   ✻

I AM A Japanese Confucian Buddhist Presbyterian from Hawaii. My mother's mother and father were born in Yamaguchi Prefecture in Japan. My father's father and mother were born in Fukushima and Gifu. They are all dead now. My husband is a Scotch Irish German Christian Scientist Puritan Agnostic. His great great great great great great great great great great great great great grandfather, John Coggeshall, became the first governor of Rhode Island after testifying in the trial of Anne Hutchinson and being forced to leave the Massachussetts colony. He is dead now too.

HERE IS A photo of my grandfather, taken when he was still a very young man. He is dressed in a white suit, his arms full of roses. There is something Wildean and un-Presbyterian about his pose, about the way he gazes languidly upon the flowers.

Here he is again with a group of friends on Mt. Haleakala. They have just been to watch the sun rise. Grandfather kneels in the front row, panama in hand, as immaculately dressed as ever.

Here is a formal portrait of him and my grandmother, taken in a photography studio. My grandmother so small and neat. Her beatific smile. Her slim legs crossed at the ankles, her hands folded in her lap. She has on a Western-style dress and a little black pillbox, such as she often wore, the net in front half-covering her face. Grandfather stands next to her with his perfect posture, his perfect suit, his arms hanging at his sides. His expression is familiar: the gaze off to the distance beyond the frame of the camera. His eyeglasses glint so I can't see his eyes. On the back of the photo someone has written, "27th Anniversary, 11/41."

A couple of weeks later, early on the morning of December eighth, the Military Police came to my grandparents' house. My grandfather, grandmother, and two youngest aunts were the only ones living there. My father was working in Honolulu and the next three oldest children were all away at college.

It was very dark, as my aunt Dorothy remembers. Everyone was roused from sleep by the sound of loud knocking at the front door. When Grandfather went to answer, he was confronted by armed Military Police who told him to get dressed, then took him out to a truck parked in the front drive. After posting a guard they went back inside and searched the house.

Grandfather was taken to the Maui County jail where he was incarcerated in an eight-by-ten cell for six months before being shipped to a temporary holding facility outside of Honolulu. Just before his departure he wrote a letter to the Maui Headquarters for Military Intelligence, asking permission for one last visit with his family. The letter says:

Dear Lieutenant Sir,

I, as an internee, hereby respectfully submit this petition for granting me your special permission to visit my home in Waikapu, only one and a half miles from here, just once, before my transference to the place designated by the Military Authority.

It is not from selfishness, but from a natural humanness, that I desire to meet my family before my long departure.

The house I have lived in for many years is where my six children grew up. The furniture, house goods, utensils, plants, orchids, and everything in it are dear to me. I hope to have my last meal with my wife, aged mother-in-law, and two young daughters. It will not take more than three or four hours [This has been crossed out in the draft, and changed to "four or five hours"]. We will use English only in our conversation under the Military Guard to be provided for me. I will not say anything regarding the War or about the Detention Camp and will observe the rules and regulations we are given to follow.

I have been a faithful resident of Hawaii for 35 years, never committed any crime of any nature, even the slightest offense. I have never been disloyal to America, the country of my six children, and the country we, my wife and I, chose for our last resting place. Now I shall be sent from my family for long duration, under the suspicion of which I have no knowledge. I realize truly the present situation of this country, so I am contented with the treatment I am now being dealt, but I fearlessly state here in the presence of our Living God that I am innocent though it is not the purpose of this letter to clarify my innocence.

I earnestly ask you for permission to visit my home, just once, at any hour of any day before my sad departure.

Respectfully submitted by

Yakichi Watanabe

The Military Authority granted him his request. A few days later, when my father went to visit him after he'd been moved, Grandfather—always the man of words—asked for a Spanish dictionary. "They are sending us to New Mexico," he said, "and I hear they speak Spanish there."

THE DAY BEFORE Bill and I are to begin our drive to Michigan, we go down to the nearest U-Haul to pick up the trailer. We talk to someone named Frank, who confirms, after looking it up in his book, that we'll be more than okay with a six-by-twelve, which is the maximum size that a Ford Fairmont can pull. He asks where we are headed and when we tell him, vaguely (because we are not sure ourselves), somewhere in the vicinity of Grand Rapids, he says, "I'm from Wyoming."

Bill and I look at each other, then he says to Frank, "That's great. There's some beautiful country in Wyoming."

Frank laughs. "If you like Dutchmen." Then he explains that he is talking about Wyoming, Michigan—a township in the greater

Grand Rapids area. "Yep, there sure are a lot of Dutchmen there."

I glance again at Bill, who is staring at the blond, blue-eyed Frank. "Are *you* Dutch?" Bill asks.

Frank says, "Hell no. I considered myself lucky when I got out."

Bill hitches the trailer to our car, and we drive back to our apartment without exchanging a word.

EARLY THE NEXT morning, with the help of Bill's son, who has driven up from southern California, we begin loading the trailer. When we are done, it is a job of engineering precision from top to bottom, front to back—each object fitting the next, like pieces in a Rubik's Cube. Bill looks at his watch and notes that it isn't even eleven o'clock; we'll be on our way even earlier than we'd planned. But when we walk around to the side, to admire our work from a different perspective, his son says, "It's probably nothing, but is the back end of the Ford always that close to the ground?" Now that he mentions it, the front end also seems a bit higher than usual, with the entire chassis sloping backward at a twenty-five-degree angle. As we stand there debating whether this is a peculiar design feature we have never noticed before, one of the other tenants in our building calls out as he walks by, "Looks like you've got more than you can handle!"

We stare after him in dismay as he strolls, whistling, to his car and drives off. Bill goes over to the manager's office and calls Frank at U-Haul, who informs him that we can solve our problem by redistributing the load. Just make sure to put the heaviest things over the axles and the lightest things up front, Frank says. Bill and his son set about unloading the trailer, while I pack the car with what we have been referring to as "odds and ends." When I am done, they take up the entire backseat, as well as most of the front. The plan had originally been to put the cat in the back, but since it is now full I will have to carry her on my lap. For the time being, I leave her on the passenger side, looking pathetically out the window.

By now Bill and his son have finished reloading. It is not as precise a job as the first time, but they have managed to get everything back inside—except for two large boxes, containing old textbooks from college. The slope of the chassis is down about two degrees, which is not that much of an improvement when we consider that the interior of the car is completely jammed as well. There is nothing to do but lighten the load. As Bill's son gets into his truck to head back down to San Diego, we are throwing our college textbooks into the dumpster at the far end of the parking lot.

Hayward is in the San Francisco Bay Area, where there are lots of hills. Each time we struggle up a hill, the inertia of the trailer pulls in the opposite direction. Whenever we hit a downhill, the trailer looms in the rearview, threatening to race full-out over the top of the car. With every bump, sparks fly; the hitch, which extends below the bumper, scrapes bottom hard. After we have gone a couple of miles in this fashion, we pull up to a dumpster in a Denny's parking lot where we empty out the backseat. Next follows a stop at the back entrance of the city library, where we leave more boxes of books placed neatly beside the overnight book return. After each jettisoning of ballast, we look hopefully at our Ford, which continues to retain its backward tilt. By now it is getting late, so we head for a friend's house in San Francisco—a drive that usually takes thirty minutes during off-traffic, without an overloaded trailer. Of course it is now the peak of rush hour.

THE NEXT MORNING, Bill takes everything out of the trailer for the third time. Our friend has kindly offered to let us store part of the load in her basement. "Then you'll have to come back and see us again," she says. I burst into tears.

Along with two large bookcases, we also leave the barbecue, more books, our entire record collection, the teak stereo cabinets, and all the sound equipment. Bill says, "There must have been a reason the first time I forgot to measure all this." After reloading the trailer with what remains, we note optimistically that the car is now tilted at an improved fifteen-degree angle, and we again proceed on our way. As we are driving on the beautiful Oakland Bay Bridge, over beautiful San Francisco Bay, I have the cat on my lap and we are gazing out the passenger-seat window, thinking mournful thoughts and watching our beautiful city falling away.

Suddenly Bill says, "Oh, oh trouble."

I say, "Like we haven't had trouble already."

He says, "This is serious. Smoke."

I look out the rear window, and there it is—a black, metallic-smelling cloud billowing out the back. We speculate that maybe if we slow down, it will get better, and it does.

I can't resist asking, "Does this mean that we will have to drive at thirty miles an hour all the way to Michigan?"

He doesn't answer.

That night we make another unexpected stop in Applegate, at a little motel with a fire-station motif.

BILL RISES EARLY and spends the morning under the hood. He closes it back up without attempting surgery; there is nothing he can do to make our Ford pull that trailer any faster. When we figure it out, we have been averaging thirty-three miles a day, including backtracking, and at this rate, we won't get to Grand Rapids for another three months.

That's when we decide to Make Our Move with Corrigan. After looking up their address in the phone book, we drive over and leave them our load. Next we go to U-Haul and drop off the six-by-twelve. Now the car behaves well, but the cat has meanwhile decided that she has had enough. As we are crossing the Sierras she begins to yowl.

"She's driving me crazy," Bill says. "Why don't you stop her?"

By now I am also weeping uncontrollably. When we don't turn around and go back, or—as the cat would prefer—stop this minute right where we are, I quit weeping and she crawls under the front passenger seat and refuses to emerge.

This is August of 1988; it's been a summer of record heat. There is drought everywhere, and the reports over the radio say that the corn crop is dying all across the Midwest. It is 115 degrees when we get to the Nevada desert. A little less than halfway, we stop for gas, and I drag the cat out from her hiding place. She is a rag; barely conscious. I plunge her into the ice chest and attempt feline resuscitation. From that point on, we decide to travel at night.

THE NIGHT IS still hot, but it is not as bad as the day. The darkness and the desert go on forever. I think of my grandfather in that other desert all those years ago. "At night," he writes, "when there is only the sound of the wind, I look out across the sand. I cannot see far, but I can feel the miles and miles of desert out there, big as an ocean. The sound of the wind is the sound of the ocean. And if I close my eyes and breathe in, I can smell the ocean and imagine myself home once again."

As we cross the Great Salt Lake I try to see it with his eyes. After spending his life on small green islands, how alien this landscape would have seemed . . . and yet, perhaps, how familiar—as if, in his desolation, he had been traveling it for a very long time.

When the bombs fell on Pearl Harbor, his place in the world, like that of thousands of others, was blown to bits. Over and over, in the letters he wrote after first being taken into custody, he tries to recover that place. Unsure of the charges against him, he protests his innocence. He has learned English, he says, "to assimilate myself to American life, in every respect." And if that is not sufficient evidence of his loyalty, none of his children has "ever visited a foreign country. They were expatriated from Japan in order to confirm their American Citizenship. I have helped hundreds of other Japanese children in their procedure of expatriation from Japan, without taking any fee."

But all of his arguments miss the point. It is precisely the means he uses to assert his innocence that proves his guilt. His knowledge of English and "American ways" had made him a leader in what had now become the enemy community. By encouraging loyal citizenship among the American-born Japanese, he merely helped to create unwanted complications. How much easier things might have been all around if the United States government had not been dealing with citizens having constitutional rights.

When he was unsuccessful at recovering his lost place, my grandfather decided, finally, to accept that too. "We can hope, someday, though not in our lives, that all people of the world will truly wake up to the Will of Our God and live, all races, harmoniously. Thy kingdom come." The most difficult journey he ever had to make was not between his home on Maui and the internment camp in New Mexico. It was not a journey measured in geographical distance, but in the space, the entire desert between two nouns: Missionary. Alien.

MY HUSBAND AND I have lived in Grand Rapids for the last eight years. It is a town of clean, well-kept streets and house-proud neighborhoods. People have conservative—most would say "family"—values and strong religious convictions, primarily of a Calvinist bent. They vote Republican. They seem to know their place in the world.

Since our arrival, Bill and I have moved three times. In our first apartment we lived across the hall from a college student with a fondness for heavy-metal music at two in the morning. In our second apartment we lived downstairs from a World War II veteran with Alzheimer's. One morning, after I'd gone to the market, the front door was ajar while I set the bags of groceries down in the kitchen. When I went to close the door, the World War II veteran was in our living room, looking dazed. I asked if he needed help, and he turned toward me. He froze for an instant, his eyes as round as saucers, then he ran out of the apartment yelling, "The Japs are here!"

And so I am.

BILL NOW HAS tenure at his college. I write and occasionally teach. We own a house in a tree-shaded neighborhood, with woods and a little lake nearby. All the men here are named Bud, Ted, Bob, Jim, Skip—and Bill adds—"Or Bill." On Saturdays in the summer, these men with one-syllable names can be heard calling to each other when they go outside to mow their lawns.

Bud, our next-door-neighbor, is eighty years old. He brings us fresh strawberries, cucumbers, and tomatoes from his garden. I give him macadamia nuts that my parents have sent me. Bud says that he too has spent some time in Hawaii. "Not like the tourists," he is quick to add. For a while, when they were going there every winter, he and his wife considered it home.

When Bill and I decide to dig up our backyard and put in flowers, Bud lends us his sod cutter. He comes over to help us dig up the sod and turn over the soil. Another time he brings us an enormous spool, made out of wood and metal, that he has constructed in his basement shop. "Thought you could use something like this for the cord on your electric mower," he says.

One day in early fall the doorbell rings, and it is Bud announcing, "It's time to get your driveway ready for winter." Bill steps outside and sees that Bud has already hauled over a five-gallon can of resurfacing material and all the necessary equipment.

"But shouldn't we do your driveway first?" Bill asks.

"Already done," Bud replies.

When I am outside working in the garden, he likes to come over and chat. He tells me stories about his travels. He talks about how he went to Egypt one time, about how he's often visited Europe.

"I like England because I can speak the language," he says. "But France . . . France is another story."

"I've been to France; it's a beautiful country," I reply.

Bud shakes his head. "The French—they just don't care for Americans." Then he looks at me, recognition dawning in his eyes. He realizes whom he is speaking to. "But they wouldn't have given *you* any trouble," he says.

The more things change, the more they stay the same.

A MEMORY COMES to me of my grandfather as a very old man in his nineties. He is in a white cotton T-shirt and long white cotton underwear, crouched on the floor of his study over a roll of rice paper, ink brush in hand. He is scribbling over and over in Japanese: Thy kingdom come. Thy kingdom come. A prayer. A hope. An unfinished notion.

Perhaps my mother's mother was right, and home is where the dead can find their way to us. If that is so then perhaps too, home can be a place on a page, made out of words.

LATELY I HAVE been feeling restless, and I find myself thinking of the road at night—of the sound of the tires rushing over the blacktop and the darkness flowing around the car. Though we don't speak of it much, I know Bill feels this too. The other morning I found him sitting at the dining room table with a Modern Language Association joblist and an opened road atlas.

"Not that we have any serious intentions. Not in this bad job market," we say.

But occasionally we look around our nice little house and express the longing to "pare things down." And whenever we are at a department store, we cannot resist stopping off at the electronics counter to check out the miniature appliances.

Make Yourself at Home

I HAVE A recurrent dream. I have bought—or rented, or acquired in some unclear fashion—a new house; and although I have not officially moved into it, I am, in the dream, visiting this house and looking around its empty rooms. Suddenly I come across some new access: a door previously unnoticed and unopened; a staircase (small, narrow, hard to climb); a passageway (dark, frightening) through which I travel with some apprehension.

I find myself, in the dream, in the dream-house, emerging into a space that I had not known existed. There are rooms that I hadn't been aware of: spacious rooms, lavishly furnished, filled with light and color, comfortable, welcoming. There are books half-open, as if someone has just left for a moment. Sometimes, in the dream, a steaming teapot and cups are on the table; clearly guests are expected.

I awake filled with a feeling of relief and exhilaration. The *house* that I entered in the dream turned out to be something more than a house.

Maybe (I am left, on waking, with this questioning awareness) it was actually a *home?*

And if so: what does that mean, exactly?

I recount the dream to my friend Trina. Halfway through it, as I'm saying, "—and then I open a door, and—" she interrupts me.

"—and there's a narrow staircase, right? And—"

"You have the same dream?"

Trina nods.

I ask my friend Nancy. I describe the dream, but she doesn't interrupt. No, she replies, when I ask at the end, she herself doesn't have that dream.

Then she adds, after a reflective pause: "But my mother always did."

THE MAIL ARRIVES, as it always does, late in the morning, and I sort it at the kitchen table. A real estate agent has sent a brochure showing a brick house in my neighborhood: a house I recognize. I walk past it often with the dog. I hadn't known it was for sale.

I read the description in the brochure with interest. Fireplace, study, glassed-in porch, two closets off the entrance hall, four bedrooms on the second floor, two more bedrooms—and another bathroom—on the third floor.

"Listen." I start reading it aloud to Martin, who is glancing through his own stack of mail.

He listens briefly, clearly curbs the impulse to roll his eyes, and goes back to reading something in his hand.

I can read his mind. He is not saying—but he is thinking: *We bought this house just two years ago. And now you're salivating over another house? One that costs a hundred thousand dollars more than this one? One with six bedrooms, even though there are just two of us? Are you out of your cotton-picking mind?*

He's right, of course. There *are* just the two of us. His four children—and my four, too—are grown, moved away, on their own. We live, as we should, for reasons of practicality and finance, in a small house.

But when I walk the dog that evening, I walk past the one that's for sale. I look at its windows, picturing the six bedrooms and which grandchild could sleep where on visits. I plan what color I would paint the living room: a deep yellow, perhaps, so that on winter evenings, when it's snowing outside and there's a fire in the fireplace, the room would glow. Bookcases would line the walls. Friends would come, stamp snow off their boots in the entrance hall, and hang their heavy coats in those two entrance-hall closets.

The house and its welcoming rooms would fill with conversation and music and the smell of cooking; I would bake endlessly, turning out pies and roasts—.

I turn the corner, the dog tugging at his leash, and the brick house with the blue door, the for-sale house, is behind me now.

But in my mind, I am once again—as I am in my dream—trying to make something imaginary into a *home.*

I SIT DOWN to work on (read: *agonize about*) this essay on the same day that I am also planning a dinner party. This would not ordinarily be a problem; I often do more than one thing at a time. I am an organized person. I make lists.

My list regarding the dinner party says things like: buy salmon, find recipe for orange meringue pie (*Gourmet,* maybe April?), and iron blue napkins. I have a different list, too, about the invited guests; it says: Kate (bringing bread); Walt? Will? (call Kate and ask his name again); Audrey and Jack (remember to return Audrey's book).

All of that under control and magnetized to the refrigerator, I sit down to make a list of the various qualities that comprise the concept "Home."

It occurs to me suddenly that I never had one—a home—and so it has never been entirely clear to me what one is, exactly.

Whaddaya mean, you never had a home? Everyone has a home.

Well, my dad was a career army officer. We moved all the time.

Well, you were born, weren't you? That's where your home was.

Okay, I'll try starting the list there.

HOME IS THE PLACE
WHERE YOU WERE BORN

MY MOTHER—AND my grandparents before her—had been born in Pennsylvania. There is a town in that state which bears my mother's maiden name, and I suppose it is connected to our forbears, to her—and to *me*—in some historical, perhaps honorific way. I am not inclined to genealogical research.

But she had gone away: was taken away, actually, by a husband who had been lured by his profession and in turn had lured her—first south to Georgia, then west almost as far as one could go, to the island of Oahu, where I was born. Hawaii was only a territory, then, not yet a state. My birth certificate, which I glance at occasionally in order to renew a passport or verify my existence, says: Township of Wahiawa, Country of Honolulu, T.H. I was born alive, without deformity, delivered by a doctor named George Prazak, and silver nitrate was put into my eyes.

The mother, age thirty, was described as Housewife by this very sexist document, which suggested that her alternatives might be "housekeeper, typist, nurse, or clerk", and the question which read "Industry or business in which work was done, as own home, lawyer's office, silk mill, etc." was answered "own home."

But surely she didn't think it really was. When she wrote "own home" in response to the question, she was new to the islands, which must have seemed so alien to her. Was she trying to make it into "Home," the way I would try later, and without success, in California, Connecticut, Florida, South Carolina?

My mother always told this story: I was a toddler and with my family was traveling by ship to New York from Hawaii, where I had been born and had lived my entire slightly-more-than-two years of life. Across the Pacific and then down to Panama and through the canal. Then up toward New York, and it began to get cold.

Walking on the deck, holding her hand, I would cry, she said. "It's too cold," I would wail. "I want to go home."

She would try to explain that now New York would be our home. Hawaii had been, and now it wasn't. Now home would be New York, which was cold this time of year.

But I just kept yowling that I wanted to go home.

My mother, telling this story for the billionth time, would shake her head. "How can you explain all of that to a two-year-old?" she would ask me, clearly feeling, still, after fifty years, that she had failed. "The whole concept of *home?*"

Beats me, Mom. How do you explain it to *anyone?*

HOME IS WHERE YOUR FIRST MEMORIES ARE

NOT LONG AGO, a publisher mailed me a copy of a newly published book, apparently one of a series of books for young readers about the individual states. The one I received was about Hawaii. There was no accompanying letter, no request for me to write a blurb or a review.

I was puzzled. But I decided to send the book on to my grandson, who had recently accompanied me on a vacation to the Islands, and I leafed through the pages to see if there would be anything in the book to interest him. Cultural history is not his thing. At eleven, he had enjoyed the water slide at one hotel; he liked the touristy midget-submarine ride at Waikiki; and he was particularly taken, in a Kauai shopping mall, by a trashy shop at which he purchased, against my boring grandmotherly advice, an aerosol can of something called "Fart Spray" as a gift for his friend Ryan back home in Maine.

Riffling the pages, I suddenly came across my own photograph and realized it was why they had sent me the book. There I was, on a page captioned "Famous People from Hawaii."

Excuse me? my grandson would say, skeptically.

Okay, I confess that sometimes, pressed into a simple answer by people playing, "Where are *you* from?" at a dinner party, I have answered, "Hawaii." I was born there, after all.

For many years I thought I remembered some of my earliest days on Oahu. I told a lot of people—sometimes even large audiences of strangers—about my first memory, and how glad I was that it was idyllic and plumeria-scented, with lapping waves at my tiny toes, and a rainbow overhead.

Then I transferred my father's old home movies to videotape, subjected a roomful of close friends to a viewing, pointed out the primal Waikiki scene, the blonde tyke with her tiptoes in the Pacific, and realized, when someone said matter-of-factly (and accurately), "That's not you, that's your sister," that I was a victim of the False Memory Syndrome.

What can I say? At least it was soft sand and rainbows instead of a Satanic ritual.

THE LIST DOESN'T work. Too many platitudes come to mind. *Home is where the heart is. There's no place like home. Home on the range. Home again, home again jiggity jiggity jig . . .*

It makes me feel punchy and ill-tempered. Alone in a friend's house while she runs an errand, I try to make coffee and can't figure out the simple mechanics of her Toshiba coffeemaker.

Home, I decide grumpily, wishing I were back at mine, *is where you know how the appliances work.*

Well, maybe not the VCR, I concede to myself, after a moment's pause.

One night a guest at my dining-room table is a Harvard professor. When I raise the question of "Home" and its meaning, the ensuing conversation requires that we wrest the hefty Oxford English

Dictionary down from its shelf and put the magnifying glass into operation.

The following noon, he appears at the front door, bearing twenty Xeroxed pages referring to the word *home.* He asks, as well, whether perhaps there could be a dialectic synthesis of Frost ("When you have to go there, they have to take you in") and Wolfe ("You can't go home again") on the topic.

I decide to think about that but both points of view seem profoundly depressing.

TWO NIGHTS LATER, at dinner with a friend who is a retired professor of early childhood education, I bring up the topic again. She refers me to early Sendak, in which Max went out into the night, wrestled with demons, and returned. "It's the classic Home-Adventure-Home theme," Marian points out.

Home-Adventure-Home. As in: Parents-Marriage-Husband? In the winter of 1956, I was living alone in southern California, a nine-teen-year-old bride, because my twenty-one-year-old husband, a Navy ensign, was overseas with his destroyer. I lived in Navy housing—a tiny apartment for which the rent was $61.50 a month, furnished. The furniture and walls were all the same odd beige, though the paint on the chunky furniture had the distinction of being "textured," as if someone had smeared oatmeal into it while it was still damp. My child husband and I had enhanced the decor with a wrinkly beige cotton nine-by-twelve rug ($29.95) from Sears and two fake brass lamps acquired through S&H green stamps. I was envious of those young couples among the neighbors who had been married a little longer and had managed to spruce up their identical housing with matching things called Early American. Driven by my embryonic, un-formed taste, I coveted their braided rugs and coffee tables shaped like cobblers' benches.

My parents wrote from the East Coast in early December and offered me plane fare so that I could come home for Christmas.

I wrote back and declined politely. Sanctimonious as all get-out, I pointed out to them that my home was now here on Ingraham Street in Pacific Beach, California. Their house might still be home to my younger brother, on vacation from prep school, but it no longer was to me.

I hung an ersatz southern-California wreath on my front door and felt like an adult.

My boy husband sent me two things at Christmas. One was a photograph of himself on the ship, showing the muttonchop whiskers he had grown. I looked at the stranger in the snapshot in absolute horror and wondered how I could have married someone so repulsive.

The second thing was a telegram. It had three sentences, only one of which I recall. "My thoughts are with you," it said. (Later he explained that they were each allowed three free sentences, to be chosen from a list. "My thoughts are with you" seemed preferable to many of the others.)

I crumpled both the telegram and photograph, ate some leftover tuna casserole at the beige textured kitchen table, and went to bed with a copy of *Pride and Prejudice* left over from an English course in my sophomore year of college, which I had completed just six months before. Maybe I turned the radio on. Maybe there were Christmas carols playing.

I do know that tucked away in the top drawer of the (beige, oatmeal-textured) desk in the living room was a small box that my mother had given to me when I was married. It contained another leftover with about as much appeal as two-day-old tuna casserole. It was the remaining engraved cards that my mother—a proper colonel's wife of the old school—had had made for me, announcing that after such-and-such a date, I would be AT HOME TO CALLERS at such-and-such an address.

I was, the Christmas of 1956. But it certainly didn't feel like Home.

It sucked, if you want to know the truth.

I E-MAIL MY daughter and ask her what "Home" means to her. Maybe I want someone else to suffer. Maybe I want a small paean to motherhood (mine) in response. Maybe out of desperation I am simply killing time.

I expect to wait a while for her reply. At this point I've been agonizing for some days, myself.

But her response through cyberspace is almost instantaneous. "Safety, nutrition, comfort, and a place to read," appears on my computer screen, with my daughter's name beneath.

List-making must be genetic.

1942. PENNSYLVANIA. WHEN I think of Pennsylvania, I think of green. I don't know why. It isn't like the neurological condition of synesthesia, which causes people to taste shapes and smell words. (Though I envy synesthetes, actually, and wish I could taste peppermint each time I see a triangle, or that I could identify the character of individuals by that method. The friend who hit me up for a large loan: I should have smelled spoiled milk, seen puce, and known that he'd hit the road with my check in his hand and never be heard from again.)

It is simply that the place comes alive for me, and the life it takes on is damp green with dewy summer mornings, with grass-stained bare feet, and with sugar peas sold from a basket by a local farmer at the back door.

When World War II began, my mother took her children home. Home for her was Pennsylvania. And it has always felt green.

Safety, Nutrition, Comfort, and a Place to Read

Grandpa's house seemed huge to me. I know now that it was not unusually large; but at four I had come from the two-bedroom Brooklyn apartment where we had lived after we left Honolulu. In contrast,

Grandpa's house seemed immense.

For one thing, it had two living rooms and I had never been inside a dwelling-place with two living rooms before. They weren't even *called* living rooms, at Grandpa's; the one to the right of the front hall was called the parlor, and the one on the left was the library.

The library, needless to say, was walled with bookcases. People read: to themselves, to one another. The grown-ups read to me, and when they closed that book, they read aloud to each other and I listened to that reading, too.

The dining room was huge, and meals were formalized affairs, with food passed by maids summoned from the kitchen by a buzzer under Grandmother's foot. Even mashed potatoes seemed more interesting when they had specks of nutmeg sprinkled on top and were served from a silver bowl.

There were two flights of stairs. My two previous one-story places of residence had no stairs at all. But Grandpa's house had two separate sets: the front stairs, with three distinct turns and a massive grandfather clock on the first landing. There was a banister, too. In *Eight Cousins,* which my mother read to my sister and me, children actually slid down a banister and seemed to enjoy doing so. But it seemed like a dangerous, probably uncomfortable enterprise, one of which my fastidious grandmother would disapprove because it would not only be noisy but would reveal my underpants. So I never attempted a slide.

It was the other set of stairs, actually, that appealed to me. The "back stairs," they were called, and they were to be used by the servants. Completely enclosed, leading from the kitchen to an upstairs hall, they had doors at top and bottom. With both doors closed, the staircase was impenetrably dark. I tortured myself by sitting on those stairs with the doors closed, terrified by the blackness, smothered by it, almost panic-stricken, until eventually a maid, sent to find me, or perhaps simply transferring freshly ironed sheets to the upstairs linen closet, would open the door at the bottom and a wedge of light would slice its way in and save me in my huddled, delicious fear.

"Whatever are you doing there?" she would ask, and she would shoo me along to some well-lighted, more acceptable place.

"Playing," I would mumble in reply. But I wasn't, really. I was testing myself in some smug, unfathomable way. I was passing the test, too.

Safety and Comfort

1943. I was five when I set fire to the house. Just for the record, it was unintentional.

It was winter, shortly before the January birth of my brother. My mother had washed my hair, an undertaking that involved, in those pre-nonstinging-shampoo days, a lot of bargaining, pleading, whimpering, and wiggling. By the time my hair was washed, rinsed, and combed, and I was standing beside my bed, scowling, in my nightgown, my very-pregnant mother was thoroughly sick of me.

She turned on an electric heater and told me to sit in front of it until my hair dried so that I wouldn't catch cold. Then she went off to do something in the hall. I seem to remember that she and the maid were sorting ironed laundry by the linen closet.

I obeyed, but it was boring. I began to fool with my dolls, heaped on a little wooden dolls' bed under the window. Aimlessly I rolled up the cotton blanket covering the assortment of Shirley Temples and Betsy-Wetsys. Then I poked the end of the cylinder into the electric heater. There was no malicious intent. I was five, remember?

When the little doll blanket erupted in flames, I tried to undo the catastrophe with a sort of "Rewind" mentality. *I didn't mean for this to happen, and maybe if I go back and start over, maybe it won't have the same scary ending.*

I put the burning fabric back onto the little bed filled with dolls.

The little bed was directly under the organdy curtains, which took no time at all to ignite.

Then the memory becomes blurred into a noisy panic, with people running and screaming. Someone lifted me and ran.

No one died. No one was even injured except the dolls, which were scarred with blisters and smelled of scorch for the remaining years of their existence. I think there was a lot of repapering and painting, maybe installation of a new window, and certainly there would have been serious curtain replacement.

No one blamed me. I don't think I ever told them that I actually poked the fabric into the coils of the heater. My mother was a—"It was my fault, I never should have—" kind of mother, and she took the heat every time the story was retold. It became the "Remember just before Jonny was born and the house caught fire" family tale, instead of the "Remember when Lois set the house on fire" story that I knew to be true.

The two strongest feelings that come back to me now are the desperate fear when I saw the flames, and the immense, overwhelming relief when someone picked me up and ran with me out of harm's way.

Safety and Comfort

1944. A porch on the side of Grandpa's house was furnished with wicker rockers, a wooden swing, and a hammock; it was shaded by slatted blinds that were drawn on summer afternoons. The light filtering through was tinted pale green by ivy and the air outside buzzed with the sound of locusts.

While grown-ups napped in the heat, I played on the porch with my sister and a few neighborhood children. We propelled the swing sideways until it thumped the porch pillars and a maid appeared at the screen door to warn us about the noise. We wrapped ourselves in the sides of the hammock and tipped ourselves over until we fell, sprawling and giggling, onto the rush-matted floor of the porch. We read and played Lotto or Fish.

Once we trapped a neighborhood toddler, someone's little sister, in the hammock and took off her training pants in order to examine the rather uninteresting folds of her no-longer-private parts. I felt, on the occasion of that experiment, vaguely bestial but immune from prosecution.

Safety and Comfort

1945. In the local college's Biology building, across the street from Grandpa's house, there was a certain window through which we could peek if we leaped and grabbed the just-beyond-reach sill and then scrambled up the rough stucco wall, skinning our knees in the process. There was a certain amount of bravado and tenacity required, an imperviousness to pain, and an enormous desire to glimpse once again the murky, mysterious jars on the shelf in that room. They were said to contain dead babies.

I was the smallest of the neighborhood children and had to be boosted by someone for my abbreviated glimpse. I could see the jars, lined neatly on a metal shelf, but their contents were blurred and could have been the leftover chicken soup in my grandmother's refrigerator, or perhaps some dill pickles from Mr. Barnhart's store. I squinted, trying to distinguish some pale floating legs or arms, or a ghastly face with wide-open, startled unborn eyes, but it was no more than murky fluid.

Lying, I convinced myself it was true. "Yes," I said, when they lowered me back to the damp grass at the building's foundation. "I saw toes. And fingers. They looked like this." I held my hand limply and let my fingers dangle the way I was certain dead ones would.

"I saw one with two heads," Tony, a buck-toothed neighborhood boy, said solemnly. "They're all deformed. That's why they're in the jars." Tony's father was a doctor, so we respected his report.

"I saw the two-heads one, too," someone else announced, and we all nodded, convincing ourselves that we, too, had glimpsed attached and matching faces floating side by side, staring eerily back at us.

"One is half-boy, half-girl," Tony added knowingly. We were silent, each of us trying to form a picture of that in our minds. I remembered the tidy, organized little bouquet of genitalia on the toddler we had de-pantsed on the porch, and couldn't relate it to something floating gray and dead in a glass jar.

"I have to go home," someone said, and we all agreed that yes, it was late, almost suppertime, time to go home now, and we fled across the campus lawns, away from the uncomfortable secrets of the dim room through the window.

Grandpa's house was well-lit and the windows were draped with lavish brocades. No one would ever trouble to shinny up those walls and peek inside; even if someone did, they would view only clean, orderly, well-arranged things: nothing deformed, nothing afloat, staring, reminding you of what you might once have been, or could be yet.

Safety and Comfort

1946. A child around the corner, a little girl named Judy, had skin that fell off in flakes and left oozing sores on her wrists and elbows. Her face had a pointed, foxlike shape and her eyes, which seemed too small and half-asleep, had an imploring, needy look.

She was my age and people wanted me to play with her. "Why don't you go over to Judy's house?" my mother would ask when I complained of nothing to do on summer afternoons.

But I was afraid of Judy. I was afraid of her slitty eyes and the pieces of skin that clung to her sweaters like discarded insect wings.

"Maybe later," I always said. Then I went out into Grandpa's yard, taking one of his freshly ironed handkerchiefs from the stack in the laundry room, and carefully trap bumblebees on dandelion blossoms. I lowered the handkerchief over them like a parachute falling in folds, breaking the dandelion off at the stem so that I could hold the angry, buzzing package in my hand. I paraded around the yard, carrying it like a bride holding carnations at her waist. I felt dangerous and cruel, a person with a treacherous weapon in my fist. If evildoers entered the yard—or people with too-small eyes and crusted, oozing skin—I could press my malicious corsage into their flesh.

"Would you quit messing with those bees? You're going to get yourself stung and then you'll be screaming into the kitchen for me to take care of it." The cook, out on the back steps to deposit some empty milk bottles in the collection box for the milkman, would sigh in exasperation.

I shook the bee loose and went on to a safer occupation—Pick-up-Stix or Parchesi with my sister on the porch—secure in the knowledge that I had the capacity for warfare and the knowledge of weapons close at hand.

Safety and Comfort

1947. Invited to a neighbor child's house overnight, I shook my head smugly and replied, "No, we don't do that," when the girl knelt by the side of her bed to say her prayers. I watched her bowed head with distaste while she intoned something pious to Jesus. There was something about the fakely humble way Peggy knelt that angered me. I knew that her father chopped the heads off of the chickens penned beside their garage. It didn't seem to me that their family deserved the right to pray, and I didn't like the way they did it, and I wanted to go home but was too timid to demand it.

But I slept in the bed next to hers with a feeling of self-righteous superiority and left immediately after breakfast. Carrying my little plaid suitcase, I walked smugly the half-block back to my grand-father's Episcopalian house where a quick grace before dinner sufficed as celestial communication. It felt good to be back home where things were done properly.

Safety and Comfort

Why does it mostly seem to be summer in that green memory of Pennsylvania? There were winters, too: fires in the parlor fireplace after dinner, the deep reds and blues of the oriental rugs (replaced by pastels in summer, when the curtains and slipcovers appeared, as well, and lightened the rooms with their pale pinks). In winter there was black bean soup on Sunday evenings, with sliced hard-boiled egg floating on top beside a thin slice of lemon.

Summers, the soup was chicken-corn, the kernels still attached to one another, oddly intimate, like a row of false teeth. The ice man came, his shoulder protected by a mat, his chunk of ice dripping on his back.

Winters, it was the coal man, and the special chute from his truck to the basement window, and the crashing of the coal as it slid. The milkman was all year, and the trash collector, too, with his wagon pulled by a horse down the alley behind Grandpa's house. And the ashman, lifting the heavy cans of ashes from the furnace.

Where did those people live? The men who collected and delivered. I wonder that now, but didn't, then. They lived some other place, some alien neighborhood far from ours.

Fresh from hearing Mother read *My Friend Flicka* aloud, and from a Saturday afternoon watching *National Velvet* with my sister at the theater on Main Street, I begged the trash collector for a ride on his horse. He didn't answer, just looked at me in astonishment as if I had taken off my clothes, stood on my head, and sung in Chinese. He slapped the reins lightly on the bony back of the horse and plodded down to the next house, leaving behind my embarrassment at having asked mingled with the wonderful odor of warm horsehair and sweat.

My mother laughed when I told her I had asked. She volunteered to read *Black Beauty* next.

I understood about the trash collector's horse, that it was a nag, not a steed; that it would never prance or have fire in its eyes, like

Flicka. But I knew it was all there was, at least for me; it was as close as I could get. I would have been willing to settle for a half-block jounce on a bony back and could have pretended the rest.

Settling for what there was: that was part of home, too.

Safety and Comfort

Home was a kind of fortress for me. There was so much to protect, always, and so much to protect it *from*. It amazed me sometimes that adults—my mother, my grandparents, even my sister, just three years my senior—lived their entire lives apparently unaware of this. They perceived Judy as an ordinary girl, albeit with terrible eczema, and didn't perceive that she was python-like and dangerous. They knew nothing of the monstrous creatures floating in encapsulated horror in Mason jars just across the road.

They thought the Hobaughs' dog, Sandy, in the yard down the street, was overweight and smelled bad. And that was true. But they were curiously blind to the most terrifying fact about that obese, pungent little mongrel.

Sandy had once eaten a dead rat.

Ever since that time, Sandy's saliva had been poison. How could it not be? On hot summer afternoons, when Sandy lay panting on the Hobaughs' porch, he dripped wet strings of poison into swirls on the wooden floor. To walk barefoot near Sandy meant certain hideous death.

I was the only one who knew.

Watchful, attentive, alert to hidden dangers, I guarded my grandfather's house and its occupants throughout my childhood.

Home guarded me in return, and kept me safe.

1995. IT IS more than fifty years since the day that I set fire to my grandfather's house. But I am again standing beside my bed, wearing a nightgown. This time, a telephone to my ear, I am listening to the news that my older son, at the peak of his happy, golden life, has been killed in a godawful accident.

I feel like the five-year-old who stared in horror as flames licked at the organdy curtains. *There is no way to undo this; and I am not brave enough, not strong enough, to get through it . . .*

In 1942, someone's firm and solid arms grabbed me, held me tight, and moved me to a safe place so that I would survive. Now I have to do it for myself. In my mind I open a door, determinedly climb a perilous stair, and find with relief the rooms that have been waiting. There are steaming teacups filled to the brim; and open books, half-read, are waiting on a table.

Safety and Comfort

My son is there, his blue eyes twinkling and a broad grin of greeting on his face.

My mother is smiling as she looks up from reading *The Yearling* aloud to a little pigtailed girl: the same little girl who yearned to ride the trashman's horse. I can join them any time. The place is called Memory. I settle in and feel very much at home.

Bios

SANDRA BENÍTEZ, of Puerto Rican heritage, spent her youth in Mexico, El Salvador, and Missouri and now lives in Edina, Minnesota. Her first book, *A Place Where the Sea Remembers*, won a "Discover Great New Writers Award."

ROSELLEN BROWN, who lives in Houston, Texas, is the author most recently of *Before and After*, a literary novel that uses a murder to question the nature of violence in society. She also wrote *The Autobiography of My Mother*, *Tender Mercies*, and *Civil Wars* and two collections of short stories: *Street Games* and *Banquet: Five Short Stories*. Her poetry is collected in *Some Deaths in the Delta and Other Poems*, *Cora Fry*, and *Cora Fry's Pillow Book*.

lucille clifton, Maryland's most famous poet, is the author of, among others, *Good Times: Poems*, *Good News about the Earth*, *Good Woman: Poems and a Memoir 1969–1980*, and more than twenty books for children, including those about Everett Anderson, a lovable boy who lives in New York City. She was born in Depew, New York.

KATHRYN HARRISON, who lives in a Brooklyn neighborhood called Park Slope, is the author of *Thicker Than Water* (a *New York Times* Notable Book of 1991), *Exposure*, and the more recent *Poison*. She was raised in Los Angeles.

MARCIE HERSHMAN wrote *Tales of the Master Race*, which chronicles the moral corrosion of Germany's Aryan middle classes during World War II, and *Safe in America*, in which three generations of a Jewish family suffer losses emanating from the Holocaust and AIDS. She lives in Brookline, Massachusetts and grew up in Cleveland.

ARLENE HIRSCHFELDER, from Chicago, is the coauthor of *The Native American Almanac* and the author of *Happily May I Walk* (winner of the National Council for Social Studies and Western Heritage Award), *Rising Voices: Writings of Young Native Americans*, and *The Encyclopedia of Native American Religions*. She lives in New Jersey and on Martha's Vineyard.

ERICA JONG, a New Yorker who also lives in Connecticut, is the author of *Fear of Fifty*, a midlife memoir; six novels: *Any Woman's Blues, Serenissima, Parachutes & Kisses, Fanny, Being the True History of the Adventures of Fanny Hackabout Jones, How to Save Your Own Life*, and *Fear of Flying*; seven volumes of poetry including *Becoming Light: Poems New and Selected*; and a children's book, *Megan's Two Houses*.

MAXINE HONG KINGSTON, who grew up in the Chinatown of Stockton, California, teaches at the University of California, Berkeley. She won the National Book Critics Circle Award for *The Woman Warrior: Memoirs of a Girlhood among Ghosts*; she wrote the novels *China Men* and *Tripmaster Monkey: His Fake Book*. She is now the most-taught author on American university and college campuses.

LOIS LOWRY won the 1994 Newbery for *The Giver*, a stunning book about a supposedly utopian society, and is the author of ten Young Adult (YA) books about Anastasia Krupnik and several about Anastasia's genius brother, Sam. She wrote, among many other YA novels, the award-winning *Number the Stars*, which tells the historically correct story of the many Danes who saved their Jewish neighbors during World War II. She lives in Cambridge, Massachusetts, and in an 1840s farmhouse in rural New Hampshire.

JILL MCCORKLE, a native of Lumberton, North Carolina, lives near Boston. Her best-known novels, *Tending to Virginia* and *Ferris Beach*, and a collection of short stories, *Crash Diet*, often mirror the effects of southern childhoods on her characters. Her newest novel is *Carolina Moon*.

CAROLE MASO'S latest novel is *The American Woman in the Chinese Hat*. She is the author too of *Ghost Dance*, *The Art Lover*, and *Ava*. Maso, an Italian-American from New Jersey, lives in New York City's Greenwich Village and often in France.

MARY MORRIS comes from Illinois but she too now lives in Brooklyn, New York. Morris is the author of four novels *(Crossroads, The Waiting Room, A Mother's Love,* and *House Arrest)*, two story collections *(Vanishing Animals* and *The Bus of Dreams)*, and two travel books *(Nothing to Declare* and *Wall to Wall)*.

MICKEY PEARLMAN is the editor of five anthologies, including *Between Friends,* and the coauthor of *Tillie Olsen* and *A Voice of One's Own*. She is the author of *Listen to Their Voices: 20 Interviews with Women Who Write* and of *What to Read: The Essential Guide for Reading Group Members and Other Book Lovers*. She grew up in Florida and lives in New Jersey.

MEG PEI, an Italian-American now living in Chicago, was raised on Long Island. She wrote *Salaryman*, the story of a Japanese middle manager who comes to America; it won the Friends of American Writers Award in 1993.

MELINDA WORTH POPHAM, originally from Kansas City, lives in Los Angeles. In *Skywater*, which won *Buzzworms's* Edward Abbey Award for EcoFiction in 1990, she writes of coyotes in the Sonoran desert of southwestern Arizona.

FRANCINE PROSE lived until recently in rural Crumville, New York, but grew up in decidedly urban Brooklyn. She is the author of *Bigfoot Dreams, Women and Children First* (short stories), *Hungry Hearts, Household Saints, Primitive People, Judah the*

Pious (winner of the Jewish Book Council Award), *Hunters and Gatherers*, and the forthcoming set of novellas, *Guided Tours of Hell*.

DANI SHAPIRO, a New Yorker from New Jersey, is the author of three novels: *Playing with Fire, Fugitive Blue,* and *Picturing the Wreck.* She is a contributing editor at *New Woman* magazine and has been published in the *New York Times Magazine, Glamour,* and *People.*

JANE SHAPIRO, who lives in Princeton, New Jersey, is the author of the novel *After Moondog,* which was a finalist for the *Los Angeles Times* Book Prize. Her journalism and short stories have been published in the *New Yorker,* the *New York Times, Mirabella, Ms, Harper's Bazaar,* and the *Village Voice.*

JULIE SMITH now lives in New Orleans, where she was formerly a reporter for the *Times-Picayune.* She is the Edgar Award-winning author of *New Orleans Mourning,* of *The Axeman's Jazz,* based on a real-life serial killer who terrorized that city in 1919, and of *House of Blues.* Her latest mystery is *The Kindness of Strangers.*

SYLVIA WATANABE, a Japanese-American born on the Hawaiian island of Maui, now lives in Grand Rapids, Michigan. Her first collection of short stories, *Talking to the Dead,* was nominated for the PEN/Faulkner Award. "Where People Know Me" (from *Between Friends*) was nominated for a Pushcart Prize.

A Note to the Reader

We hope this book has energized you to think about those places you have called Home. We'd like to hear from you.

MICKEY PEARLMAN
c/o Michael Flamini
St. Martin's Press
257 Park Avenue South
New York, New York 10010